INTELLIGENT M&A

INTELLIGENT

M&A

Navigating the Mergers and Acquisitions Minefield

Scott Moeller
and
Chris Brady

BICENTENNIAL
1807
WILEY
2007
BICENTENNIAL

John Wiley & Sons, Ltd

Other Wiley Editorial Offices

John Wiley & Sons Inc., 111 River Street, Hoboken, NJ 07030, USA

Jossey-Bass, 989 Market Street, San Francisco, CA 94103-1741, USA

Wiley-VCH Verlag GmbH, Boschstr. 12, D-69469 Weinheim, Germany

John Wiley & Sons Australia Ltd, 42 McDougall Street, Milton, Queensland 4064,
Australia

John Wiley & Sons (Asia) Pte Ltd, 2 Clementi Loop #02-01, Jin Xing Distripark,
Singapore 129809

John Wiley & Sons Canada Ltd, 6045 Freemont Blvd, Mississauga, ONT, L5R 4J3,
Canada

Wiley also publishes its books in a variety of electronic formats. Some content that
appears in print may not be available in electronic books.

Anniversary Logo Design: Richard J. Pacifico

Library of Congress Cataloging-in-Publication Data

Moeller, Scott.
    Intelligent M&A: navigating the mergers and acquisitions minefield/Scott Moeller and
Chris Brady.
        p. cm
    Includes bibliographical references and index.
    ISBN 978-0-470-05812-1 (cloth : alk. paper)
    1. Consolidation and merger of corporations.   2. Business intelligence.
3. Consolidation and merger of corporations—Management.   4. Organizational
change—Management.   I. Brady, Christopher, 1947–   II. Title.   III. Title: Intelligent
mergers and acquisitions.
    HD2746.5.M64 2007
    658.1'62—dc22   2007020422

British Library Cataloguing in Publication Data
A catalogue record for this book is available from the British Library

ISBN 978-0-470-05812-1 (HB)

Typeset in 11.5/15pt Bembo by SNP Best-set Typesetter Ltd., Hong Kong

This book is printed on acid-free paper responsibly manufactured from sustainable
forestry in which at least two trees are planted for each one used for paper production.

To Daniela
who gave me the inspiration for this book and support
during many M&A deals
SM

To Anita
who has supported me through all the changes
of the past year
CB

CONTENTS

INTRODUCTION

In the realm of corporate activity, mergers and acquisitions (M&A) have played a defining role in shaping the corporate landscape over the past century. Given the breathtaking pace at which M&A transactions transform corporations and the sheer scope and scale of modern-day deals, it is no surprise that the work of investment banks and corporate finance boutiques has come to dominate the headlines. Yet, for all the bravura of M&A, such transactions also carry a high degree of risk as a result of the premiums paid and the organizational upheaval caused. The lament heard after most failed deals is that certain elements were not known, indeed it will often be claimed that they could not have been known. Any intelligence specialist will tell you that all things are knowable – it is merely a question of how badly you want to know and how hard you are prepared to work to acquire that information.

For definitional clarity, when we talk about 'business intelligence' (often called 'competitive intelligence,' particularly in the US) we are referring to the 'business intelligence function' not the hard and soft information systems that have identified themselves as 'b systems.' The function itself (sometimes called 'corporate intelligence') is a vital aid to managerial decision making in any industry and at any time. By furnishing companies and other organizations with detailed and timely information about the commercial and competitive environment, the 'art' of intelligence enables companies to determine more accurately where they have been, to orientate themselves in the present, and to plan for the future.

No more so than in the field of mergers and acquisitions, where so much risk attaches, business intelligence acts as a robust yet dynamic tool, providing company executives and other decision makers with the capability and wherewithal to make the necessary rational business decisions that will enable them to lead their organizations towards achieving their desired corporate objectives. By systematically acquiring and analyzing data, information, and knowledge, business intelligence makes a significant contribution not only to establishing but also to maintaining a long-term competitive advantage. This is especially critical in the often-hostile 'heat of the battle' of an acquisition takeover.

The idea for this book emerged from the normal office banter in the room the two authors shared at Cass Business School in London. Chris Brady teaches an MBA course on Business Intelligence which draws on his own experiences as an intelligence analyst during his service in the Royal Navy. Scott Moeller teaches a course in Mergers and Acquisitions that attracts more students than any other elective in the business school, and builds on his many years in the investment banking and private equity worlds. We had opportunities to overhear discussions that the other would be having with students, faculty, and industry practitioners. We realized the interconnected nature of the two fields we each studied and decided to connect our two courses for the benefit of the students. The natural extension of that decision was to extend the result of our collaboration into the book you are now reading.

This book shows that by employing sufficient and first-rate intelligence as part of an M&A process, companies are able to achieve a higher degree of commercial success from those transactions. We will provide examples where, unfortunately, the inverse is also true, when companies ignored obvious and sometimes not-so-obvious intelligence possibilities. In the bear pit of corporate finance, to enter into the realm of high risk/high reward deals other than with one's eyes and ears wide open is undoubtedly to tempt fate. In this day and age, only the bravest (or the most foolish) would willingly or knowingly do so. It is intelligence that provides the information that the eyes and ears transmit to the brain.

Using business intelligence techniques in a takeover is not simply a matter of doing some things better, such as due diligence where business intelligence techniques are already widely used. Instead what is required is a change in approach or method from the inception of the deal idea through to the post-merger integration which often takes years, if not decades, to complete. In fact the bottom line regarding the common ground of business intelligence and acquisitions is that management must work to ensure that the process from start to finish is linked in a meaningful and productive way. Understanding the value of intelligence requires a change in mindset for most executives and organizations.

One successful example that we shall be discussing is that of Johnson & Johnson who proactively work to link their takeover actions with their strategic intent at every step of the way. We shall see how, instead of merely focusing their attention on clinching a deal, they remain absolutely committed only to pursuing targets that are continuously relevant to their strategy; they then follow through their actions such that the expected value from the deal is created.

As we turn towards our conclusions, it will hopefully have become clear that business intelligence in all its shapes and forms adds '... color and context to the M&A environment ... ,' as the Corporate Development Director of Friends Provident plc told us. This serves to oil the cogs of the M&A machine and enables deals to be maneuvered towards a satisfactory conclusion for all the parties involved. It is increasingly clear that the role of business intelligence – both unmistakeable and irreplaceable – has the opportunity to transform the mergers and acquisitions marketplace, providing a pole star for participants, a focus for questioning, and a useful steer for information gathering. While ignored in the future at the peril of any participants in an M&A deal, business intelligence – however discreet and reserved – must constitute a core element that will drive successful transactions. Without it, modern M&A activity - defined and shaped by the complexity of our modern financial and commercial environment – would be entirely different. We are already seeing evidence of this in the greater success of deals conducted in the current merger wave since 2003.

At his trial in January 2004, Joachim Funk, the former Board Chairman of Mannesmann (now part of Vodafone plc) casually referred to hostile M&A deals as being somewhat '... reminiscent of a battlefield ... ,' no doubt a telling and perceptive description of the scene after many corporate transactions. Others are fond of quoting Sun Tsu and Machiavelli or generals such as Napoleon and Patton. Yet, while corporate language is replete with military jargon (such as 'strategy' and 'tactics'), nevertheless, it is the use of intelligence in a commercial context – enabling companies to leverage their superior knowledge and insight to prevail over their rivals – which provides the greatest parallel between the universe of the soldier and that of the businessman. Those same military leaders were careful to note that they only acted when they felt they had the necessary intelligence at hand, and action without the necessary intelligence was reserved for either the inexperienced or desperate.

In any M&A transaction, company executives – like the generals in the midst of a military battlefield – ultimately need to rely on extensive intelligence as an aid to ensure that campaigns are waged, fought, and won for their shareholders with the greatest probability of success. Indeed, given the abundance of corporate outfits and private equity houses chasing the same limited number of deals, intelligence becomes not just 'a nice to have' but a fundamental and indispensable tool without which contestants should not consider entering the M&A 'ring.' Summed up by a journalist at the *Guardian* as '...the commodity that really matters in the knowledge economy...,' intelligence enables companies to get ahead of the game at the very moment that the corporate stakes are the highest.

This book is structured to provide an introduction to the mergers industry and the emerging field of business intelligence. The book then works through an M&A deal from the beginning when the deal is only a strategic idea through to the post-merger period. In each phase, we show how business intelligence techniques can be applied to improve the likelihood of a deal succeeding, not just in progressing to the next phase, but in being successful for managers, employees, shareholders, and other stakeholders of the companies. We are practitioners, so we have included in each chapter a number of illustrative case studies from our own experience and those of others. Accordingly, this book is designed to provide ideas to develop further and is not heavy on proscriptive to-do lists. At the end of the book, we've added a chapter to provide some hints about how a manager can personally best survive a merger, either from the target or bidder's side.

As also shown by those case studies, each deal is unique. We have tried to provide examples from many industries, although geographically they concentrate on the UK and the US. We believe that these examples will be very helpful for anyone engaged in the M&A field, especially to provide ideas from outside your own industry. We have also provided an extensive bibliography to steer readers to further examples and discussion. For many of the topics in this book – such as strategy, company valuation, and negotiation – an entire library could be built of books written about those subjects that we have only been able to discuss within the context of the intersection of business intelligence and the mergers and acquisitions field.

We are indebted to a number of people in producing the research and text of this book. Two of our MBA students at Cass Business School, Robert Gershon and Tamara Kanafani, helped us with researching the role of business intelligence in mergers and acquisitions; a number of other students and faculty too numerous to mention have also provided case studies or inspiration for sections of this book, but special note and appreciation go to Lisa Abshire, Ekaterina Chalova, Alina Chapovskaya, Debi Davidson, Maslin Istaprasert, Yulia Korotkikh, Richard Odumodu, Otaso Osayimwese, Marianna Prodan, and John Richardson of Cass Business School, David Welsh of Drexel University and Chris Mouchbahani. Catherine Stokes has made sure that what is in our thoughts has been reflected properly on paper. And our families have been understanding in the time that we spent with the manuscript and not with them. Thanks to all.

CHAPTER 1

THE NEED FOR INTELLIGENCE IN MERGERS AND ACQUISITIONS

Mergers and acquisitions are an integral part of the global strategic and financial business landscape, whether one is part of the acquiring company, the target, a competitor, an advisor (including investment bankers, accountants, lawyers, and many others), an investor, a regulator, or someone living or working in the neighboring community.

Although fluctuating widely from periods of peaks and troughs of merger activity, the baseline size and growth of mergers is clear. In fact, the 'slow' period of activity in 2002 was well in excess of the 'peak' of activity in the late 1980s.

Yet despite this impressive trend, mergers and acquisitions are often misunderstood and misrepresented in the press and by those who are engaged in each transaction. Deals, especially when hostile, cross border, or among large companies, might be front-page news (and interestingly there are some days when *every* story covered on the first page of the *Financial Times* is about an acquisition), yet there is a great deal of conflicting evidence as to whether they are successful or not. Our own research has shown an improved performance of companies that make acquisitions, especially in the merger wave that began in 2003.

That said, there do seem to be some inviolate truths about M&A deals:

1. Many fail to deliver the promised gains to shareholders.
2. Boards, CEOs, senior managers, and advisors pursue deals for personal reasons.
3. Deals have a momentum of their own and this means that they don't get dropped when they no longer make sense.
4. The deal doesn't end when the money changes hands; in fact, that point marks the start of the most difficult stage of a deal, the tough integration process that few get right.
5. Success with one deal doesn't guarantee success in the next deal.

Some M&A failures have been dramatic. The AOL/Time Warner deal lost 93% of its value during the integration period as the internet service provider merged with the publishing company in an attempt to combine content with delivery. VeriSign, another internet-related services company, lost $17 billion of its $20 billion acquisition of Network Solutions in 2000, and its stock fell 98%. It is not just the fallout from dot.com failures that have lost money following a major acquisition, as another classic example of failure – and one where the very basic elements of business intelligence were ignored – is Quaker Oats, a food and beverage company founded in 1901. In the brief case study which follows, look at the first word of the penultimate paragraph. It is the key identifier of an intelligence failure. The word is 'following.' Incompatibility of cultures is one of the biggest post-acquisition killers.

Quaker Oats

On November 1, 1994, Quaker Oats acquired Snapple for approximately $1.9 billion, becoming the third largest producer of soft drinks in the United States.

The Quaker Oats Company had been founded at the start of the 20th century, and its most famous product, Quaker Oats Cereal, originated in 1877. At the time of the initial acquisition, Quaker Oats was one of the leading manufacturers of cereal products in the United States, but it had also diversified into baby food, animal feed, chocolate (in Mexico), and honey (in the Netherlands). One of its most successful recent diversifications had been the acquisition in 1983 of Gatorade, a sports drink company. Under Quaker Oats' ownership, Gatorade had grown tremendously. This success contributed to the feeling within Quaker Oats that, because its main business was mature, it should focus on 'investment in brands with high growth potential and divestment of lower growth, lower-margin businesses', as stated in its 1995 Annual Report.

Snapple was a trendy, slightly eccentric company, founded in 1972 by three entrepreneurs (two window washers and the owner of a health food store). Under the brand name 'Snapple' (acquired in 1978), their product line had grown by word of mouth to be one of the best-selling fruit drinks lines in the northeast United States. They also sold iced tea drinks, which had been added in 1987.

Where Quaker Oats was an old-line national company, Snapple was a 'New Age' company run as a regional family business. However, as such, Snapple did not have the resources to continue to expand, and with increased new competition from the largest soft drink manufacturers (Coca-Cola and Pepsi), they looked for someone to acquire them.

Quaker Oats thought that there were important potential synergies between Gatorade and Snapple. On the surface, it appeared that they could share distribution channels (reducing costs) and they had complementary geographic areas. Quaker Oats also hoped that its conservative culture could be invigorated by Gatorade.

Following the acquisition, it was determined that the pricing strategy was different for the two product lines, the distribution different (Gatorade used a warehouse distribution system whereas Snapple used a single-serve, refrigerated delivery system) and, most importantly, the cultures were not compatible (affecting integration, advertising, and many other areas where coordination was required). In addition, in the quarter just prior to the acquisition, Snapple had experienced a 74% drop in sales on a year-over-year basis, a fact that was only told to Quaker Oats a few days before the deal was finalized. At the same time as sales volumes were decreasing, the cost of integration and national rollout under Quaker Oats was rising.

Less than three years later, in 1997, Quaker Oats sold off its Snapple division to Triarc Corporation for $300 million.

One challenge in trying to determine success of an acquisition lies in how to define 'success.' Is it shareholder value? If so, over what period? Or should one look at sales growth? The ability to retain key customers? Employee retention? Cost savings? And how would the company or companies have performed if they had not merged? Perhaps as some have suggested, success should be defined by the publicized goals of the merging companies themselves and then measured against achieving those stated objectives.

No matter how measured, a fair degree of consistency has emerged in the results of studies that have examined M&A 'success' through the 20th century. Essentially all of the studies found that well over half of all mergers and acquisitions should never have taken place because they did not succeed by whatever definition of success used. Many studies found that only 30 to 40% were successful. Yet most companies that have grown into global giants used M&A as part of their growth strategy.

This paradox raises the following questions:

- Can a company become a large global player without having made acquisitions?
- Is organic growth sufficient to become a leading global player?

The challenge for management is to reconcile the low odds of deal success with the need to incorporate acquisitions or mergers into their growth strategy. Figure out how to beat the odds and be successful in takeovers. This is where business intelligence techniques are essential.

Prior experience may not be a predictor of success, although some studies have shown that acquirers do better when making an acquisition that is similar to deals they have done previously. Here again the need for specific intelligence is central. Many studies have shown that relatively inexperienced acquirers might inappropriately apply generalized acquisition experience to dissimilar acquisitions. The more sophisticated acquirers would appropriately differentiate between their acquisitions. In a deal that will be discussed later, VeriSign appears to have failed with its 2004 purchase of Jamba AG despite having made 17 other acquisitions in the prior six years, many in related internet businesses. Intelligence cannot, therefore, be taken for granted.

DIFFERENT TYPES OF MERGERS AND ACQUISITIONS

There even is some confusion about the terminology used. Many have questioned whether all mergers and consolidations are really acquisitions. This is because the result – sometimes as much as a decade later – is that the staff, culture, business model, or other characteristics of one of the two companies becomes dominant in the new, combined organization.

Name changes reflect merger realities: Morgan Stanley

This reality of a merger can often be reflected in the name change. For example, in 1997, Morgan Stanley and Dean Witter Discover 'merged.' Although the new company was renamed 'Morgan Stanley Dean Witter,' within several years it was renamed just 'Morgan Stanley.' In a power struggle at the top in the initial years after the merger, the former head of Dean Witter (Jack Purcell) dominated and the former president of Morgan Stanley (John Mack) left to become the head of a rival investment bank, Credit Suisse.

That was not the end. In 2005, eight years after the original 'merger', a palace coup of former Morgan Stanley managing directors forced the ouster of Purcell and reinstated Mack as head of the bank.

This was not a unique situation even for the brokerage industry, as over decade earlier in 1981, the commodity trading firm Phibro Corp had acquired Salomon Brothers to create 'Phibro-Salomon,' yet the Salomon managers ultimately prevailed and the company was renamed Salomon Inc. Salomon was later acquired again, and today is part of the global financial powerhouse Citigroup, although rumors consistently arise that Salomon may again be independent.

Although one therefore should be careful in using the terms 'merger,' 'acquisition,' and 'consolidation' and other related words, in practice these terms are used interchangeably. Additionally, 'takeover' is a term that typically implies an unfriendly deal, but will often be used when referring to any type of merger or acquisition. In this book, we will most often use the term 'merger,' even when the transaction could be or has been structured as an 'acquisition.'

The three major types of mergers/acquisitions are driven by different goals at the outset and raise different issues for the use of business intelligence.

- **Horizontal mergers** are mergers among competitors or those in the same industry operating before the merger at the same points in the production and sales process. For example, the deal between two automotive giants, Chrysler in the US and Daimler, the maker of Mercedes cars and trucks, in Germany, was a horizontal merger.

  In horizontal mergers, the managers of one side of the deal will know a lot about the business of the other side. Intelligence may be easy to gather, not just because there will likely be employees that have moved between the two companies over time in the course of business, but the two firms will also most likely share common clients, suppliers, and industry processes. These deals often include cost savings as a principal deal driver, as it is more likely that there will be overlaps and therefore redundancies between the two companies.

- **Vertical mergers** are deals between buyers and sellers or a combination of firms that operate at different stages of the same industry. One such example is a merger between a supplier of data and the company controlling the means through which that information is supplied to consumers, such as the merger between Time Warner, a content-driven firm owning a number of popular magazines, and AOL, the world's largest internet portal company at the time of their merger. There is often less common knowledge between the two companies in a vertical deal, although there may still be some small degree of common clients and suppliers, plus some previously shared employee movement. Depending on the perspective of the firm, the vertical merger will either be a backwards expansion toward the source of supply or forwards toward the ultimate consumer. The 2003 acquisition of TNK (a Russian oil company with large oil and gas reserves but little western refining capability or retail marketing) by BP (which had declining reserves and strong global marketing and refining operations) is one such example. We will visit this acquisition again.

- **Conglomerate** mergers are between unrelated companies, not competitors and without a buyer/seller relationship (for example, the 1985 acquisition of General Foods, a diversified food products company, by Philip Morris, a tobacco manufacturer). Conglomerate mergers do not have a strategic rationalization as a driver (although often cost savings at the headquarters level can be achieved, or in the case of Philip Morris, it wished to diversify risk away from the litigious tobacco industry). This type of merger was common in the past, but has fallen out of favor with shareholders and the financial markets, although when they do occur, they can benefit greatly from the more creative uses of business intelligence. For example, detailed scenario planning involving simulations based on high quality information can identify unforeseen issues that can drive such deals and provide a logical rationale.

Deals are either complementary or supplementary. A complementary acquisition is one that helps to compensate for some weakness of the acquiring firm. For example, the acquiring company might have strong manufacturing, but weak marketing or sales; the target may have strong marketing and sales, but poor quality control in manufacturing. Or the driver may be geographic: when Morgan Stanley made a bid to purchase S.G. Warburg in

1995, it wanted to complement its powerful position in the US market with Warburg's similar position in the UK and Europe. A supplementary deal is one where the target reinforces an existing strength of the acquiring firm; therefore, the target is similar to the acquirer. A good example of such a deal would be when one oil company buys another oil company, such as the aforementioned 2003 deal when BP purchased a controlling interest in TNK, a Russian oil company with large oil reserves.

THE MERGER WAVES

Merger activity tends to take place in waves – a time of increased activity followed by a period of relatively few acquisitions. Each wave has been stimulated by events outside the merger world, but which have had a significant impact on the level of merger activity. Each wave is sharply distinguished from earlier waves with creative new ways of consolidating companies and defeating the defenses of targets, although each wave built on the merger techniques and other developments from the previous wave.

There is also the tendency, as with the military, of preparing to fight the last war's battles. Just as the Maginot Line couldn't stop the Third Reich's panzers as they rolled through Belgium and into northern France, it is not sufficient for a company to have out-of-date takeover defenses. Strategic initiative or power does not guarantee success to the bidder, as the United States learned militarily in Vietnam in the 1960s and in Iraq in the 1990s and 2000s. The parallel in business usually means relying too much on a large checkbook and first mover 'advantage' as Sir Philip Green discovered in 2004 when trying unsuccessfully to take over Marks & Spencer.

Merger activity can be likened to the Cold War arms race where one country's development of new weapons stimulates the development of more sophisticated defensive systems, thus forcing the first country to make further advancements in their offensive weapons to remain ahead. In the M&A arena, as acquiring companies have developed more sophisticated tools to make the acquisition of companies more certain, faster, easier, or less expensive, the advisors to the target companies have designed stronger defenses for their clients. These defenses have then stimulated further activity to create better acquisition methods. Just as with the arms race, the process becomes more complicated and expensive for all the players.

Knowledge of previous takeover techniques is therefore important for any bidder or target – and is a critical aspect in the application of business intelligence. The development of these tactics has concentrated in the six major merger waves since the beginning of the 20th century, and focused during much of that time on the United States as the largest and arguably the most open M&A market in the world. In most cases, the new developments in M&A were first tried in the US and then 'exported' to other countries or regions, although before the 1990s the major economic regions had waves somewhat different to the US but often driven by similar factors. Since the 1990s, the merger waves have been truly global.

The **first** merger wave took place from 1897 and continued through 1904. It started in the United States after the Depression of 1893 ended, and continued until the 1904 stock market crash, with a peak between 1898 and 1902. This merger wave featured horizontal mergers (over three-quarters of all mergers then) often resulting in a near monopolistic industry in the consolidating industries: metals, food, oil, chemicals, trains, machinery, and coal. It was therefore also known as the 'monopoly merger wave.' Some of the companies formed from this wave in the US have remained global powerhouses and included: Dupont, Standard Oil (controlled 85% of the US domestic market), American Tobacco (controlled 90% of its market), General Electric, Eastman Kodak, and US Steel (controlled 75% of its market). There was a similar trend in other markets, particularly Germany, France, and Great Britain.

The **second** merger wave was from 1916 until the Great Depression in 1929. The growth of this merger wave was facilitated by cooperation among businesses as part of the Great War (World War I) effort, when governments did not enforce antitrust laws and in fact encouraged businesses to cooperate. For the first time, investment bankers were aggressive in funding mergers, and much of the capital was controlled by a small number of investment bankers (most notably J.P. Morgan). The role of investment bankers in driving the deal market continues today.

Over two-thirds of the second merger wave acquisitions were horizontal, while most of the others were vertical (thus, few conglomerate mergers). If the first merger wave could be characterized as 'merging for monopoly,' then the second wave could best be described as 'merging for oligopoly.' Many of these mergers created huge economies of scale that made the firms economically stronger. Industries that had the most mergers were mining, oil, food products, chemicals, banking, and automobiles. Some of the companies created in the US in this period were General Motors, IBM, John Deere, and Union Carbide.

The **third** merger wave occurred from 1965 to 1969. Many deals in this wave were driven by what was later determined to be the irrational financial engineering of company stock market earnings ratios (similar in many ways to the exuberance of the dot.com era 30 years later). This wave was known as the 'conglomerate merger wave,' as 80% of all mergers in the decade 1965–1975 were conglomerate mergers. A classic example of such a merger is the acquisition by ITT of companies as diverse as Sheraton Hotels, Avis Rent-a-Car, Continental Baking, a consumer credit company, various parking facilities, and several restaurant chains. Clearly, ITT would not be able to integrate these companies at the production, business, or client levels, so there was little in cost savings or strategic rationale that drove the deals despite claims of management efficiency at the headquarters level; instead, the growth of ITT was blessed by the market with an award of a high stock price!

One reason for such conglomerate mergers was the world-wide growth after World War II in stronger antitrust rules (or the more vigorous enforcement of existing antitrust and monopoly regulations), thus forcing companies that wanted to expand by acquisition to look for unrelated businesses. The beginning of the end was the fall of conglomerate stock prices in 1968.

Inco vs ESB and Colt vs Garlock

Most deals during this early post-war era were friendly. The first significant hostile takeover in the US by a major firm was in 1973 when Inco (a mining company, originally named International Nickel Company) acquired ESB (a battery manufacturer, originally known as Electric Storage Battery); significantly, Inco was represented by Morgan Stanley, at the time the leading M&A advisor. Inco was successful in acquiring ESB, and this deal changed the rules of the game where the large investment banks would now get involved in hostile bids. Note that the first hostile bid in the UK was in 1958 and 1959 when British Aluminium was acquired by Tube Investments and its American partner Reynolds Metals; the bidders were advised by S.G. Warburg.

Another deal, Colt Industries' lightning raid of Garlock in 1975, brought hostility to an all-time high. The new development in this deal was that Colt took the hostile negotiations public and advertised heavily, forcing Garlock even to hire a public relations firm, which may be common today but would not have been done in the early 1970s. Famously, its advertisements accused Colt of launching a 'Saturday Night Special' (a term used in the US to denote unregistered hand guns purchased for immediate use in crime) which entered the M&A vernacular as a description for a takeover offer that is open only for a short period of time, thereby forcing target company shareholders to make a quick but not fully informed decision.

The **fourth** merger wave was from 1981 to 1989. During this wave, hostile deals came of age. Generally, the characteristics of this merger wave were that the number of hostile mergers rose dramatically, the role of the 'corporate raider' developed, anti-takeover strategies and tactics became much more sophisticated, the investment bankers and attorneys played a more significant role than they had since the second merger wave, and the development of the high yield ('junk') bond market enabled companies to launch 'megadeals' and even purchase companies larger than themselves. This last trend contributed to the high number of leveraged buyouts with excessive use of debt and companies going private. Assisting this merger wave was relaxed antitrust enforcement, especially in the US under President Ronald Reagan and in the UK under Prime Minister Margaret Thatcher.

The **fifth** merger wave (1994–2000) was characterized by consolidations of industries and globalization. The dot.com boom and bust also occurred during this wave. Many 'strategic' consolidations unfortunately failed to deliver on promised gains, such as lower costs and greater synergies, and ended with the decline in stock prices worldwide beginning in 1999/2000. Nevertheless, there were a large number of significant deals during this wave, in the following industries:

- Oil (BP/Amoco, Exxon/Mobil, Total/Petrofina).
- Financial services (Citicorp/Travelers, Deutsche Bank/ Bankers Trust, Chase Manhattan/J.P. Morgan).
- Information technology (Compaq/Digital Equipment, Hewlett Packard/Compaq).
- Telecommunications (Mannesmann/Vodafone, SBS Communications/Ameritech).
- Pharmaceuticals (Glaxo/Wellcome).
- Automotive (Daimler Benz/Chrysler).

The **sixth** merger wave began in 2003, less than three years following the end of the previous cycle. Merger waves therefore are occurring on a more frequent basis with a much shorter quiet period. This sixth merger wave has been truly global and has seen more focus on strategic fit and attention to post-merger integration issues. It has been heavily influenced by the corporate governance scandals of the early years of the new millennium and the resulting laws and regulations that have been passed – most notably the Sarbanes–Oxley Act in the United States. Success for these deals has been largely driven by three factors, as shown in Figure 1.1, which comes from a presentation that Towers Perrin developed together with Cass Business School.

An additional change in the sixth merger wave has been the rise in activity by financial buyers (hedge funds, private equity funds, and venture capital funds) who therefore do not and cannot have strategic interests as the primary driver. These funds purchase large stakes in companies and then either purchase the remaining part of the company or force a reorganization through the exercise of their shareholder rights. In some cases these share-holder actions have stopped deals from taking place where the funds exerted pressure on management as they felt they could achieve higher returns in other ways, such as the return of cash to shareholders in the form of a special dividend or where the intrinsic growth potential of the company was seen to be

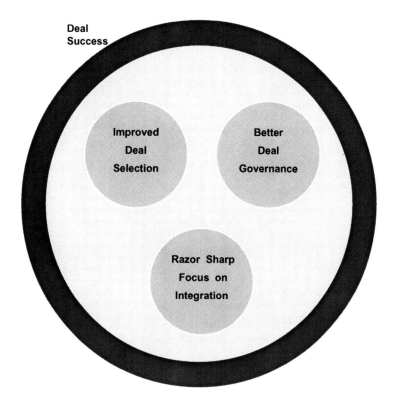

Figure 1.1 Sixth Merger Wave Success Factors.

excellent. This was the case in early 2005 when the Deutsche Börse was forced to withdraw its proposed takeover of the London Stock Exchange, despite the fact that the board of the Deutsche Börse had already approved the deal. More on this deal later.

Unlike previous merger waves, more companies have been successful with their acquisitions than not, although it is not clear whether this trend will continue. As shown in Figure 1.2, our analysis, in consultation with Towers Perrin, of shareholder performance in deals during the 1980s and 1990s was negative when compared to the market, whereas the performance of deals in the recent merger wave is thus far better than the market.

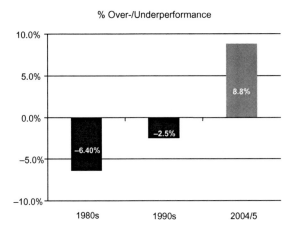

Figure 1.2 Average Deal Performance vs the Market.

History will repeat itself, and one way in which this happens in M&A is the reasons and rationale driving the deals. Just as understanding the history of M&A is helpful in planning today's deals both offensively and defensively, understanding the reasons behind a deal are also critical.

Pharmaceutical industry consolidation: AstraZeneca's acquisition of Cambridge Antibody Technology

As one pharmaceutical industry expert told us, 'No large pharma will be successful if they do not have a proportion of their pipeline coming from external sources. Most big pharma have around 30% of their pipeline in collaboration deals. Years ago the big pharmaceutical players thought they could exist on their own but they realized not. Merck were one of the last ones to realize this and had to get into trouble first . . . in the early 1990s Merck was "the" pharma company but they thought they could do it alone and look at them now. They have been hungry for deals in the last few years and have licensed a lot . . . All large pharma are saying the same thing

"The World is our Research Laboratory" . . . of course, they are all mad!'

AstraZeneca was the UK's second largest pharmaceutical company. Its acquisition of Cambridge Antibody Technology (CAT), the UK's largest biotechnology company, began with an alliance. The relationship between the two firms had started, in 2004, with AstraZeneca taking a 19.9% equity stake in CAT. According to the CAT website, they arranged a strategic alliance for the 'joint discovery and development of human monoclonal antibody therapeutics, principally in the field of inflammatory disorders, including respiratory diseases.' It was decided that CAT would be responsible for antibody discovery, manufacturing process development, and the supply of material for exploratory clinical trials. AstraZeneca was responsible for translational biology, clinical development programs, regulatory filings, and commercialization.

The results of the cooperation were encouraging and promised more for the future. Six discovery projects, one pre-existing CAT discovery program adopted into the alliance, and five new programs all had progressed on schedule by June 2005.

Building on the success of this existing collaboration, the companies decided to move further. On the morning of May 13, 2006, the shareholders of CAT woke up to some incredibly good news. AstraZeneca announced it was ready to pay an unprecedented 70% premium to acquire the remaining 80.1% of CAT's shares that it did not already own. AstraZeneca proposed paying 1320 pence per CAT share, higher than even the most optimistic analysts had expected, thus valuing the all-cash deal at £702 million.

AstraZeneca's purchase of CAT was a strategic step to secure operations in the biopharmaceutical market segment, build up future capabilities, strengthen its own positions, and limit access of competitors to the technologies it considered critical.

REASONS FOR M&A DEALS

Some of the reasons to acquire or merge may have started to become clear from the earlier discussions in this chapter, such as the need to control a source of raw materials in a backwards vertical acquisition, as BP announced when it acquired TNK. But it is usually necessary to dig deeper than the press statements from the parties involved. Very often the publicly stated reason is quite different from the underlying strategic rationale (assuming such a rationale really existed).

Numerous theories have been put forward regarding the reasons for mergers and acquisitions. Whether '. . . caught up in the "thrill of the hunt," driven to complete deals as a result of internal company politics, management bravado, or the need to boost divisional key performance indicators in order to reach bonus targets . . . ,' as suggested to us by Sarah Byrne-Quinn, Group Director of Strategy and Business Development at Smith & Nephew, deals are often motivated by personal and financial as opposed to strategic considerations. Either way, to avoid peripheral issues taking center stage, organizations need to remain open minded when pursuing a deal, building teams to question assumptions on an ongoing basis and to remain focused on the overall strategy for the company, while being motivated by the underlying 'quality' of an acquisition at the right price for an organization.

There are often multiple reasons given, sometimes conflicting and overlapping. Generally speaking, the most common reasons used to justify a merger or an acquisition are claims of market power, efficiency (in various forms), pure diversification, information and signaling, agency problems, managerialism and hubris, and taxes. Each of these is discussed briefly in the box.

Drivers to deals

- Size matters: many, if not most, deals are driven at least in part by the desire of management to gain more **market power**. These acquisitions are designed to increase influence through size and market share, tempered by the regulatory constraints of monopoly rules and regulations.

- **Basic efficiency** arguments claim synergies from an M&A deal and are best shown by the equation $2 + 2 = 5$; that is, the value of the newly merged firm is greater than the combined value of the individual firms prior to the merger. Thus, this theory is really a 'growth' theory from both the shareholders' and managers' perspectives. More than any other factor, this one is used as an argument to shareholders that they should approve a deal. Although often independently verified, in most deals it is the bidder's analysts that will provide the 'proof' of these future synergies for both revenues and expenses.

- A clever claim, that is most often hidden or only discussed within the bidder's consortium of insiders, is that there is **differential managerial efficiency**. This means that the bidder believes they have much better ('more efficient') managers than the target. Therefore, after the merger, the target's management efficiency will be raised to the level of the acquirer's as the bidder takes over senior management positions or trains the target's management to be better. If this could be true, then the merger increases efficiency and creates shareholder wealth. This would be most likely where firms are in related businesses. Difficult to prove? Almost certainly. Common? Yes.

- **Operating synergies** take place when deals are done to achieve economies of scale where size matters or economies of scope where the efficiencies come from allocating expenses over a wider variety of activities. Mergers of scale and scope must be carefully constructed so as not to grow to a size where there are diseconomies of scale and scope; in other words, where the company becomes top heavy and inefficient. Typically in a merger situation, management of the acquiring company will emphasize the cost synergies such as reduction in operating costs, elimination of duplicate facilities, and reduction in various departments (marketing, purchasing, sales, and so on). However, just as important should be the revenue increases from the merger, which are often overlooked.

- **Financial synergies** arise if the internal capital market of the newly combined firms is considered to be more efficient than raising capital externally. This relates to the transfer of capital (money) from low to high return businesses. There is also the potential for increased debt capacity with lower borrowing rates if the company's credit rating improves due to the merger (although more commonly the credit ratings will be lower immediately following or even preceding a merger due to the uncertainty associated with the deal).

- The **strategic response** theory of takeovers focuses on the idea that a merger can be driven by a need to realign the firm in response to a changing external environment. The driver is therefore outside the company and may be due to product life cycles (where products or services are maturing, such as mobile phones where the growth rates began declining in the early 2000s) or product/service replacement (for example, when broadband began to replace dial-up modems for internet connections in homes).

- Individual companies may be **undervalued** or not valued properly by the stock market. Some mergers therefore take place when the market value of the company before the merger does not reflect the full potential value to the acquiring company. Perhaps the value of the target was correct when it was a standalone company, but for a bidder taking into account some of the above factors (such as operating synergies and management efficiency), the value of the company could be much greater to that particular buyer. If the deal is a horizontal deal, the acquiring company may have better information than the financial markets about the long-term potential of the target in terms of competitive positioning, product development, sales, and so on. The problem here is that even if the acquirer has more information, they may fail to turn it into intelligence because the systems do not exist to do so. Often, knowledge will slosh around an organization without being adequately managed in order to deliver added value.

- **Pure diversification** can be valuable in its own right and may in fact also be faster and more efficient than growth through internal means. Diversification is often preferred by the existing management of the acquiring company, especially in situations where the existing markets (and therefore opportunities) are mature. Of course, shareholders can diversify much more efficiently and selectively than can the company itself, so what is best for the management and employees of the bidder may not be in the best interest of the stockholders.

- One ploy sometimes used is called **'information and signaling.'** Just by making an offer, additional value is created as the target is put into play. This assumes and follows the empirical evidence that most target company share prices rise when a new bid is received. If the offer carries new information (and the fact that there is an interested bidder may be sufficient new information), then the increase in share price may be permanent. But even when unsuccessful, it may result in a revaluation of the target's share price. In any case, the target management is now

> sensitized to the fact that they could be a takeover target and may work to make the company more efficient in response.
>
> • Since it is almost impossible for shareholders in public companies to replace inefficient or poorly performing management, where **agency problems** (separation of ownership by shareholders and control by managers) exist – as in most public companies – acquisitions can be a solution. This is similar, therefore, to the differential management efficiency discussion above. Acquisitions are a discipline to managers when other, internal, mechanisms of corporate control have failed. The threat of being acquired can often be sufficient to assist in solving the agency problems.
>
> • **Managerialism and hubris** drive deals all too often. Managers are interested in size ('big = better') and do deals to increase the company size and therefore their personal power, compensation, perquisites, and so on. Managers are often overly optimistic in evaluating mergers, due to pride, 'macho' culture, or hubris, and do not learn from the past when most deals end in failure.
>
> • **Tax considerations** are sometimes the impetus to merge – but rarely the only reason; there may be tax-minimizing opportunities in some mergers.

PUBLIC SECTOR MERGERS

Although the focus of this book and the examples shown are heavily from the private sector, the principles discussed apply to public and non-profit sector mergers as well. Certain differences should be noted. It would be a rare public sector deal that was hostile, as these mergers are often the result of both long consultation periods and, at least in the democratic world, a long process driving toward consensus. That isn't to say that public sector mergers cannot be driven by one individual – such as New York City's Mayor Rudolph Giuliani's three attempts to merge two health departments in the State of New York which were ultimately legislated in November 2001. But even when initiated by one individual or group, the ultimate decision usually follows a democratic process.

Public sector mergers are becoming more common. This is largely in response to budget pressures and the increase in demands for accountability that have forced governments and non-profit organizations to improve their performance and achieve key targets to satisfy the public demand for their services, as shown in the example from the UK's NHS in the box.

Mergers and acquisitions within the National Health Service in the UK

The National Health Service (NHS) runs the lion's share of hospitals, primary care facilities, ambulance services, and many other services in the health sector in the UK. In recent years, there has been a significant effort to upgrade the standards of health services in the NHS through the creation of Foundation Trusts, with standards originally modeled after the private sector.

As part of this upgrade, the UK government has been encouraging NHS Trusts to merge. This is expected to be especially attractive to the government when a well-run trust – which has already achieved Foundation Trust status – would merge with a trust that has been in trouble, either on financial grounds, because there has been a clinical failure, or because it has otherwise missed key government targets in terms of standards.

The first such merger has taken place between the Heart of England Foundation Trust and Good Hope Hospital. This had the approval of the Strategic Health Authority and the boards of the two organizations. The support of Monitor, the UK regulator of the Foundation Trusts, in all such mergers was conditional on the outcome of risk evaluations assessments. The deal is expected to allow for the improvement of health services in the region around Birmingham served by the two NHS organizations.

As with private sector acquisitions, public sector mergers can also be triggered by external shocks. The terrorist attacks in the United States on September 11, 2001 led to a reorganization within the federal government of the US where some 22 departments (including border patrol, immigration screening, and airport security) were combined to form the Department of Homeland Security. This was akin to a similar reorganization that took place in the US after World War II when the War Department became the principal component of the newly created Department of Defense. These mergers were driven by demands to improve the quality of management and services as well as the need to increase efficiency, coordination, accountability, and cost savings.

Merger of the UK Foreign Office and Commonwealth Office

The Foreign Office was formed in 1782 originally as the Foreign Department. In 1919, Lord Palmerston merged it with the Diplomatic Service and again in 1943, it merged with the Commercial Diplomatic Service and the Consular Service. These changes were in response to the increasing complexity of the management of foreign relations, such as an increase in embassies throughout the world and the expanding demand for passport issuance as greater numbers of people traveled.

The Commonwealth Office was formed from a merger of the Commonwealth Relations Office and the Colonial Office in 1966. This was driven by a change in the status of the former British colonies after World War II. Most of those colonies were now independent and the Colonial Office was no longer needed. The Colonial Office had been set up in 1660 from the Council for Trade and Plantation, so had a history even longer than the Foreign Office.

The new office – the Foreign and Commonwealth Office – was formed in October 1968, having taken seven months to complete. It was driven by the need to increase efficiency and eliminate overlapping roles with the changes in the nature of the former colonies and other countries. It was an amicable deal, and both organizations supported the combination. Given that both had long histories of prior mergers, it was seen as just another step in a long line of change, although naturally there were significant differences in drivers to the most recent merger.

CONCLUSION

From whichever perspective one views M&A activity – whether economic, strategic, financial, managerial, organizational, or personal – corporate takeovers should permit firms and organizations to promote growth and offer savings while achieving a significant and sustainable competitive advantage over their rivals within the global marketplace. With new geographic and service markets opening at an unprecedented pace, the evolution of the competitive landscape means that acquisitions must be made in order for the company to succeed in filling the product, geographic coverage, and talent gaps. As such, an acquisition provides senior management or a board of directors with the opportunity to grow more quickly than would otherwise be possible, with access to new customers, new technologies, greater synergies, and the power that comes with size. It is also an adrenaline rush for all involved at the top, despite the possibility that many will be made redundant including some senior managers driving the deal.

M&A deals are risky. A full merger or acquisition should be attempted only as a last resort. (We will briefly discuss the alternatives to M&A later in Chapter 5.) Full integration may take years to complete, and therefore the benefits may be a long time coming. Current employees, customers, and suppliers may be neglected. There's the tendency to overpay when acquiring another company, not just because of the auction effect if there are multiple bidders for the target, but also because the sellers are motivated to get the highest price possible and they are the ones who know their own company best – where the skeletons are hidden and which assets are most valuable. For bidder and target alike, it is critical to use business intelligence efficiently. There are many areas where mistakes can be made in the acquisition of another company.

Merging or acquiring can be a threat to the current shareholders or a great opportunity. The outcome is never preordained. It is necessary to crawl carefully through the minefield, using as much intelligence as possible to avoid the potential and often very real dangers.

CHAPTER 2

BUSINESS INTELLIGENCE

At the time of writing, there are two stories in the business press which perfectly illustrate the need for quality business intelligence in the M&A process. First is the ongoing saga of EMI's troubles. Its two most senior executives have been dismissed, costs have been drastically cut and management slashed. All this shortly after EMI had rejected an offer from the private equity firm Permira to acquire the company at more than 300 pence per share. The share price has fallen to 245.25 pence per share despite the continuing takeover speculation. The *Wall Street Journal* suggested that Permira refused to increase its bid just before Christmas 2006 because of the surprisingly poor showing of the new Robbie Williams and Janet Jackson albums. Major investors such as Fidelity and Schroeders have offloaded EMI shares.

The EMI restructuring is an implicit admission that it had failed to anticipate a marketplace that now includes YouTube, MySpace, and, more importantly, iTunes. This was a classic case of an intelligence failure. Intelligence failures generally occur, despite the wealth of information available, because of a lack of a systemic intelligence function and consequently a lack of suitable analysis for decision makers to draw upon. All the players in the EMI game appear to have been surprised by entirely predictable events. In business there is no such thing as a pleasant surprise; any surprise is worrying because it indicates weak intelligence systems. To quote Sun Tsu from the *Art of War*, 'it will not do to act without knowing the opponent's condition; and to know the opponent's condition is impossible without intelligence.'

The second story concerns Hewlett-Packard's boardroom spying/pretexting scandal which claimed its first conviction when a private investigator pleaded guilty to using illegal intelligence-gathering activities in collecting information on board members. There will almost certainly be a domino effect which could claim the already disgraced former HP chairman, Patricia Dunn.

What the EMI and HP stories teach us is that intelligence should be at the very heart of all corporate endeavors and often is not. If the US auto industry, which itself is in considerable danger, had heeded Sun Tsu's advice it would not have been stuck with a truck and SUV (sports utility vehicle) strategy while Toyota and Honda were seducing the American public with hybrid cars. The US manufacturers failed adequately to create, maintain, or use properly functions within their organizations responsible for monitoring, analyzing, and predicting the external environment. Most of the companies external sensory functions were either not working or not registering at the policy level. According to two Wharton professors, George Day and Paul Schoemaker, the reason Ford's external antennae were not working was because the President and CEO, William Clayton Ford III, was not a 'vigilant leader' but rather an operational leader ('more controlling, focused on efficiency and cost cutting, and doesn't explore outside potential'). In fact, they argue that the variety of roles that Bill Ford took upon himself, when he ousted Jaq Nasser, meant that he was not sufficiently competent at either the internal (operational) or external (vigilant) sides of the business.

The reason this conversation is significant for M&A activity lies in the title of Day and Schoemaker's book – *Peripheral Vision: Detecting the Weak Signals that will Make or Break your Company*. A recent global workforce research study shows that less than half of employees believe that they are in safe hands and that their executives are taking steps to ensure the long-term success of their organizations. For example, it seemed as if virtually every sales floor staff member in the retailer Marks & Spencer knew that customers wanted to use their own credit cards, everyone that is except the management; just as for years, American soldiers returning from Vietnam told of an 'unwinnable war' and nobody except Clive Sinclair even considered the possibility that the C5 electric vehicle could succeed.

How, then, should organizations avoid such catastrophes? The answer is by staying in close touch with the external environment.

When the devastating tsunami struck Indonesia in 2004, two groups emerged relatively unscathed: they were indigenous tribal people and animals. They survived because they had instinctively moved to the safety of higher ground. They detected even the weakest signals because their senses were so acute and active. Because they recognized an existential environmental threat and also had a healthy respect for what the environment can do, their antennae were permanently up. They understood that if they ignored the environment, it could do them serious harm. Corporations that ignore the balance between external and internal demands are almost certainly doomed to the equivalent of business tsunamis. We may have just seen EMI's version. The success of organizations engaged in M&A activity should start, therefore, with the external environment in which M&A will take place.

> ### Viable Systems Model
>
> In the late 1960s and early 1970s, Stafford Beer, one of the giants of cybernetics and systems theory, developed an all-encompassing organizational model which he entitled the Viable Systems Model (VSM). The model was based on what Beer called 'a management system which we know, first-hand, to be admirable and survival-worthy: the human nervous system.' In 1999, Bill Gates wrote in his book, *Business at the Speed of Thought*, that 'to function in the digital age, we have developed a new digital infrastructure. It's like the human nervous system.'
>
> Both recognized the value of using the human nervous system as a model for dealing with complexity. However, while Gates was attempting to sell what we would today refer to as business intelligence (BI) technology, Beer was trying to sell a conceptual solution to the organizational problems of simultaneously dealing with internal issues while engaging with the external environment. Beer recognized that a system, any system (perhaps especially a business), could not simply look inwards but must also be adaptable, responsive, and pro-active in its relations with its environment.

THE INTELLIGENCE SYSTEM

The way in which the most successful organizations do this is by honing the performance of what Beer refers to as 'System Four,' the 'intelligence' system. In the VSM, System Four is the function responsible for all things 'external and future.' The other functions are responsible for 'policy' (System Five), 'coordination' (System Two), 'operations' (System One), and 'monitoring' (System Three). So, whereas System Three is concerned with 'internal and present,' System Four ('intelligence') is only concerned with 'external and future.' Additionally, and this is where Beer's view of the intelligence function differs from most, he sees that function as not only responsible for information incoming from the environment but also for projecting information into the environment. So, for Beer, marketing, PR, and advertising would be part of the intelligence function. It is also our view that such a function is an integral element of the M&A process.

For anyone in the government or military, of course, this is not unusual. In those organizations, intelligence has always had a dual collection/dissemination role, albeit often confused with disinformation. Incidentally, disinformation is also important in M&A and the experienced practitioners of M&A are expert users of disinformation, although it will often be referred to only in the context of 'signaling' the market about intentions. Deceiving potential targets and other players in the game is an essential skill. For business, however, the idea of a wholly coordinated and integrated intelligence function is not universally accepted – or at least in modern business it appears not to be.

Ironically, in the late 16th and early 17th centuries, it was considered essential. The East India Company, for example, employed what might be considered the father of economic intelligence. Richard Hakluyt was appointed, in 1602, 'to set down in writing a note of the principal places in the East Indies where trade is to be had.' It was an obvious appointment because Hakluyt had already published *The Principal Navigations, Voyages and Discoveries of the English Nation*, a tome which consisted of over 500 reports collated from other reports delivered by the complete gamut of European travelers, from explorers to pirates and colonists. These reports provided data on navigation, geography, resources, politics, and economics from every corner of the known world.

BUSINESS INTELLIGENCE INDUSTRY

Of course, in the modern era, such intelligence activities are largely outsourced, usually on an ad hoc basis. Indeed, there is a modern company named after Hakluyt which claims its primary activities are to 'promote commerce by the provision, supervision, and facilitation of business activities engaged in the research and supply of information for the use of commerce, trade, and industry in the UK and elsewhere.' The *Financial Times* in 1995 described it as a 'body established to give British companies the inside information they need when contemplating big ventures in foreign countries.' If that sounds a bit like traditional Foreign and Commonwealth Office (FCO) old boy networking in 'foreign' lands, it is because that is precisely its nature.

However, while the business intelligence industry might have started as an adjunct to the FCO in the UK, there are now more professional outfits providing a much more business-like approach to the intelligence function. The Knowledge Processing Outsourcing sector globally generated £200 million in revenues in 2006 which represented a 59% increase from 2005. Frost & Sullivan estimate that the figure will reach £2.5 billion by 2010.

Whether traditional or modern, the intelligence function remains the same – to be the eyes and ears of the organization,

---

Deloitte's Business Intelligence Business

Deloitte, for example, have grown their business intelligence business from the 'one woman and her dog' of several years ago to a 50+ unit accounting for significant turnover in 2006. Emma Codd, the lead partner, estimates that the majority of Deloitte's intelligence business is deep due diligence in the emerging markets of the former Soviet Union. For this, she needs operatives on the ground who can be contracted on an ad hoc basis to provide targeted information as and when required. The operatives at the center need to have the attributes of the insatiable learner – for two reasons. First, that is the job; second, there aren't any ready-made courses designed for the intelligence business.

to gather and, more importantly, analyze information which provides a competitive advantage. Of course, examples of failures to engage are numerous. Notwithstanding the classic and well-documented cases such as Marks & Spencer and IBM (initially missing the personal computer market), there are others that make the case for external engagement just as powerfully. As previously mentioned, there are also the failures of the big US auto companies to see 'green-ness' as a business opportunity, record companies to see the internet as a channel for piracy, and internet gambling companies to see that the US Congress would actually legislate against its activities.

Why, then, does it appear so difficult for organizations to engage with the external environment? First, as most observers agree, there is a perception of greater complexity in the modern business environment. Getting to the other side of that complexity clearly involves greater knowledge of the environment but also greater knowledge of how to deal with complexity. Again, it is worth returning to the middle of the last century for advice. This time to the writings of Ross Ashby, who even had his own 'law' – Ashby's Law of Requisite Variety. The essence of the law is captured in Ashby's contention that 'only variety absorbs variety.' Substitute the mid-20th century use of the term 'variety' with today's 'complexity,' and you will better understand his 'law.' What this means is that there should be a balance between the environmental complexity and the complexity of the organization seeking to control that environment. This can be done either by expanding (amplifying) or contracting (attenuating) the complexity in one or more of the parts. Justin King, CEO of the large UK food retailer Sainsbury's, put it in 21st century language when he said: 'Strategic advantage is still there. In a more complex environment, equally complex strategic solutions are necessary.'

General Electric and Microsoft, for example, can be characterized as organizations that expand their complexity to meet the complexity of the environment. They acquire and/or grow the diversity of their organizations. This requires extreme sensitivity to environmental dynamism. The acquisitive gazes of the traditional media companies at new media outlets such as the internet and mobile phones are clear examples. They need such a foothold to enable their content to remain king. They need to increase the 'variety' of their own organizations.

How they do that is the stuff of strategy, of course. That is why when a company such as Friends Reunited came on the market in 2006, a variety of content specialists such as News-Corp, Trinity Mirror, the *Daily Mail*, ITV, and BT immediately began to hover. Thus, Virgin needs NTL to get into TV, NTL needs Virgin's brand and mobile phone capabilities, and suddenly the group can provide the quadruple offer (pay TV, mobile phone, traditional phone, and internet). So, BSkyB buy Easynet (a broadband internet provider) and ITV buys Friends Reunited. All such deals are attempts to amplify complexity in the organization. Interestingly, BSkyB's acquisition of ITV shares was aimed at restricting NTL/Virgin's complexity. Conversely, other organizations are offloading businesses in order to concentrate on what they perceive as 'core' businesses. These businesses are effectively contracting the environment with which they intend to engage. According to Ashby, either solution can work; what cannot work is an imbalance in variety.

The second reason why organizations fail to engage with the environment is that they do not believe it is necessary. They become complacent. They believe that their approach has worked, is working, and will, therefore, continue to work. They fail even to observe the environment, much less respond to it. Again, the US auto industry is an obvious example.

Finally, and perhaps most significantly, organizations simply fail to give sufficient thought and resources to intelligence as a function. To quote the work of Sun Tsu again, 'the reason the enlightened leader and wise general conquer the enemy, and their achievements surpass those of ordinary men, is foreknowledge.'

However, Sun Tsu also points out that unwise leaders often choose to limit the effectiveness of the intelligence function by according it too little value and consequently too few resources – 'to fail to know the condition of opponents because of a reluctance to give rewards for intelligence is uncharacteristic of a true leader . . . uncharacteristic of a victorious chief.'

WHAT'S OUT THERE?

Having a highly effective intelligence function would enable even those organizations that do observe the environment to increase their chances of survival and prosperity whether through a period of organic growth, acquisition, or post-merger integration. They could more accurately detect external threats which include the obvious market concerns, such as how competitors are behaving, but equally is concerned with aggressive competitors, criminals, and environmental changes. Corporate fraud, identity theft, reputational damage, computer spying, and the vulnerability of online commerce, for example, are all issues that must be addressed. In 1999, cyber-crime losses in the US ran at somewhere near $250 million; in 2007, it is expected to be closer to $3 billion. Attempted ransom attacks on companies such as Yahoo and eBay, where the essence of the business is the technology, are obvious targets although, to be fair, companies that rely primarily on their technology mostly take adequate precautions.

However, evidence suggests that many other businesses are still complacent about cyber-crime, particularly such dangers as the theft of corporate data and consumer data theft. The open nature of the internet and the rapid turnover of innovative net technology mean that new channels are constantly being opened up for the cyber-criminal. It is estimated that a majority of web servers are still vulnerable to hacking attacks. Such threats are not two, three, four years old and now under control; they are current and ongoing. The good news, according to a source at the British National Hi-Tech Crime Unit, is that avoiding such traps is relatively easy – 'don't take the bait.'

Easier said than done. The reason criminals thrive in cyber-space is not the technology, but the people. Most of us are either inexperienced with modern technology or just plain ignorant. We do not have sufficient knowledge to sense vulnerability. John Naughton of *The Observer* told a great, possibly apocryphal, story which makes the point precisely. According to Naughton, he supervised a project team at a nuclear installation. Apparently, the guys there ran a competition to see who could get into the site with the most ridiculous security pass. The winner was waved through using a box of John West sardines. Of course, this may just be a story but it is one with which we can all identify.

Irrespective of the quality of technological security, human beings will mess up; they will use predictable passwords, they will stick those passwords in open view, they will talk in public places; human beings will be unaware of the dangers of 'drive-by' hacking – that is hacking into laptops using wireless connections in public places such as Starbucks.

Added to simply human inadequacy is criminal activity, another human failure. In early 2005, for example, a British immigrant in the US was jailed for 14 years for his part in a $100 million identity theft scam. Philip Cummings did not use 'spyware' or 'phishing,' instead he simply stole the information as it crossed his desk as part of his work on the helpdesk of the US company Teledata Communications. He downloaded the data onto a laptop and passed that laptop to a criminal gang. The gang, in turn, drained the accounts of as many as 30 000 US citizens.

The point is, no matter how sophisticated hackers are, they need access like any other thief; the easiest way to gain access is for somebody on the inside to open the door. Also, memory sticks and MP3 players make data theft relatively quick and easy. No anti-virus software, anti-spyware software, or firewall can protect against the insider. And don't think that insiders are passive until activated by nasty outsiders. They can be planted in an organization. As Callum McCarthy, the chairman of the UK Financial Services Authority, has stated, 'There is increasing evidence that organised criminal groups are placing their own people in financial services firms so that they can increase their knowledge of firms' systems and controls, and thus circumvent them to commit their frauds.'

Not only can such activities cause enormous commercial damage, they can also cause major reputational damage.

Bank of Ireland CEO quits over 'adult' websites

The Bank of Ireland had outsourced their IT function to Hewlett-Packard in 2003. As reported by Reuters, in early April 2004, a limited audit of internet usage was extended to include the CEO, Mike Soden's personal computer. The audit found that he had accessed an adult website. The results were leaked to the press. Within two months Soden was gone.

Consider the case of the former Bank of Ireland CEO, shown in the box above. Who extended the audit? Who leaked the results? An employee disaffected by the outsourcing move? A board rival? In one sense, it is irrelevant; what is relevant is that this was external damage perpetrated from the inside. This could be particularly damaging while an M&A deal is being negotiated. For example, consider what unauthorized and commercially sensitive information a disaffected employee in the finance or payroll departments, much less in sales or research, could reveal during a hostile bid or an M&A due diligence process.

Clearly, the Bank of Ireland case was malicious but, returning to human frailty, most reputational damage results from the deadly combination of carelessness and the e-mail, as shown in the box below.

> **Danger of e-mails**
>
> Between 1999 and 2001, Henry Blodget, one of Merrill Lynch's top analysts, sent e-mails that described a company as a 'piece of junk;' unfortunately, it was a company Merrill had categorized as a 'buy.' Blodget became one of the first bankers to be hoisted by the e-mail petard when the US Securities and Exchange Commission banned him for life and extracted a $4 million fine. He wasn't, and won't be, the last.

This case didn't occur during merger or acquisition negotiations, but if it had, it could have scuppered the deal. Remember Nick Leeson's $1.6 billion fraud in 1995. That led to the downfall of Barings Brothers and its ultimate acquisition by ING Bank for a mere £1. Leeson had concealed trades, but the Bank of England had concluded that both internal and external controls (intelligence) failed to detect this.

While we have concentrated here on malicious external threats, the same intelligence function would also be responsible for scanning the environment for generic market threats and M&A opportunities. Environmental scanning will be dealt with in more detail later in the chapter. It is clear that engaging with the environment is not a benign, nice-to-do activity; it goes to the very heart of the survival of the organization and it is essential that the entire workforce understands the significance of the activities.

HOW DO WE PROJECT THE COMPANY'S MESSAGE INTO THE ENVIRONMENT?

In reality, the above explanation about the intelligence function should be common-sense, notwithstanding the fact that few organizations take it as seriously as they should. However, as noted earlier, what the Viable System Model also promotes is the idea that the intelligence function should not only be responsible for data incoming from the environment, but should also have responsibility for projecting information into the environment. At its simplest, this entails sending messages about the organization's identity (brand), intentions (strategy), and activities (products). It can, of course, also include disinformation, spinning, and black ops.

Looking at the brand issue, for example, indicates why Beer believed the projection and collection of knowledge from and to the environment should be integrated. The way in which 'brand' is projected into the environment is as important as the way it is protected from the environment. As demonstrated earlier, reputation can be easily damaged and must be defended. A damaged reputation can cut millions from a bid price and seriously weaken bargaining positions. However, that protection must start with the manner in which the messages are sent. This is what differentiates VSM. Using the VSM approach entails simultaneity of protection and projection. The one informs the other. Thus, analysis of the environment (traditional research) can identify opportunities for marketing, sales, and negotiators. It also enables the organization to build trust by activities such as corporate social responsibility (CSR) and sponsorship, as well as other previously disconnected activities. What could be more similar to a traditional intelligence activity, for example, than viral marketing – it's a classic propaganda exercise.

The beauty of VSM is that it co-locates these activities under a single function which naturally generates sharing and naturally eliminates siloism. This is, of course, the very claim made by business intelligence (BI) systems vendors. Corporate performance management (CPM) is the latest of such 'products.' As Oracle pitched it on their website in May 2005, 'CPM aims to underpin corporate performance and governance by delivering timely, accurate, relevant, accessible information to every desktop. It gives a company a single, x-ray view through the entire organization. . . .' No problem, then. Performance and governance dealt with by an expensive IT system. And, of course, this one will be the one that actually works. The fact that, by most estimates, as much as 80% of CRM (Client Relationship Management), BI, or CPM capacity is never used is too easily ignored. The answer to the question of how best to engage with the external environment may not be to install a costly BI product, but to create an organizational intelligence system, a System Four. But how?

REVIEW

The first thing to do is initiate a review of the components of the company's external interaction. This does not need to be a six month formal review carried out by a consultant and costing a fortune. A day's facilitated brainstorming with the senior management team, fully engaged (which probably means off-site), should suffice. The objective would be to identify any gaps in the external provision, any disconnections between the components. If, however, the company is similar to one of the over 50% of Fortune 500 companies which has an intelligence input into the development of their strategies, then the review will deal with the existing effectiveness of that input. As stated, the review process need not be complicated or expensive, but it will be resource intensive and the resource will be the brainpower and thinking time of the senior management team, and not just for the day of the brainstorming.

Prior to the brainstorming, divisional heads must access the latent knowledge stored in their staff. Here, we recommend a revolutionary technique – ask them and listen to the answers. Not by e-mail or fax or memo, but in person. And make the questions simple: 'what extra information would make a big difference to your numbers if we were able to provide it?' 'Where do you think we might find it?' 'What's stopping us getting it?'

Collate the results of that process and the resultant document becomes the foundation of the brainstorming. When Allan Leighton joined the Royal Mail as the new CEO he did not visit his office for at least a week; he was too busy out asking questions of the workforce. The same applies to the due diligence process in an acquisition, as we will discuss in a later chapter.

The other early issue the review must address is that of outsourcing. Is the intelligence function compatible with outsourcing? The answer is that like most functions it can be outsourced. In fact, the fastest growing outsourcing business is what is referred to as KPO (knowledge process outsourcing). India has, again, led the way. A variety of small companies with, on average, about 30 employees have sprung up to satisfy the intelligence needs of the large corporates. Indeed, General Electric has taken a large stake in one such company, GECIS, which is the big kid on the block. Others, such as Office Tiger and Fractal Analytics are also doing great business. These companies have bought access to virtually every database on earth and with their teams of highly educated graduates they can respond to what is referred to as activated or targeted intelligence requests almost immediately.

STRUCTURE

Having identified the gaps or inefficiencies in the company's established intelligence system, remedies must be implemented. For example, if the intelligence system is viewed as the conduit without which other systems cannot succeed, then consider co-locating the marketing, IT, and R&D under the direction of a single head, the chief intelligence officer (CIO) perhaps.

Of course, structural change is not enough on its own. There must also be a cultural shift. Most importantly, there need to be transparent rewards for sharing information. An organizational check in virtually any company will almost certainly find that it actually rewards hoarding information. For example, imagine getting the sales teams together and asking them to fully share client information. Now imagine the response. Precisely how to change the culture from hoarding to sharing will be particular to each organizational situation, but this is an area where it is clearly worth expending serious thinking time. Without changing this cultural mindset and engendering a thirst for intelligence, developing the intelligence products is pointless.

Products

It may be that internally advertising the product range can actually stimulate recognition of the value of those products and change the culture. Essentially, there are seven intelligence products that a mature intelligence function can provide:

1. Immediate intelligence
2. Continuing intelligence
3. Technical intelligence
4. Analytical intelligence
5. Internal intelligence consulting
6. Activated intelligence
7. Counter-intelligence

IMMEDIATE INTELLIGENCE

This is intended to provide end-users with intelligence within a 24-hour time frame. It is usually collected from open sources and passed to the user without any significant, or in some cases no, analysis. It is either requested on an 'alert' basis or is part of a 'daily briefing' delivered via e-mail, intranet, or hard copy. Given that this product is resource intensive, it may be sensible to outsource to one of the fast-growing KPO firms mentioned earlier in the chapter.

Ashish Gupta, the country head of one of them, Evalueserve, describes the service they provide as, 'research on tap.' KPO companies employ knowledge workers who become the out-sourced intelligence function for banks and consumer product companies, for example. KPO can provide the analysis upon which early decisions concerning M&A are based when all the data sources are external to the target as no contract has yet been made which would allow internal due diligence to start. The labour-intensive report compilation can also be outsourced which would free up the expensive time of London- and NY-based investment bankers to concentrate on other value-added activi-ties, including the face-to-face meetings to generate deal flow. It would also have the added benefit of physically separating the research and trading functions at the heart of many recent finan-cial scandals.

The National Association of Software Services Companies (NASSCOM), the Indian trade association, estimate that the KPO industry will be worth $17 billion by 2010; that is a 15-fold increase. If true, it means that your competitors will probably be using it. Although the KPO option has been included in this section on immediate intel, it should be obvious that it can also be used for most of the intelligence products that follow.

CONTINUING INTELLIGENCE

In contrast to the 'quick and dirty' intelligence provided by the 'immediate' product, the 'continuing' product is rigorously researched, analyzed, and documented. Delivering this product entails continuous monitoring of the competitive environment – competitors, trends, and irregularities – in fact, anything that can add competitive advantage. Continuing intelligence is rarely actively disseminated; rather it becomes an element of the intel-ligence database from which decision makers can draw informa-tion. Of course, it is necessary for the holders of the database to advertise its value and availability to the internal market. This is a powerful reason for fully integrating the intelligence function. By so doing, the users can influence the content of the database on an iterative process. An M&A deal originating anywhere in the organization will therefore know of its existence and even be experienced users. This is a true competitive edge in the vicious world of M&A where every advantage needs to be taken.

TECHNICAL INTELLIGENCE

Traditionally, this has been an area of intelligence seen as competitively neutral. The idea was to maintain technological competitiveness and to manage R&D and new product development projects effectively. However, the environment has changed because the modern consumer is much more sophisticated and now views product content in technological terms. Technology is not simply the way in which corporations adapt to market demands; rather it is a significant product attribute. It is not the fact of having a car that functions which adds competitive advantage, but the technology inside the car which differentiates it.

Consequently, the way in which organizations pick up technology signals from the environment is as crucial as their technological prowess. One group of researchers (Schattzel, Iles and Kiyek) suggested that a 'firm's capability to receive technological demand signals from buyers, its technology demand receptivity (TDR), influences its response to those signals and, thus, influences R&D, as well as new product development efforts and, consequently, its overall industry competitiveness.' In the past, this has been done by keeping a close eye on technologies emerging from research institutes or universities; sponsoring chairs, for example, has enabled companies to get early sight of developments.

The future will require that even with research, siloism is no longer acceptable. Depth of knowledge will be required across industries which are liable to converge and therefore drive further mergers and acquisitions. Imagine, for example, the convergence of TV, the internet, and the gambling industry. Online poker will eventually converge with TV poker, computer game poker, and real poker. The organization which imagines that convergence and monitors the technology to enable it will be the one to benefit first and possibly most. This will be in spite of the recent legal restrictions imposed by the US. In fact, these restrictions have made creativity even more important.

ANALYTICAL INTELLIGENCE

In a sense, the early warning receptivity necessary for technological competitiveness precisely mirrors one part of the analytical product so essential to an organization's survival. The first part of the analytical process is to provide advance warning of emerging opportunities and/or threats. In its simplest form, this might be 'intelligence alerts.' However, such an interpretation of an early warning system fails to understand the true value of the product.

What actually needs to happen is two-fold; *first*, the intelligence analysts must develop a comprehensive list of potential indicators and a capacity for doing so effectively to the *second* phase which consists of scanning the environment. In that way, as the environmental signals begin to arrive they can be immediately checked against the dashboard of indicators previously developed. Each M&A deal will have its own dashboard, designed and developed specifically for that transaction.

Absorptive capacity

Organizations need to develop what has become known as 'absorptive capacity.' Cohen and Leventhal, who originated the concept, argue that 'the ability of a firm to recognize the value of new, external information, assimilate it, and apply it to commercial ends is critical to its innovative capabilities.' It is, therefore, essential to understand the sources of an organization's absorptive capacity. These range from the traditional R&D function to the diversity of expertise within an organization. The research shows a clear and direct correlation between the organization's prior related knowledge and its ability to absorb new externally generated knowledge. Thus a failure to invest in developing diversity of knowledge may actually impede future development in a particular area. The conclusion must be that what we, in this book, refer to as the intelligence function and business innovation are completely interdependent and symbiotic.

If that is the case, then the manner in which the holders of diverse knowledge interact internally becomes of vital concern to the business when trying to absorb external information. Clearly, such recognition reinforces the anti-silo imperative that we have argued is needed for technological innovation. Organizations must, therefore, put in place procedures to enhance 'absorptive capacity.' These can include communication and knowledge-sharing routines between departments and partners.

Environmental scanning

However, to leverage fully its absorptive capacity, an organization must also be actively seeking greater knowledge. This is where environmental scanning is so important. The Indonesian tsunami avoiders mentioned at the start of the chapter may do this instinctively but firms must do it consciously. According to a survey conducted by the Fuld-Gilad-Herring Academy of Competitive Intelligence more than 65% of 140 corporate strategists interviewed admitted to being surprised by as many as three high-impact competitive events in the past five years. Such surprises

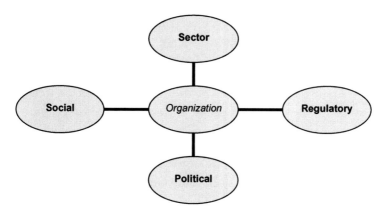

Figure 2.1 Organizational Environment.

can only be avoided by continuous scanning of the environment. The significant environment for any organization consists of the four subsets, indicated in Figure 2.1, which continually impact that organization.

Sector: Naturally, sector-specific information is central to competitive intelligence requirements. Data in this sphere should include competitor analysis, technological developments, customer activity, supplier details, and potential targets or attackers.

Regulatory: Regulatory issues such as financial reporting rules or foreign ownership laws can have huge commercial ramifications. Rupert Murdoch's entry into the US to expand his global media empire, for example, was fraught with regulatory obstacles, many of which were overcome with US citizenship. Internet gambling is another obvious example of an industry desperate for regulatory intelligence.

Political: Knowledge of political factors including local, regional, and national economic climates should be a prerequisite of the decision making process. The attempt by the United Arab Emirates-owned P&O to acquire US ports in early 2006 was ultimately thwarted by political reaction. An earlier and more sensitive intelligence assessment may have contributed to the development of a different entry strategy that would have delivered a more favorable result.

Social: Similarly, social concerns, such as shifts in ethnic, gender, age, or national characteristics, could massively affect a company's ability to operate and prosper in a particular environment.

In *Peripheral Vision*, mentioned earlier, Day and Schoemaker have developed what they refer to as a 'strategic eye exam.' This is 'a diagnostic tool for evaluating and sharpening companies' peripheral vision.' The exam tests an organization's strategy, the complexity and volatility of its environment, its leadership orientation, awareness of its own knowledge management systems, and its structures and incentives. An awareness of an organization's peripheral capability, the authors argue, allows companies to scan the environment more effectively for such surprises as that which befell P&O's US acquisition strategy.

Perhaps the most important advice to emerge from their book is the simple device of concentrating on 'open' questioning. Answering a question such as 'What will the world look like in 2020?' is of an entirely different order to a quantitative question such as 'What are our sales figures for Q1?' Both have their place but a predominance of either can be dangerous.

Scenario planning

Having scanned the environment and separated the signals from the noise, how does the analytical product then add the most value in mergers and acquisitions? The answer is by scenario planning. The first thing to realize is that the process of scenario planning is the consequence of a culture obsessed by the future – its risks and opportunities.

Another company famed for its extensive usage of scenario planning is Shell. Using their own jargon, Shell's scenarios team is tasked to 'help charter routes across three interrelated levels; the

Scenario Planning at Samsung

At Samsung, for example, scenario planning is enshrined in what is referred to as their VIP (Value Innovation Programme) House. The house is where the Samsung product managers, researchers, engineers, and assorted others 'live' while solving problems and/or planning projects. The reason that this house is considered so important is because Samsung believes that 70–80% of 'quality, cost, and delivery time is determined in the initial stages of product development.'

Samsung's CEO and Vice Chairman, Jong-Young Yun, is clear about one thing: 'The race for survival in this world is not to the strongest but to the most adaptive.' Like the tsunami tribes and animals, he views the business world as an environment of existential threat and potential disaster. The VIP house provides his disaster avoidance radar.

Jet Stream level of long-term trends, uncertainties, and forces: the Weather Systems that reflect specific features of key regions; and the Turbulence of market level factors.' To get a feel for the Jet Stream level, go to www.shell.com/scenarios. Whether a scenario planning function is structured as a Samsung hot-house or a highly centralized Shell-like group, the point is to monitor simultaneously the past, present, and future. In all instances in addition to the expected, it is essential to attempt to imagine the unimaginable. From those imaginings, scenarios must be built such that when a 'new' scenario presents itself, it is recognizable.

If a company cannot afford the infrastructure to deliver such comprehensive reports as part of their acquisition planning, then use alternative means. The US National Intelligence Council, for example, provides free scenario projections on their www.dni. gov/nic site. Although generic in nature, this site is a good jumping-off point at the start of the merger planning process.

Also, because humans find it difficult to calculate probability rationally, a company's intelligence function can use the power of the bookmaker. Daymon Runyon, paraphrasing Ecclesiastes, said that 'The race might not be to the swift, not the battle to the strong but that's where the smart money goes.' By using trading (e.g. www.intrade.com) and/or spread-betting (e.g. www.cantorindex.com) sites, a company can see how the world really views the likelihood of specific events and, significantly, how their own company is viewed by the market. In 2003, an insensitive but smart analyst at DARPA (the Pentagon's Defense Advance Research Projects Agency) proposed setting up a speculative futures market on terrorist attacks. Notwithstanding the obvious temptation for real terrorists, the idea was sound. Getting people to bet real money on future events focuses the thinking of those people and saves the inordinate costs of expensive computer models. There really is wisdom in crowds.

Companies could actually create their own internal speculative markets to leverage the knowledge contained within the organization. By allowing employees to bet on specific questions (using company money for real returns), an efficient market for ideas can be created. More real, more relevant, and more fun than a 'suggestions box'! Apparently, the pharmaceutical company Eli Lilly has used this approach to predict the success of drug research with remarkable accuracy, and there is no reason to doubt its applicability to the M&A market as well.

INTERNAL INTELLIGENCE CONSULTANCY

Many companies fail to utilize their intelligence analysts as fully as they might. Embedding analysts within internal M&A teams allows the analyst to provide targeted and timely intelligence to the group. Another internal function that the intelligence community can provide is the establishment of educational seminars to a variety of users to provide product and service visibility, and to promote the value added by the intelligence function. Employees are then better prepared for the intense period of an M&A deal when 'education' may seem an unlikely luxury.

ACTIVATED INTELLIGENCE

If the internal community recognizes the value of intelligence products, it will naturally generate 'activated' requests. These are requests generated by both formal and informal observation of the environment. A casual reference in the business press or an overheard remark can require some speedy intelligence.

Activated intelligence only appears at the request of a client and is tailored to that client's needs. The most obvious situation during which such intelligence is needed is leading up to or during an M&A deal. In such situations, the role of the intelligence function is to provide speedy, targeted information. It is essential that an intelligence expert therefore be embedded in any M&A team. After the M&A deal closing, the intelligence community will review, analyze, and debrief the relevant teams. The consequent reports and any other documentation will form part of the organizational knowledge base for future M&As, as will be discussed towards the end of this book.

COUNTER-INTELLIGENCE

The final product, if it can be so termed, is counter-intelligence. This function covers activities undertaken to protect the company. It is as important to secure your own proprietary information as it is to find out about others. The vulnerability of organizations, both human and systems based, has been discussed elsewhere and it is the role of counter-intelligence to minimize any damage done by competitors or maliciously driven intrusions.

Damage limitation may seem a low-level ambition but it is realistic. Breaches of security will happen and the smart intelligence worker will attempt to predict those breaches and respond immediately when that prediction occurs. Knowledge of the inevitability of failure must be integrated into strategic decision making at the most senior level. In an M&A deal, for example, it is prudent to assume that confidential discussions will be leaked to the target or the press. This doesn't mean one expects this to happen – nor should it mean that the company should be less vigilant in trying to prevent it from happening – but it does mean that a plan is in place in case it does happen.

Technology can also be used illegitimately to spy, bug, or invade. It is not unusual now for the senior officers of major corporations to have their offices, homes, and vehicles regularly swept for bugs.

HOW SHOULD THE INTELLIGENCE PRODUCTS BE DELIVERED?

Having educated the M&A team and in fact the entire organization to the range of products available, the individuals using that business intelligence will also need to be satisfied as to how those products are manufactured and delivered. Although the analysts deliver the products, they rely on others for the production of the raw material – information. This is the job of the intelligence collector. The collectors' work is done either technologically or by human intervention. Technology can come in any form. Technologically enhanced intelligence gathering can be simple CRM (customer relationship management), RFID (radio frequency identity) tagging, CPM (corporate performance management), data mining, or video mining. Ideally, for the organization, it is a combination of these systems which will provide an almost complete breakdown of an individual consumer's behavior.

> **Wal-Mart's customer data**
>
> At the last count, Wal-Mart had in excess of 500 terabytes of customer data stored at its Bentonville headquarters in Arkansas. Like us, you may not know what a terabyte is. Well, to put Wal-Mart's data volume into perspective, the entire internet is estimated to hold fewer terabytes than Wal-Mart holds. Using its financial muscle, Wal-Mart is also driving its major suppliers to RFID tag items. The plan, according to some analysts, is for the supplier to own each product until it is sold. These items therefore never actually come onto the Wal-Mart balance sheet.
>
> As Wal-Mart builds up its knowledge of what goes into your shopping trolley, it can aid the positioning of goods as well as the pricing of complementary goods. For example, in the flu season, the store might discount cold medication and place it strategically near to complementary goods such as orange juice or broth products on which they *increase* the margin.

Intelligence gathering by human intervention also has the capacity for illegitimacy. Falsely representing oneself (as in the recent scandal of Hewlett-Packard's 'pretexting' to trace boardroom leaks), phantom interviews, and intrusive networking are all used to gain information. Ironically, however, most information is fairly easy to come by without subterfuge, although the really important information will definitely require digging and may require cash.

CONCLUSION

Knowing that knowledge of the external and future is an essential component of any M&A strategy is one thing; organizing, structuring, and convincing the rest of the company to see intelligence as a core function is something else again. This is, perhaps, the most important cultural shift that an organization needs to make. Easy steps such as providing an intelligence hotline or intelligence website, asking for help around the organization, creating a virtual intel community, and interacting positively with the sales force can all begin to adjust the climate; changing the culture takes much longer but must start with these simple behavioral alterations. By failing to coordinate and prioritize the intelligence function, companies increase the risk of failure in any endeavor but perhaps most significantly in the M&A game. Risk assessments rarely recognize that the biggest risk to an organization is the failure to harness the intellectual potential, which exists within the company, to look out and forward.

CHAPTER 3

DESIGNING THE ACQUISITION PROCESS

*B*usiness intelligence techniques can effectively be used at all stages in the takeover deal process. Some points in the process (such as due diligence) will *appear to* fit more naturally the traditional view of business intelligence, but effective use of the techniques outlined will assist in improving the success rate at all stages of a deal from when a takeover is first proposed through to the continuing integration of the two companies years after the deal has been consummated.

The term 'appear to' is used above because even traditional due diligence has often been unfocused and therefore unsuccessful. This was certainly true in the case shown in Chapter 1 when Quaker Oats did not find out about the drop in sales of its target company (Snapple) until several days before the deal was announced, despite the ability to check with suppliers, grocery stores, and industry analysts about the sales of Snapple's drinks. Quaker Oats did not need to rely on Snapple to get this information and even if they had received that information in a timely fashion directly from Snapple, they should have verified it with other external sources. As shown in that case, Quaker Oats could also have conducted better due diligence on the differing distribution systems used by its own Gatorade division and the target, Snapple.

STEPS IN A DEAL

Although each acquisition or merger deal is unique, in general the merger process usually involves the steps shown in the box below. The buyer's perspective differs from the seller's, but both largely need to follow these steps. Steps overlap and in some deals there will be a loop back to an earlier stage. Some steps will be brief in certain deals, whereas in others a seemingly unimportant step will gain much greater importance. Anticipating the likely stages and timing will assist greatly in planning the deal. In certain situations (such as unexpected hostile bids), some of the steps may be shifted or even ignored due to time constraints.

Stages of a typical takeover (buyer's perspective)

1. Corporate strategy development: determine if acquisition or merger is the appropriate strategic move; develop long list of possible candidates.
2. Organize for the merger/acquisition: select project leader, form different teams, identify outside advisors, and so on.
3. Specific deal pricing and negotiation:
   – identification of final acquisition candidate(s);
   – valuation and pricing;
   – negotiations between both managements.

4. Structuring and approval:
   - structuring the deal;
   - due diligence;
   - arrange financing;
   - approval by common stockholders;
   - file papers and obtain approvals with jurisdictions in which each company operates;
   - closing.
5. Post-merger integration (integration planning should start with Step 1).
6. Post-acquisition review.

Although it is more common for buyers to initiate a deal, targets can also put themselves up for sale. Sellers initiate deals most commonly when they are experiencing some difficulty: financial difficulties including anticipated growth needs that cannot be funded through earnings, succession issues (especially with private companies where there has been a strong founder or start-up entrepreneur), or even legal issues (where the company has been the target of a major lawsuit, for example). It is critical to determine the underlying reasons because they are not always stated. The stated reason may in fact be a minor factor with the real driver left unspoken. Understanding these reasons is an important business intelligence responsibility.

Stages of a typical takeover (seller's perspective in an open auction)

1. Corporate strategy development to determine if the division or company should be sold.
2. Preparation of the expected pricing and expected deal terms.
3. Organization for the merger/acquisition: select project leader, form different teams, identify outside advisors, and so on.

4. Development of 'long list' of possible buyers and discussions with those companies.
5. 'Short list' stage with limited due diligence inside the seller.
6. 'Preferred bidder' stage with almost unlimited due diligence and strict confidentiality agreements exchanged.
7. Deal finalization:
    - arrange financing;
    - approval by common stockholders;
    - file papers and obtain approvals with jurisdictions in which each company operates;
    - closing.

Targets may not even know that they are being sold. Investment bankers and other advisors keep lists of companies that are possible targets and then take those lists to companies that may be interested in growth through acquisition (or may only be interested in making sure that a competitor doesn't get their hands on the target).

Company-specific Deal Processes

Different companies and different deals may have different processes, but the basic elements above are contained in all deals. For example, General Electric has been a serial acquirer: in 2006, it purchased over 50 companies. Over many years, it had developed a deal process designed to support its six major business areas: commercial finance, infrastructure, industrial, healthcare, consumer finance, and media (NBC Universal). Figure 3.1 shows the deal process for the Human Resources (HR) area, and other areas have similar and related processes.

SELLING APPROACHES

Once a seller has done the strategic review to determine whether to put itself or a division up for sale and has engaged the appro-

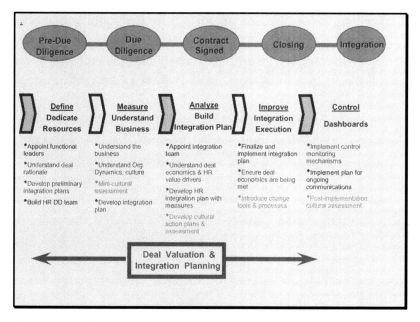

Figure 3.1 M&A HR Deal Process Overview at General Electric.

priate advisors to support the sale including intelligence special-ists, there are three major approaches to selling with each having unique advantages and disadvantages.

1. Public or open auctions are preferred when there are 'trophy' assets and confidentiality issues are unlikely. The advantages include an ability to show to shareholders that the best price has been achieved for the company/division as the largest possible market of potential buyers has been targeted. However, such auctions can be very embarrassing for man-agement and the company (with impacts on reputation, sales, and employee morale). There is also the risk of competitors seeing information that is better kept confidential. These public auctions also are difficult to control and sometimes develop a life of their own. Public auctions are often required for assets that governments privatize, such as the recent sales of state-owned telecommunications and power companies.

2. Limited private auctions approach a limited number of parties and are useful where there is a small number of relatively easily identifiable potential buyers. This is a preferred route of the major investment banks. The advantages in these limited private auctions are that they usually maintain a good level of confidentiality and less public and internal embarrassment if the auction were to fail. Nevertheless, there is a high level of skill required to build the 'feeding frenzy' required to get the highest price, although an experienced advisor should be able to generate this interest and avoid the risk of a limited private auction becoming a bilateral discussion if that isn't what is desired.

3. Bilateral discussions are useful where highly confidential issues exist (such as client lists or intellectual property), where there are only a limited number of potential purchasers, or when speed is required. Such discussions by their nature have a reduced effect on customers, employees, and suppliers, but are rarely the best way to achieve the highest price for the company or division being sold. It may therefore be very difficult to justify such bilateral discussions to the owners or shareholders of a company.

Marks & Spencer bilateral sale of its credit card business

When Marks & Spencer (M&S) sold its credit card business to HSBC in the middle of its defense against Sir Philip Green, it was accused of selling the business at a 'fire sale' price, despite a sales figure of £762 million.

In the heat of the takeover battle, Stuart Rose was hired as CEO of M&S to defend the company from the unsolicited bid. He needed to gain instant credibility. Additionally, he needed to demonstrate to his shareholders that he had a strategy for the business that focused on the core retail business and not financial services. He also needed to raise cash to fund a promised dividend and to show the market that M&S was willing to make tough but rapid decisions. One of Rose's ways to demonstrate his new focussed strategy was to act decisively in selling the credit card business quickly, even if the bilateral nature of the sale did lead to accusations that M&S could have obtained a higher price for the unit.

Assuming an open auction or limited private auction, a 'long list' of companies to participate in the auction or discussions needs to be identified. The advisors will usually look both vertically and horizontally in the industry, consider whether management may want to buy the company or division, whether there are financial buyers (such as hedge funds or private equity firms, and visit companies that may have expressed an interest in the past or recently attempted and failed in another purchase. The use of intelligence techniques to develop this list will be discussed later as it is important that potential bidders not be missed, nor is it useful to waste time on those who would not make it through the process. Indeed, the M&S case has some ironic echoes. As discussed in the previous chapter, for years, M&S operated in an externally ignorant cocoon.

The long list of companies is then prioritized and those most likely to bid are given confidentiality agreements before continuing the discussion. At that point, an information memorandum developed in the preparation phase is distributed to the interested companies and their advisors. Some potential bidders will be uninterested and drop out.

Then the deal moves into the 'short list' stage where each short-listed company is given further information. Three to seven bidders are ideal in this stage. Four to six weeks for this stage is again common, assuming that there is not a regulatory need to do the deal more quickly because of public announcements.

Tactics are important and the need for good intelligence on the bidders is critical: for example, does each buyer get information specifically requested or does each buyer get all the information in aggregate? This dissemination of information is often done in a document or data room, and again there are tactical decisions to be made as to where the room is located, how access is gained, how often can potential bidders gain access, is some or all of the information online, and which advisors can participate. Other due diligence efforts will take place as well, including meetings with management, visiting sales offices and manufacturing plants, talking to clients, interviewing financial staff, and so on. Through all of this, the companies that didn't make the short list must be kept informed in case any or all of the short-listed companies drop out of the bidding.

Lastly, there is the selection of the winner – the 'preferred bidder.' From this point, that bidder will get exclusivity to further information and the level of confidential information disclosed is higher. The losers again may need to be kept warm in case the preferred bidder declines to make a final offer or if there are problems in closing the deal. Here again, constant intelligence monitoring is often neglected. The complacent period surrounding perceived victory is very dangerous. Ultimately a sale and purchase agreement will be negotiated and the final contract agreed and signed. Certain conditions may have been entered into the agreement, such as regulatory issues, the ability to arrange the necessary financing, and final shareholder approvals (often in a special general meeting of shareholders).

TIMING

Although the timing can range from days (in the case of some private companies) to several years (most notably when there are regulatory issues involved and multiple jurisdictions), an 'average' deal can be completed in four to six months.

There is no set duration for the first stages of strategy development and organization. Some companies have corporate development departments that continually scour the market for potential acquisitions and advisors tasked to do the same (and to be 'on call' in case a deal becomes active). These companies can respond quickly to an opportunistic bid or an unsolicited takeover attempt.

Assuming no external pressures, the proper amount of time to be allotted to the preparation and pricing would be four to six weeks. This is adequate to gather the information and conduct the analyses necessary. The larger and more complex the deal – and the larger the deal team – the longer the time required. Acquisitions of private companies also can take longer as less information is in readily available format in advance.

Regulations can represent the most likely reason for a deal to be delayed, although proper intelligence gathering and analysis should highlight where this is likely to take place. According to one study by the consultants, McKinsey, approximately 40% of all US deals involved detailed requests from regulators for information and almost 4% ultimately had a legal challenge, thus delaying the closing considerably beyond the initial target date.

MANAGING THE PROCESS

This merger process can and should be managed from both the buyers' and sellers' sides and, ideally, coordinated between them. Unfortunately, all too often the process itself becomes the manager, especially when there is an inability to decouple from the deal once it is under way. These so-called 'runaway deals' are when the momentum of the deal takes charge and when executives and advisors get embroiled and lose objectivity.

The following issues should be considered to avoid this problem:

1. It is important to remember that the deal can change during the process.
2. In early stages, there is only limited knowledge of the target, so be willing to change opinions.
3. The process should allow for withdrawing from the deal at any stage.
4. Public and external pressures will interfere with the internal process.
5. There is a tendency to postpone ambiguities until after the deal has closed, but this is dangerous. Any uncertainty about significant items or insufficient information should be resolved before the deal closes (and optimally much before that).

The deal itself creates a potential, but this must be managed in order to realize it. Value is created only in post-merger integration, although it depends on price as well.

Yet with all the best planning and advisors, no deal will ever proceed exactly as planned. Perception may be more important than reality. As President Dwight Eisenhower said of his time leading the Allied forces in Europe in World War II, 'In preparing for battle I have always found that plans are useless, but planning is indispensable.' Among other reasons, he must have known that the very act of planning would enable him to react more swiftly once the battle situation shifted.

The intelligence function used effectively is a tool which can guide the team to gain the most from perceptions about the roles and abilities in the takeover battle of the company, its advisors, and the competition. If used correctly it helps to maintain a clear understanding of the principal current perceptions surrounding the prospective deal, and since the role of intelligence is an iterative process, it ensures that the changing moods and dynamics of these perceptions are incorporated into the planning and deal process.

Questions needing answering include determining which perceptions are the most widespread, which are the most powerful, which are likely to be developing, and which are losing favor. Crucially it allows the team to understand its own position and how others perceive them and vice versa. Along with the motivations for advisors driven by their billing models (whether fixed fee, time based, or as a percentage of the deal size), their perceptions need to be monitored.

The process is dynamic. There needs to be constant monitoring of the changes in the environment that then enables a company to take advantage of certain perceptions, limit the damage of others, and even to ensure that perceptions are moving in a direction that will provide benefits when it is possible to influence them. However, in order for this to be done successfully, the most important factors at play must be understood.

One executive in a major global investment bank described how important it is to gauge shareholder attitudes in cases where the management are accountable in their decisions to the shareholders. 'Always make sure you know who gets to make the decision: what are their attitudes and perceptions surrounding the issue? That way you can make sure to play the right card in the right way and at the right time.' He further highlighted that the decision making process usually goes through various levels, and as such actions need to be targeted according to the perceptions at each stage of the decision making ladder.

Lastly he described how those who make the final decision are often made up of certain groups, so, for example, when dealing with shareholders, corporate shareholders will hold very different opinions and perceptions than private individuals. Depending on the size and overall stake, a different approach will need to be targeted at the important groups. Thus whatever the

> ### Rating agency perceptions
>
> During 2002, a US-based bank was forced to divest an acquisition in Eastern Europe that had only just been completed, due to the pressure placed on them by one of the credit rating agencies. Despite the acquisition making economic and strategic sense, the bank was forced to sell as quickly as possible in order to stop their bond rating from being downgraded.
>
> The reason behind this was that the rating agency felt that the bank should be seen as simply focusing on improvements within the US at that point in time, rather than to be seen as turning their energy away from the problems in their core home market during the economic downturn following the bursting of the dot.com bubble. As such the need to withdraw from their expansion into Eastern Europe was driven purely by the rating agency's fear of how the market would perceive the expansion, rather than due to any actual threat that the bank was making a bad business decision.
>
> In this case the bank clearly overlooked the rating agency as a major stakeholder (or even, as some companies do, as an advisor) until the rating agency took them by surprise following the announcement of the deal. The agency had the power to control the bank's actions with a threat which the bank could not afford to ignore.

context, the groups that hold varying degrees of power always need to be identified, understood, and managed accordingly. As shareholders, these are the people who will ultimately determine the fate of a deal at that phase of the takeover process.

The example in the box clearly illustrates the need to identify who has control or influence over the key decisions at all levels. Perhaps if the bank in the example had realized in advance what the perceptions of their rating agency were, they could have reassured both the market and the agency, and carried out some further actions to prove their commitment. In this way they might have been able to retain the profitable acquisition and their Eastern European expansion plans, rather than rushing out under the panicked enforcement of their rating agency about the acquisition, which resulted in immediate losses and left them missing out on a major growth opportunity. Another example where a stakeholder perception was ignored or where the intelligence function failed was Deutsche Bank in its acquisition of Bankers Trust in 1999: that deal was delayed by several months and almost prevented completely by the surprised (at least to Deutsche Bank and its advisors) insistence of the New York State regulators that the issue of the payments to Holocaust victims by the German government be resolved before approval would be given for the acquisition.

LBOs/MBOs

Certain types of deals will bring with them particular problems. This is certainly true for management buy-outs (MBOs) and related structures (such as management buy-ins – MBIs). These are a subset of leveraged buy-outs (LBOs) which utilize a high level of debt to buy the target company. This structure distinguishes them from the most common type of merger or acquisition transaction where one company acquires another company, or two (or more) companies decide to merge into one, usually in exchange for stock or cash.

The perception that there is a significant potential for conflicts of interest in management buy-outs is due to the fact that managers in public companies are fiduciaries for stockholders, charged with the responsibility for maximizing the price shareholders get from selling the company or division, but in the case of an MBO, they are also the buyer and therefore have an incentive to minimize the purchase price. An example of this was the relatively low offer in the form of an MBI by a management group led by Ross Johnson (an inside manager) in the RJR Nabisco LBO deal in the late 1980s which was then quickly surpassed by KKR, who ultimately purchased RJR Nabisco in the largest LBO of that decade.

Directors are prohibited from favoring a management bid over another bid. To avoid charges of insider trading in an MBO, management must disclose all material and non-public information or refrain from trading in the stock of the company. Full disclosure by management is an effective defense against such allegations.

In an MBO, an internal management team has arranged the leveraged purchase of the company, and with an MBI it is a group of managers from outside the company that have arranged the LBO. Graphically, the different types of LBO can be as shown in Figure 3.2.

In any type of LBO, the cash is borrowed using the target's assets and expected cash flows. Debt is therefore secured with the assets of the enterprise being acquired. This is why the financing is often referred to as 'asset-based lending.' Therefore most LBOs are in capital-intensive industries that have assets that can be used as collateral for debt; they don't take place as often in service industries where there are fewer fixed assets.

Although the LBO deals that gain the most attention in the press often involve an entire company being taken private in

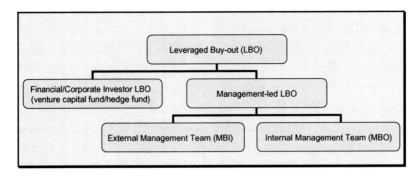

Figure 3.2 Types of Leveraged Buy-outs.

a leveraged financing, many LBOs involve a purchase of a division of a firm rather than the whole firm. The end result of such LBOs is that the business division becomes a private company rather than a public company or part of a public company. One common example is when a corporation decides that a division does not fit into its plans and wishes to divest, and a management team or investor group decides to purchase the division.

Why do LBOs make sense? By going private, the separation of ownership and control is eliminated; managers focus even more attention on eliminating costs and this often creates the extra earnings capacity necessary to service the very high levels of debt incurred in the purchase. Management in most LBOs are clearly incentivized to work harder to increase sales and revenues, make cost cuts that have been previously overlooked, and generally 'sweat' the assets.

The capital structure of an LBO may also lead to greater efficiencies. Management equity in LBOs is on average higher than in publicly held companies. Those managers have greater incentives to monitor revenues and expenses more closely than the widely distributed equity base typical for most public firms. There is also more focus on the cash flow, and correspondingly no longer a need to focus on quarterly earnings for securities market reporting to outside investors. This focus on cash flow is critical to the success of a highly leveraged firm, as it is cash flow that is needed to service debt, as opposed to earnings per share to pay dividends or satisfy equity analysts. Firms that have been taken private in an LBO even try to minimize taxable income to lower taxes, thus to increase after-tax cash flows.

Increased debt can therefore be a benefit to corporations, despite the perception of many analysts to the contrary. Debt can be a useful constraint that causes firms to be more efficient. High cash flows and low debt payments can lead management to make less efficient capital investment decisions in a public company.

With increased debt after an LBO, there is less freedom to waste money.

In fact, the characteristics that make a company (or division of a company) a potentially desirable LBO candidate are also what many would consider the factors to describe a well-run company (see box). The perception externally that a company has these characteristics will make it more likely to be an acquisition target – often unsolicited.

Factors that make a company attractive to be an LBO

- Stable cash flows so that the debt servicing can be predicted with some accuracy.
- Experienced management, especially when the management will be retained (as is often necessary to squeeze the most profits and cash flow from the company).
- Room for significant cost reductions (LBO employee cutbacks are greatest at the administrative layers).
- High equity interest of owners so that the deal can be done on friendly terms.
- Limited debt on balance sheet so that this unused capacity to borrow can be used in the purchase.
- Separable non-core businesses that can be sold after the deal to reduce the debt load.

LBO funds make the bulk of their money when a company in their portfolio does a reverse LBO. This is when a company that has gone private in an LBO goes public again at a later date. It is somewhat obvious (from the manager's perspective) that a good time to do the LBO is when the market is down and the company is cheap; after the market has started to recover and the company's major problems are cleaned up, the company can go public again or be purchased by another firm.

Examples of some famous money-making reverse LBOs

Harley Davidson (the famous motorcycle manufacturer) almost disappeared before being taken private by 13 executives who bought the company from AMF Inc. in an LBO in 1981 for $81.5 million. Shareholders put in just $1 million. When the company was relisted on the stock exchange five years later in 1986 (and seven months earlier having been within four hours of being foreclosed by its lead lender, Citicorp), the equivalent share price was over 40 times the price paid by the investors that took them private.

Another famous example in the 1980s was Gibson Greeting Cards. In 1982, a well-known LBO firm, Wesray, headed by the former US Treasury Secretary William Simon, purchased Gibson for $81 million ($58 million in cash and the assumption of $23 million in liabilities), with the investors putting in just $1 million of their own money. Eighteen months later in 1983, Wesray took Gibson public in a share offering at $330 million where Simon received $66 million on his own investment of around $330 000.

Highly leveraged funds and internal management teams are only two potential buyers other than the traditional strategic corporate buyer, but as can be seen from the example of the LBOs above, there is significant money to be made from deals that can be structured properly.

HEDGE FUNDS AND VENTURE CAPITALISTS

The competition for deals has heated up in the most recent merger wave with private equity and venture capital houses now a major driving force in the market and at some times have overtaken corporate buyers as the most dominant group of buyers. This competition for deals has the potential to raise the price of target companies – emphasizing once more the need to have full business intelligence to allow for sharp-pencil valuations and the information to provide to shareholders that the valuation was appropriate. It is also worth noting that as competition increases, the need to complete speedily increases also; and speed enhances the chance that something will be overlooked. A classic intelligence failure.

More recently another dimension has been added to the M&A field provided by the ever-increasing hedge fund community. Hedge funds have given corporates some support by acting as arbitrageurs in M&A deals; by securing stakes in companies that are undervalued, they bring companies into play but also provide corporates a chance of competing against well-funded private equity funds.

The hedge funds have deep pockets with good liquidity from which they can outbid private equity firms. Indeed, while they are considered a threat by private equity firms, their role as arbitrageurs is even more important. Understanding their role is critical in any deal, and there will be some examples later where the hedge funds have influenced the outcome of some very high profile transactions.

BUSINESS INTELLIGENCE IN THE M&A PROCESS

Clearly corporate strategies have been forced by the private equity world to use ever more structured and disciplined moves directed at realizing value from acquisitions. There is no doubt that over the last few years, corporations have become much more sophisticated in their approach to deal making and implementation. This push towards more robust processes has also been driven by the increasing accountability and transparency required of boards. Corporate boards are increasingly required to bear more responsibility and become more involved in assessing risk management practices; conversely, senior executives are facing more detailed questioning about their strategy and decisions. All these processes can be made extremely robust and explicit through a business intelligence approach, and with the support of such tools as Scenario Planning, which was discussed in Chapter 2.

From the perspective of business intelligence, the entire M&A deal process may rightfully be considered a 'field day' for spies given that so much critical information is unwillingly and unwittingly revealed throughout the cycle of a deal. Whether stolen or mistakenly given away by staff, the loss of confidential and critical information to rivals is costly to any firm in any marketplace at any time. Divulging competitive information to another player can ultimately inflict serious damage on a company if a deal is not signed, allowing an 'acquirer' to walk away with a significant amount of useful information on a competitor that can subsequently be turned against them. Thus, whether entered into for genuine commercial reasons – or as a tool by which to gather information on competitors – the M&A process may result in the loss of confidential and critical information to various parties, requiring vendors to resolve first what should be revealed to whom and when throughout the process.

Whether carried out by trusted insiders, business partners, employees, or even government officials, espionage and the loss of business intelligence to competitors can and does often play a central role in the entire M&A process as people try to access information by a variety of means for their own advantage.

Given the state of flux that parties to an M&A deal often find themselves in, it should come as no surprise that companies become easy targets for exploitation in one shape or another. Indeed, one case in point that demonstrates this vulnerability was the acquisition of DLJ by Credit Suisse First Boston (CSFB) in 2000, when prospective buyers – able to view production figures for the target's sales staff – selectively lured away individuals to the detriment of CSFB. Likewise, the acquisition of Bankers Trust by Deutsche Bank in 1999 also resulted in a large number of high level departures from the combined firm with whole teams being poached to work for rival banks.

Clearly, given the level of business intelligence 'victimization' within the M&A process and the significant vulnerability of firms to the loss of critical information exposed as part of the due diligence process, companies need to protect and guard their assets more carefully, preventing unnecessary leaks and slips throughout the M&A process. This will be covered in greater depth in Chapter 7.

While adhering to certain tenets of secrecy (such as confidentiality agreements, non-disclosure agreements, project code names, secure data rooms, and information divulged on a 'need-to-know' basis), nevertheless many of the parties connected with a material corporate event such as an M&A deal may also profit from information seepage. While bankers and other advisors may wish to build up tension or interest in a deal through leaks to prospective rivals in order to inflate a target's auction sale price (thereby also achieving a larger commission-based fee for themselves), others, including potential acquirers, may also wish to release non-public information to the outside. The business media are forever trying to scoop potential M&A deals for their headlines. They serve as a vehicle by which parties to a transaction can leak stories in order to test out institutional shareholders' response to a potential deal.

Information leaks

An example of an alleged leak of deal terms involved United Dominion, as reported in *CFO Magazine* in 1996. Having undertaken extremely quiet negotiations about the potential acquisition of a company and having made a discreet offer at a 30% premium to the target's (then) trading share price, United Dominion found the potential acquisition's shares gradually trade upwards towards the level offered – possibly on account of leaks from a number of sources inside the target who wished to impede the deal from progressing, as there were no other business or market explanations for the share price rise. Thus, unsure as to whether or not it could trust the target to remain silent while the machinations of the deal advanced, United Dominion withdrew its offer – causing the target's share price to return once again over a short period of time to its original pre-negotiation trading level.

In another example, a medium-sized private storage company attracted the attention of two businesses simultaneously, who made a joint approach. The first exploratory meeting established some common ground and reasons to move forward, although there was still some uncertainty about the nature and timing of the acquisition. In view of the nervousness of the storage company owners, next steps were agreed on a very cautious basis, starting with a non-disclosure agreement (NDA). Within 24 hours of that first meeting, the deal was aborted acrimoniously following a major breach of the NDA by one of the interested parties.

All in all, as these examples clearly demonstrate, given the level of leakages involving M&A deals and their effect on vendor and target share prices, it is no wonder that executives (when it is in their favor!) try everything they can to prevent such 'porosity' – including the use of in-house expertise whenever possible, reducing the amount of pre-deal work, and the drafting of confidentiality agreements between parties. Of course, there will be times as well when well-placed 'leaks' of information or even the inference that such leaks may take place will serve one of the parties in the negotiation.

CONCLUSION

There isn't a time during the takeover deal process when it isn't necessary to be alert to the changing external and internal environments through the effective use of the business intelligence techniques discussed earlier. Many M&A practitioners have understood the value of these techniques and the value of employing managers and staff experienced in their use, but have usually limited their application to the due diligence process. This is a mistake. Competitive advantage can be gained by applying these techniques throughout the deal process and in any type of merger or acquisition, whether friendly or hostile, whether structured as an acquisition or a management buy-out, or whether familiar as in a merger with a close competitor or alien as with a diversification into an area where the company has no prior experience.

CHAPTER 4

CONTROLLING THE ADVISORS

Although the ultimate responsibility for the success of a deal will rest with the board of directors and senior management, in most mergers there are a large number of advisors necessary to bring the deal to completion. Some of these advisors may be involved from the first step in the planning process through to closing (and possibly even beyond), whereas other advisors will play a much more limited role during a very specific part of the merger process.

An example of the deal group from General Electric is shown in Figure 4.1. Some of these team members will be internal, others external, and for GE as with many firms, there will be a mix where, for example, the in-house legal team will be advised on the deal by external legal experts. Typically, the larger the company and the more frequently it engages in acquisitions, the more likely the existence of an internal team. Even in these cases, external advisors will be used when there are multiple deals

Figure 4.1 The GE 'Deal Team.'

simultaneously taking place or when a deal is outside the immediate area of experience or expertise of the team (say, in a new geography or product line).

ADVISOR ROLES

The financial advisor is typically at the center and acts as the experienced coordinator of many of the other advisors and their activities. (Some experienced serial acquirers such as General Electric or Siemens will act as the coordinator.) The financial advisor naturally gives general financial advice but also drafts some and coordinates all documentation, controls other advisors and often the client, advises on target valuation and deal pricing, manages the overall strategic direction of the offer, and lends its reputation to the transaction. There can be two financial advisors: an investment bank doing the M&A advisory work and a lending bank providing and coordinating the required funding for the purchase. The financial advisor will often play both roles as well as the role of stockbroker. The roles also differ depending which side of the deal the bank is advising, and both the bidder and target will have their own financial advisor. There can also be more than one financial advisor to each side, and in these cases the financial advisors must coordinate among themselves.

When an **investment bank** represents the buyer, they will do some or all of the following:

- Find acquisition opportunities, such as locating an acquisition target or merger partner when the deal is not originated in-house.
- Evaluate the target from the bidder's strategic, financial, and other perspectives; valuing the target; providing 'fair value' opinion.
- Develop an appropriate financing structure for the deal, covering offer price, expected final price including expenses of the deal, method of payment, and sources of finance (such as debt, equity, or cash).
- Advise the client on negotiating tactics and strategies for friendly/hostile bids or, in some cases, negotiating deals on behalf of the client.
- Collect information about potential rival bidders.
- Profile the target shareholders to 'sell' the bid effectively; helping the bidder with analyst presentations and 'roadshows.'
- Gather feedback from the stock market about the attitudes of financial institutions to the bid and its terms.
- Help to prepare the offer document (especially the 'front end' (rationale) of the offer document), profit forecast, circulars to shareholders, and press releases, and ensuring their accuracy.

When representing a target, the activities are different:

- Monitoring the target share price to track potential offers and provide an early warning to the target of a possible bid.
- Crafting effective bid defence strategies.
- Valuing the target and its divisions; providing a fair value opinion on the offer.
- Helping the target and its accountants prepare profit forecasts.
- Finding white knights or white squires to block hostile bids (discussed further in Chapter 6).
- Arranging buyers for any divestment or management buy-out of target assets as part of its defensive strategy.
- Negotiating with the bidder and its team.

Solicitors and lawyers will draft legal agreements and documents and also the 'back end' (details) of offer and defense documents. They give general corporate and regulatory advice and sometimes offer tax advice. They would do the legal due diligence in identifying any potential legal and regulatory showstoppers to the deal. These might include antitrust investigation by the Competition Commission in the UK, the European Commission, or the Federal Trade Commission in the US. The lawyers would prepare the bidder's case in such investigations.

Accountants draft the 'middle bit' (numbers) of the offer documentation and provide the 'independent' financial information as required (typically three years); note that it is management, not the accountants, that produces the financial forecasts. Accountants will give tax advice (when lawyers don't) and often take on the bulk of due diligence. Many accountancy firms have specialist consultancy divisions as well that may be involved in specific areas such as compensation and benefits and other human resources issues.

Human resources consultancies have an increasingly important role in supporting the target or bidder. From a bidder's perspective, it is critical to know the strength of the target's senior and even middle management teams. The bidder needs to know as well whether those people will stay with the new company and what incentives will be required. There may be other personnel-related issues as well, such as redundancy requirements, union contracts, pension deficits, and many cultural issues to consider. Likewise the target has an interest in knowing how it will be treated in the new organization.

Stockbrokers are the eyes and ears in the market for both the bidder and target. They are the principal line of communication with institutional shareholders and because of their knowledge of the markets and the investors, they provide input on valuation and pricing. They may also organize other banks and brokers should it be necessary in raising additional funds. They may sometimes liaise with regulatory authorities on the strict requirements of regulatory filings. The investment bank may also act as the stockbroker, as noted earlier.

Public relations advisors help with the selling message to multiple audiences, including not just the shareholders who will ultimately determine whether the deal is acceptable, but also to management and staff of both companies, customers, suppliers, and the general public. They may organize various campaigns through press briefings, one-on-one or group presentations, and other media events.

There are numerous other advisors as well, including:

- **Consultants** of all types advising on topics such as strategy, specialized due diligence, governance, post-merger integration, security issues, and so on. These consultants can also form 'clean teams' to assist with early negotiations (discussed later in Chapter 9).
- **Registrars** who control shareholder lists and organize communications with shareholders and share transfers on both sides.
- **Receiving banks** who will take in offer acceptances and ultimately pay out the consideration to the target shareholders.
- **Printers** for the myriad documents required.

Some of the advisors related to business intelligence gathering will be discussed in greater detail in later chapters, as will corporate intelligence consultants in Chapter 7 on due diligence.

The different art of Middle Eastern M&A

The National District Cooling Company ('Tabreed'), a publicly-listed company in the United Arab Emirates (UAE) in the Middle East had decided to pursue a service expansion acquisition of an electrical engineering servicing and management company in the UAE ("Ian Banham & Co."), owned and managed by the CEO.

Beyond the usual acquisition price, earnouts, negotiations and legal agreements, there were several unique aspects to the deal:

1) Being retained by the seller but also advising the buyer
2) Negotiating with the owner and manager seller although the owner also had to strike a deal with his 'silent' local majority local shareholder partners; such 'silent' (or 'mute') partners were necessary to obtain a local operating license but actually had no say in running the business
3) Finding a local employee who was a citizen of the UAE with an engineering license at the local acquirer, Tabreed, that would officially acquire the target shares under his name, as under local law the buyer/owner needed to have a local engineering license which was very difficult to obtain.

Different countries: different customs and different art of M&A.

ADVISOR SELECTION

The selection of advisors is itself a strategic decision. Certain advisors have the reputation and experience which makes them the first choice in an industry. Others will be the leading specialists in particular aspects of a deal – for example, Goldman Sachs, one of the largest M&A investment banks, is particularly well known for its defense of targets in hostile bid situations. If a bidder therefore knows – as it will! – that it will be launching a hostile bid, then it might be advantageous for that bidder to engage Goldman Sachs as its advisor. In this way, it will force the target to choose an investment bank that may not have as much experience. This assumes, of course, that the advisor is not already on a retainer or has recently represented the target. It should also be obvious that the bidder is at an advantage in choosing its advisors; targets will typically be responding in the heat of a battle with more severe time pressures and limited choice as the bidder will have set the stage.

HOW ADVISORS ARE PAID

How advisors are paid is an important factor in understanding how they operate. When representing buyers, financial advisors typically charge a retainer, a management fee, and an abort fee in addition to (in the case a deal is successful) a straight percentage of deal size/consideration. Sometimes the fee can be time based for a limited number of months, which is then set off against the success fee if the deal does complete.

Financial advisors representing the target have found it more difficult to structure a 'success fee,' and thus the fees in these instances tend to be time based or as a fixed percentage of deal size. A success fee is more difficult to structure because of the potential conflicts of interest. Accountants and lawyers are also typically time based and often will agree to a cap (with 'get-out' clauses in case the deal develops along lines much differently than anticipated).

Despite their expense – often as much as 5% of the total deal size – our research has shown that the inclusion of a financial advisor is good for buyers because the advisors increase shareholder wealth by finding bidders or targets with greater value, providing advice on premiums, identifying liability concerns (including demonstrating to shareholders that they did the most they could to achieve the best deal for the shareholders), providing local knowledge in the increasingly complex cross-border deals, and because of their competence demonstrate a higher probability of a deal's successful completion.

ADVISORS AND BUSINESS INTELLIGENCE

Each of the advisors can play an important intelligence role, although often each advisor's actual role is limited to their traditional functions. Accountants check and produce the numbers, but if asked, can provide important information about the industry and other companies in the market. Investment banks may drive the overall process and be responsible for the valuation, pricing, and negotiation, but are also important reservoirs of information about the market, and competitors. They have Chinese walls that operate to keep information from one deal being used on another, but the general experience of the senior investment bankers themselves is often enough to provide a client with information that otherwise could not be obtained.

Both large, global consultants and small boutique advisors are renowned for their ability to seek out non-public information about client and customers. There is a demonstrated willingness of employees, suppliers, and clients to provide information for no other reason than having been asked. Often it is difficult for a company to ask this information directly, because they would need to identify who is asking. Consultants, on the other hand, do not need to disclose their clients unless asked – and frequently are just not asked! Why people are so willing to divulge confidential information to experts is not always clear, but what is clear is that many will do so for no other reason than that someone has asked them.

Some specialist consultants focus specifically on due diligence work and intelligence gathering. One or several steps up from the detectives made popular by Hollywood, these consultants can be masters at finding information that is otherwise difficult to obtain. Although there are those that operate on the wrong side of generally acceptable ethical and moral principles (granting that these may differ by culture, country, and individual), there is also much that can be done for targets or bidders by these investigative firms on the totally right side of the law. Selection of such consultants is therefore a key factor in successfully obtaining the information required.

CONCLUSION

Once a deal is announced and even if there are only rumors of a deal, advisors from all professions will descend upon the two companies merging. Each will have a unique and often compelling marketing pitch describing how the deal will proceed better (read: cheaper, faster, more efficiently, with less distraction to the core business, with greater long-term performance, with fewer redundancies, and so on). This is why there is one intelligence omission that you may have noticed. *Do not forget to employ (internally or outsourced) your intelligence function on your advisors.* No matter how reputable the advisors or how much work in the deal is conducted by the external consultants, the board, senior managers and employees are the ones who will live with the result for years. This responsibility cannot be delegated.

CHAPTER 5

IDENTIFYING
THE BEST TARGETS

T he reasons for carrying out M&A activity are clearly dependent on the context of the business, the dynamics of the environment, future strategic intents, and the personal motivations of senior management. Some companies, for example, may need to acquire in order to increase their market share, to expand quickly into new markets, to gain access to scarce resources, to keep up with their competitors, to reduce their number of competitors, or even just to increase their sales growth or profitability. So, for example, private equity firms by and large only look for targets with operational and/or financial inefficiencies that can be turned around. In the case of some large industrial firms that have stated that they seek to achieve a double digit growth, they can only do this through consistent acquisitions as they operate largely in mature industries.

Whatever the case is, these motivations will define the approach taken to acquisition planning: each company must make their corporate development strategy explicitly and directly based on these motivations. In this way, they will have clear working guidelines split over different time lengths about their strategic intent, where they would wish to expand, and even where they would like to divest. This strategy must be both realistic and personalized to the company. It will identify where there are holes that must be filled with acquisitions or mergers.

STRATEGIC vs OPPORTUNISTIC DEALS

As noted earlier, all mergers and acquisitions should be based on a sound corporate strategy. It is therefore critical that managers and boards do not get caught up in the 'merger game' with the 'thrill of the chase.' Unfortunately, strategy is often forgotten or misused in making acquisitions, thus contributing to the poor success rate of mergers.

There is often a distinction made between strategic and opportunistic acquisitions, with the assumption that the latter are inherently bad. This need not be the case, as opportunistic acquisitions will frequently be the driver to the development of a new strategy, the acceleration of an existing strategy or just the chance to make money. Both types of acquisition can be successful or unsuccessful, often depending on how the deal is completed and the effective use of intelligence. Intelligence is actually the key variable in opportunistic endeavors. This follows the adage that luck is where preparation meets opportunity. The intelligence function is at the heart of preparation.

Management's role is absolutely fundamental to the amount of success that can be achieved in a deal. An empowered management is paramount in any business situation; within the context of M&A, if management is able to assess choices critically based on an informed, flexible expertise, then chances are that success will be more forthcoming. Indeed what truly separates the wheat from the chaff are those individuals who are able to make the best choices in the most efficient and effective way. In this respect, experience working for the intelligence function is an excellent development milestone in improving the skills of management and their performance.

Indeed, the speed and flexibility that come from being on the ball are certainly of direct relevance to M&A where the deal process has become much faster and the competition much harder to beat. It is for this reason that opportunistic acquisitions are often necessary – if by 'opportunistic' is meant a deal that had not been anticipated in the strategic planning process.

Ideally, companies need to be both strategic and opportunistic in all their activities, including M&A. Just as a salesman would not ignore unanticipated requests from a client or a phone call from an unsolicited customer, a company should not ignore a deal to buy another company offered to it by an advisor. Furthermore not only are strategic and opportunistic approaches not mutually exclusive, but rigidly rejecting or following either one to the exclusion of the other will engender certain weaknesses in a company which would limit the amount of overall success that could potentially be achieved. Therefore, advisors and internal managers should be encouraged to identify potential acquisitions even if there is only remote relevance to the company's strategy immediately identified: this is a critical element of the business intelligence process.

This is driven as well by the fact that all major business decisions, acquisitions included, generally take place as a result of multiple factors coming together; moreover in practice things can only be taken advantage of when they are in some degree available. It is much more useful to pursue an informed decision-making process which can flexibly respond to any new changes, be they problematic issues or opportunities (often they are both at the same time).

What is required is an effective balance of advanced planning with opportunism on the basis of comprehensive and continually updated knowledge and expertise. This is fundamental to maintaining competitive advantage by allowing businesses to respond quickly to changes in their environment. In the M&A context, when a target or a critical piece of information has suddenly become available or a change has occurred which can make it available, the company can make a sensible decision as to what course of action should be taken; if one has a plan then one can assess in which cases to deviate from it, but the plan itself should never be the defining force.

It is neither realistic nor prudent to say that a company should not pursue a possible opportunity simply because of its sudden appearance. This also applies to the opposite case where control risk measures should be considered. Either way, the informed decision made at this point should simply be in reference to what the next step taken should be, with an idea of what possible steps could then follow in various directions. The company should also be in control of that decision making process and avoid the tendency to let the advisors drive the decision timing.

Opportunism in the aftermath of the Cold War

Following the fall of the Berlin Wall in 1989, investment in armament companies fell completely out of vogue. The private equity firm, the Carlyle Group, bought up the majority of several armament companies at two times cash flow only to sell them further down the line in the 1990s at eight to nine times cash flow at a time when military operations in Kuwait, Iraq, and elsewhere were rising. At the time of Carlyle's initial investments, most other investors were avoiding armament companies, whereas Carlyle acted quickly to secure the companies before another group of investors realized that the fall of the Wall didn't mean that military operations were consigned to the dustheap of history.

At any point in the M&A process, the acquirer should be prepared to step away from pursuing the deal or to consider other options. Indeed, this skill is very much reliant on a strong lateral thinking scope for alternative courses of action, clear business acumen unclouded by hubris and deal momentum, and courage to pursue what sense dictates. At a formal process level, review points and 'time-outs' should be planned into the process to make sure that management can walk away from a deal at any time prior to closing.

The willingness to accept opportunism does not reduce the need to do proper target identification. In fact, the prior identification of appropriate targets will assist in the ability to act quickly when a potential target becomes available, either because of a raid by another company or corporate events such as poor earnings, change in management or shareholding, product development, or whatever.

Put simply by Sarah Byrne-Quinn, Group Director of Strategy and Business Development at Smith and Nephew plc, '... good M&A is where opportunity meets strategy...' and success or failure can often be decided in the strategy planning sessions that occur months, if not years, before deals actually take place.

ROLE OF STRATEGY

In reference to finding a possible target, management can therefore make quick, informed decisions based on their knowledge of their own capabilities, corporate strategy, the state of the market, an understanding of the business of the target, and current key stakeholder perceptions. From this point they choose whether to act on the opportunity or to attempt to buy more time in order to carry out some more research on key determinants. Further on, this can be achieved through securing the target by way of an exclusivity agreement or establishing the company as preferred bidder in an auction by offering a solution that better meets the target's needs and which outrivals the competition.

M&A deals are by definition a means to an end. They should never (but sometimes do) drive strategic situations and choices. Embedded within strategy even when opportunistic, mergers and acquisitions should help firms to change the competitive structure of their industry, operating within a framework that enables them to utilize their unique resources and capabilities best. Thus, whatever the business strategies that a company employs to its competitive advantage, the establishment of acquisition objectives should be firmly rooted within an entity's 'grand design,' helping to promote its strategic goals and objectives.

It is also important to note at this point that an inefficient strategic planning process and understanding at a company can make it very difficult to have an efficient mergers and acquisitions process. The two are inextricably linked. Part of the reason is that strategy is important as a screen for potential acquisition candidates. If the number of candidates increases to too high a level, they cannot be properly and efficiently assessed.

SCREENING CANDIDATE TARGETS

The screening of candidates will typically include the following criteria, but the actual criteria used may differ for each acquirer and even for each deal:

- Industry and the target's position in it.
- Size of the business: sales, assets, market value.
- Strategic capabilities.
- Profitability and other financial factors (including levels of debt).

- Risk exposure, including the cyclicality of the business, any significant legal or regulatory issues (including monopolies), inherent risks to the products, and so on.
- Asset type, whether buying the whole company or just a division only, real estate, natural resources, or people.
- Intellectual property: patents, client lists, supplier relationships.
- Management quality and the likelihood that they will remain with the company.
- Current ownership.
- Culture and organizational fit.

Two filters need to be applied when screening the list of potential targets: first, what the company itself is capable of achieving with available resources and second what the competition is doing and which way the market is moving. It is important that the company chooses its strategic intent on a balanced analysis of these two dynamics, since if it only follows the first it risks losing touch with the market's needs, and if it only looks at the latter, it risks jumping on the acquisition bandwagon and misjudging both what will be of real use to its development strategy and also what it will be able to make use of given its current situation, skills, and resources.

Need for candidate screening

The founder of one corporate venture capital fund noted that in one year (2000–2001), over 700 companies were assessed and 50 in detail but yielding only 13 investments. Other private equity firms confirm that the typical ratio of targets to investments is 40 or 50 to 1.

> VeriSign looked at over 120 companies before purchasing Jamba in 2004, and yet, as noted later in Chapter 7, the acquisition still failed to meet its strategic objectives.

To assist with the determination of the acquisition strategy, it is important to ascertain the answers to the questions below for each potential target.

- **Workable strategy?** There are several possible mistakes that can be made at this point, such as considering the target only and not the combined firm or performing static analysis and not the industry's future or the reactions of competitors, customers, and suppliers.

- **Pricing?** The acquirer must set a 'walk-away' price so that all the benefits will not be bid away in the heat of the process. As we will see later, such pricing is an art, not a science; it is dynamic, and will change as market conditions change and is highly dependent on the quantity and quality of the data that is available. Thus the 'walk-away' price may change – up or down – as the available information changes.

- **Cultural compatibility?** Without an ability to operate as a unified firm, the best business strategy will remain unfulfilled. There must be a plan for the cultured integration of the two companies or the result will be failure or a possible destruction of value.

- **Potential problems?** Potential risks must be identified as should the alternatives to mitigate those risks. Remember that proponents of the acquisition will downplay the risks in 'selling' the idea to senior management and the board of directors. Other individuals and advisors will 'go native' on the deal as we will see later and lose their independence and objectivity. There are also predictable errors – fundamental factors that can cause mistakes that can be anticipated and therefore prevented.

- **Key managers?** One of the many key factors is who will manage the various departments in the 'new' organization. Identification of the management skills of both organizations is key.
- **Implementation plan?** It is critical to plan for the ultimate integration of the two companies, not just the closing of the deal; milestones need to be set. As will be noted later, this builds on commonalities and then moves to the differences.

The application of each of these issues will be different for each company – and often different at varying points in a company's life cycle.

Cisco

Some serial acquirers, such as Cisco, have become quite expert in ascertaining that companies they acquire fit their corporate strategy and rely on acquisitions to complement its own internal research and development.

As reported in the *ECCH Bulletin*, Cisco has had periods when it buys one to two companies per month (it bought 51 companies in the 2½-year period preceding March 2000). In its early period of rapid growth, Cisco developed a six-point blueprint for evaluation of prospective acquisitions:

1. Similar vision to Cisco.
2. Must produce quick wins.
3. Long-term win situation for all parties (shareholders, employees, customers, and business partners).
4. Cultural compatibility must exist.
5. Close geographic proximity to Cisco.
6. Friendly deals, never hostile.

There are many examples in M&A, and in the business world generally, where some important factor has been largely ignored during the planning process or in the selection of a target. The effects of this can be indirect by simply missing out on a possible opportunity in the market, as with the case shown in Chapter 3 of the US bank whose expansion into Eastern Europe was cut short by its rating agency. Or they can be extremely grave by causing direct tensions around the firm, an example being the problems at Gate Gourmet, shown in the box.

Gate Gourmet and its unforeseen labor problems

In 2006 after its acquisition by Texas Pacific, the US-based private equity firm, Gate Gourmet came up against some serious problems surrounding labor issues that resulted in a very public row both within Gate Gourmet and with its Heathrow Airport customers, the major airlines, as reported widely in the press and on the BBC.

Gate Gourmet was the principal supplier in the UK of airline food to British Airways and other major airlines. The labor problems seemed to have come completely out of the blue for the new owners, yet a very rudimentary application of business intelligence techniques would have highlighted the importance of labor issues in that industry. People rarely just suddenly erupt into protest; almost always such tensions increase over a period of time and can be foreseen, gaged, and potentially managed prior to any major upheaval. In order for this to happen, one does, however, have to be listening, reading the signs, and using that knowledge and intelligence to take appropriate steps and to use intelligence to determine the correct steps to take.

Thus it is vital for a company to know itself well – in other words, superb internal business intelligence. Top management must have a good idea of the company's strengths, weaknesses, and future potential. The latter factor would need to be assessed on the basis of a reflective and iterative process in which management reviews the company's main actions and their outcomes in various projects and prior acquisitions, and then assesses how effective they were at achieving the stated goals. This internal business intelligence enables the company to make an informed assessment of how much success it will be able to achieve in a particular area. In companies with many employees it is important to codify this knowledge so that it can be actively used to inform strategic decisions in a multi-faceted way. Often this is done in a strategy group or corporate development discussion.

Within this area, it is also important to establish how the market and wider business environment see the company. One example when it would be of use is in choosing a target and then justifying that choice to the market and other stakeholders. If there is understanding of how others perceive the company, then management will be able to use this knowledge to choose better targets and pick the best rationale to convince the market and the shareholders of the validity of the choice. Since shareholders, whether in public or private companies, are ultimately most often most interested in economic gain, be it in the short or long term, understanding their motivations can be extremely useful in improving the deal approach and tactics.

Mobicom and Freenet.de: the importance of accounting for all stakeholders

Germany's Mobicom already owned 50.4% in Freenet.de and wanted to make it a 100% subsidiary. The merger did get approval by the board and shareholders at the annual general meeting in 2005; however, in the meantime Texas Pacific bought 27% of Mobicom from France Telecom, making them the largest minority shareholder, as reported in the press.

Resentment of the new private equity shareholder resulted in a small number of dissident shareholders suing Mobicom over the approval of the merger in a bid to prevent Texas Pacific from claiming an option of a special dividend payment from the newly merged entity.

If Mobicom had realized that many of its shares were being bought by the private equity house, then it could have either taken appropriate measures, by delaying the merger for example, or it could have approached the remaining share-holders with a solution which avoided going to court.

DEAL PIPELINES

Best practice M&A demands that company managers create and maintain a pipeline of potential deals at all times. Having invested months, if not years, of time and effort in systematically culti-vating an in-depth and meaningful relationship with each poten-tial acquisition candidate, or a secret analysis of the potential target if that is the more appropriate route, first-rate acquirers more often than not get to the table ahead of their rivals and are able to act with both speed and confidence because they know exactly what they can expect to achieve through the acquisition. Thus, as Tom Ward, Corporate Development Director at Scottish & Newcastle plc, said, with an in-depth knowledge of a com-mercial scenario and by executing a '. . . clear plan for a market or a business, [the best acquirers] can manage even the most competitive of M&A situations. . . .'

Prioritized company lists of potential targets

The principal in one larger sized private equity firm described how it has lists of possible targets that are constantly being updated according to the developments of the company and the market. Within each division of the firm, these lists are categorized according to levels of 'activation' which designate how seriously the company should be considered as a possible target in respect to its own specific criteria. Then, as the level of prioritization increases, so too does the degree to which it carries out external due diligence on the market and the company, until it has stringently assessed the degree of relevance of this company to its target requirements. Based on an understanding of where this company falls short of its criteria and where it meets expectations, that private equity firm evaluates how much success it is likely to realize, and therefore whether it should pursue the target any further at that point in time and under what terms.

Another company, Cintas, a manufacturer of uniforms in North America, diligently assigns an individual from a line organization within the group to keep in touch with each and every individual prospective target, often for years at a time, ensuring that it watches for the favorable conditions to pull the trigger on talks, according to an article in the *Harvard Business Review* in 2004.

Christopher O'Donnell, the CEO of Smith & Nephew plc, said at a 2003 analyst presentation (and reported by *FD Wire*) that 'we'd like to do two or three [acquisitions] a year. . . . We have a central team, we have teams in each of the businesses, [and] at any given time we have between 20 and 30 companies that we look at.'

In the corporate venture capital fund noted earlier in this chapter, deals only proceeded when there was a senior line manager in one of the acquirer's own divisions who would approve the deal as well as contribute some divisional resources to assist with the due diligence.

ACQUISITION STRATEGY

In referring back to the merger process described in Chapter 3, it should be clear that strategy must be determined early in the merger process but then implemented at the end. The strategic intent must be identified before any discussions start between the two firms – sometimes well before but even when responding to an unexpected opportunity in the market, the strategy should be internally determined before the start of any conversation with the target or its advisors. Of course, the strategic assessment should continue to be reviewed and revised throughout the deal process, as additional information becomes available and as both internal and external conditions change (for example, market demand and competition).

The significance and importance of strategic direction and planning cannot be overstated. Indeed, one of the most prolific and common problems associated with deals and no doubt a causal factor in the high rate of documented failure is that most organizations simply do not have an acquisition strategy; rather, reacting to suggestions thrown at them by investment bankers and other professional intermediaries pitching for business, M&A activity often proceeds without being supported or underpinned by a competitive strategy model. Hence, of the prime reasons given for the shortfall in M&A results against expectations, the vast majority tend to reflect a failure to perform the required business intelligence to understand how the two companies would combine both strategically and culturally. This should be a special concern for cross-border acquisitions. For example, in just looking at some German acquirers, the cultural management difficulties encountered by Daimler, BMW, and Deutsche Bank in their foreign acquisitions could certainly have been minimized by better intelligence analysis.

BUSINESS INTELLIGENCE IN TARGET SELECTION

Major stakeholders influencing power cannot be ignored. Situations that could have been completely manageable ahead of time had the acquirers been aware of the issues, and acted on their knowledge to minimize their risk exposure, may be impossible to manage at a later point in time. Moreover this does not require much more than a certain change of attitude towards assessing the dynamics ruling the business environment.

In short, the vital thing is not to disregard information during the strategy planning stage which you might initially consider to be irrelevant, since that status might very well change. In fact one simple way to guard against this is to ensure that multiple perspectives are covered by involving as many diverse people as possible. Each will have different understandings of what is relevant, what is irrelevant and to what degree, and these varying perspectives can be used to take into consideration as many factors and dynamics as possible. For this to work effectively, the firm must nurture an ethic which embraces an open approach to the collection of information and an approach that encourages questioning. Seeking the same types of information, or only that which confirms the accepted wisdom, must be avoided at all costs.

In an attempt to ensure that M&A activity is embedded in strategy, companies should turn towards business intelligence in order to obtain the necessary insight required from a firm's market and competitive environment. It allows companies to understand their competitive positioning within the markets they serve, their strengths and weaknesses relative to significant competitors, or even the types and levels of competitive pressures being faced. Competitive intelligence feeds from corporate strategy into acquisition strategy, aiding companies to identify the right strategic approach to acquire and integrate a desirable target and to formulate the most appropriate tactics for negotiating with the acquisition's management. Whether focused on a product, geographical area, market structure, leadership, or level of concentration, business intelligence permits companies a level of foresight and insight that helps them ensure that they truly understand not only their current competitive landscape but their prospective one as well.

By assisting senior management to understand their own company's operations, strengths and weaknesses, and environmental positioning, business intelligence programs can help firms to develop a comprehensive acquisition program, derived from the opportunities and threats that emerge from environmental or industrial scanning. In short, whether as the upshot of macroeconomic analysis, detailed market research, industry investigation, or social, governmental, or cultural issue enquiry, the use of business intelligence to extract insight allows firms to understand better the industry and strategic landscape within which their potential acquisitions reside.

The use of corporate intelligence at the planning and direction stage of M&A activity is therefore critical to the subsequent success of deal flows. By side-stepping a deal-making mentality and focusing on critical questions that help review a company's position, intelligence facilitates a detailed understanding of whether an acquisition is in fact necessary and, if so, how it will fit within a firm's existing portfolio. Thus, by allowing firms to draw up acquisition criteria that potential takeover targets must satisfy, competitive intelligence systems can help to ensure that acquisition candidates will meet the organizational fit and post-merger integration criteria pivotal to deal success.

The development of 'winning' business strategies through M&A activity thus relies on management being able to make informed choices through reliable, timely, and relevant information, which smart competitive intelligence systems can provide.

In assessing the strategic fit of acquisitions, the use of intelligence tools such as benchmarking and product evaluation, market share measurements, patent research, value chain analyses, and customer evaluations allow companies to determine the opportunities – derived from M&A activity – for synergies and long-term growth.

Thus, by making sense of the vast amounts of information regarding a company's markets, environment, and direct/indirect competitors, so business intelligence provides management with the necessary insight to formulate winning corporate strategies. As the strategy and business development director of Yell, one of the FTSE 100 companies, expressed it, having '. . . a clear strategy of where a business wants to go and then building intelligence from that day forward . . .' enables companies to pre-select prospective acquisitions that will enable them not only to match but also exceed the return to shareholders offered by competitors.

BP acquisition of TNK for Russian oil reserves

In 2002 when BP admitted that production growth would be only 3% instead of the 5.5% target that the company had set, its stock price fell more than 7% in one day. Thus, BP had incentive to increase its reserves, a significant driver to its acquisition of the Russian oil company TNK in 2003. In large part because of that acquisition, BP's total resource base grew from 41 billion barrels of oil equivalent (bboe) at the end of 2001 to approximately 59 bboe at the end of 2005. The resource life of the company (an oil company's oil and gas reserves divided by annual production) increased over the same period from 33 years to 40 years.

From TNK's perspective, it had realized around the turn of the millennium that it would not be able to achieve its long-term strategic goals without a strategic alliance that would provide, among other things, access to large amounts of capital needed to develop and market its reserves. The possibilities of finding such a partner in Russia were limited, as was the prospect of increasing assets simply by buying or finding more oilfields. At that time, it appointed a financial advisor, Goldman Sachs, to find a partner and met with the major players in the global oil market.

A two-year long negotiation process ensued between BP and TNK, with significant attention paid to the structure of the deal and the due diligence, as reported by *Reuters*. The potential risks were high: not only was the industry inherently risky, but there were significant political risk issues for a major Western company investing in Russia at the time. Cultural issues also needed to be addressed if the deal would be successful post-acquisition.

The result was the purchase in August 2003 of 50% of TNK for approximately $7.7 billion. It represented one of the first international mega-deals in Russia. It was supported by the Russian government: to many foreign investors, the move by BP was risky, but from the Russian government side, it was a way to prove that major investments in Russia could be safe.

SCENARIO PLANNING

Information at the planning stage must be applied properly. Supporting this is the business intelligence tool of scenario planning as a means to develop the corporate ability to respond fast in an effective and thoughtful way. We introduced scenario planning in the second chapter on business intelligence, and planning is one place in the merger process where its use is critical. Many companies do not routinely use formalized scenario planning as a business tool, and where it is used, it is most common in large companies. It should, however, be used by all.

What makes this tool so powerful is that it is an excellent way to understand better the key drivers in a certain situation, how to prioritize them, how they could develop especially in terms of turning points, what relationships they have with each other, and what underlying assumptions are at work. In this way the scenarios can be used to evaluate what risks need to be minimized and how, and what opportunities can be sought out and to what effect. By way of a quick example, scenario planning can be used in the context of acquisition planning by taking into consideration a wide range of potential future developments that may impact the future performance of a target. Multiple scenarios can and should be built around any set of dynamics, from competitive reactions to the deal to future industry innovations, so that their effects can be forecast in terms of future performance. The pricing of the target can then be carried out based on the value implications of the most likely outcomes. The post-merger integration plan can be designed to address any strategic, management, and competitive issues.

One interviewee, in charge of M&A in a multinational pharmaceutical company, told us how they run scenarios before acquiring in order to see how their valuations hold up; while another, who is a partner in a major private equity firm, described how they run scenarios on possible targets over the whole time frame until point of exit. In fact, as the latter summarized it, 'the biggest problem we face is if our assessment goes wrong, or if we've misunderstood the position of the business, and its simply too costly to turn around.' Scenario planning as a component of a comprehensive business intelligence function enables businesses to avoid making such mistakes and also empowers them to exploit changes in the environment in a fast, effective, and cost-efficient manner. Indeed, at a very basic level as noted in Chapter 2, companies can log on to Shell's scenario planning website (www.shell. com/scenarios) or onto the CIA's or the Economist Intelligence Unit's for good quality, easily accessible first level intelligence.

Of course, scenario planning is extremely useful at any stage involving corporate decision making, be it in the exploration of which target or market to choose, or in constructing a development strategy. In both cases, the company is dealing with a set of forces in a market and an unknown future; scenario planning then allows one to understand the dynamics taking place and what the possible turning points could be in the development of various scenarios. Such an approach would also help companies build into their short- and long-term strategies alike various different possible courses of development depending on how things should pan out. The main bonus, however, is not fixing in on any particular course of action, since scenarios often depict extreme cases, but rather in involving top management in the process of discussing and exploring the issues.

By involving top management in their discussion and debate, the role of questioning will expose underlying assumptions so that an explicit understanding of the main issues involved may be built up among the management. The effect of this is to make management more astute at understanding the general situation, and more able to make fast and effective choices. Clearly in order for this exercise to be of sustainable use to management, it needs to be carried out at regular intervals in order to pre-empt any changes in the situation.

ALTERNATIVES TO ACQUISITION OR MERGER

There are very few situations where the only strategic alternative available to a company are to merge with another company or to acquire one. Companies must look at all of the other options before embarking on a strategy of merging or acquiring: mergers or acquisitions are very expensive, distracting to management and staff, and time consuming. Therefore, the strategic planning in advance of a merger must consider ways to achieve the same strategic goals without having to resort to a merger or acquisition.

What are the alternatives? They can be any of the following: internal growth, restructuring or divestitures, joint ventures or strategic alliances, holding companies or minority investments, or just doing nothing. Clear investigation through business intelligence techniques will assist in determining which would be the preferred route.

Alternatives to M&A

Internal growth is always an alternative, although often an acquisition may seem to managers a better option in order to accelerate growth or provide access to new markets, products, and management. It may also be the case that the company requires something to 'kick-start' the firm, as internal growth may have failed in the recent past. Internal growth also often does not attract the publicity of a large merger deal; for managers who seek the attention of the press and markets, a big acquisition may therefore appear better.

Restructuring and divestitures usually include the sale of a portion of a company to an outside party. There are two types of divestitures: downsizing (divesting non-profitable businesses) and downscoping (divesting non-core businesses).

The motives for both types of divestitures are many, but can be summarized as follows:

- Creating shareholder value (providing cash for other strategic investments, monetizing a growth business, providing choice for shareholders, attracting new investors, attracting more analysts, or increasing company flexibility).
- Management efficiency (where the expertise of management can be applied in a more focused organization).

- Strategic considerations (for example, focusing on core business, preparing for a horizontal merger, increasing cash flow, or allowing more dynamic development in subsidiaries, especially when still partly owned by the parent).
- Senior management's personal agendas, such as retirements or a manager's plan to head the divested division.

Joint ventures and strategic partnerships may provide some of the same benefits as a full acquisition, but without all of the costs and problems of completely integrating two companies. In a joint venture (JV) or strategic partnership, a separate entity is often created to conduct the activities of the JV. It is common for one of the partners to gain from the JV at the expense of the other, with significant intellectual property being lost from either or both sides. JVs and strategic partnerships are not long-term solutions. On average, they last about seven years, at which time one party usually takes over completely the activities of the JV. Careful attention should be paid to the terms of the agreement.

For joint ventures, such goals may include:

- Entering a new geographic market.
- Locking up a source of supply, if the JV is with a supplier.
- Economies of scale in manufacturing or marketing (for instance, in auto production).
- Technology knowledge transfer (for example, in R&D).
- Pre-empting competitors from linking with the partner.
- Speed to market.
- Overcoming political, cultural, and legal obstacles (such as entry into new geographic markets with strong local protectionism where full acquisition or a controlling position is not possible, as in some industries in China or India).

Strategic alliances may have slightly different objectives because they may be more flexible than joint ventures. They also come in wider varieties because of that flexibility: geography (global, regional, country), sectors/markets (certain products only, or a broad range), and functions (production, sales, R&D, logistics). Since they typically have a smaller financial commitment, they may enable companies to pursue goals otherwise not available. In addition, partners keep their strategic independence.

Companies must pick the strategic alliance or joint venture partner carefully, as they typically represent only a short- to medium-term strategy. What happens at the end? Eighty percent of joint ventures ultimately end up in a sale of the joint venture to one of the two joint venture partners.

Therefore, in any strategic alliance or joint venture, each company must look at the critical success factors of the deal, such as whether the partners bring complementary capabilities and market positions, how much market overlap there is (optimally minimal as the overlaps often bring insoluble disagreements), whether the deal is based on an equal balance of business strength and ownership interest, what level of autonomy from the parent companies will be allowed (yet do those companies still provide strong leadership and parental support?), the ability to build trust and confidence, and the acceptance that there will evolve a new common culture distinct from parents.

Risk factors are many as well: rivalry and distrust, changing partner strategies and priorities, possibilities for exploratory and exploitative alliances where one partner can hold the other partner hostage to the joint venture, the parent companies become too dependent on the partners, and that one partner becomes a takeover target or has a significant change in management and strategy, thus obviating the need for the JV.

Holding companies and minority investments have some of the same advantages as joint ventures and strategic partnerships. As with those, the challenge of integration is avoided. In these instances, the parent company owns sufficient stock in the target to control the target (this usually can be achieved for less than 51%, and may be possible with stock ownership as low as 10%). Typically these deals are lower cost; as the acquiring company does not have to buy 51% or 100% of the company, there is no control premium paid for the shares, they are easier to disassemble if regulators find antitrust problems or if a partner wants to terminate the relationship, and the acquirer may be able to get control without having to go through the long and expensive process of soliciting target shareholder approval. There are some disadvantages, such as the possibility of another company purchasing a similar share of the target and, in some jurisdictions, there are tax disincentives to this type of ownership (usually related to dividends).

Do nothing: Given the failure rate of mergers and acquisitions, 'doing nothing' would have served the shareholders better in a large majority of M&A situations in the 1980s and 1990s. For many companies, the strategic or financial imperative to merge/acquire is weak, and the alternative of maintaining the current situation can often be the stronger case. Sometimes the best strategic alternative is to walk away from a deal and refocus on the existing core business. Unfortunately, a merger or acquisition is often perceived as being a decisive step that demonstrates the strength of management and their willingness to take action, when in fact the opposite may be true. It is always difficult to decouple from the momentum of a deal, especially as there will be internal and external proponents arguing for completion.

ORGANIC GROWTH

As an alternative to a merger or acquisition, organic growth is usually less risky. This is also known as 'business as usual.' As it builds on what the company already has, senior management should be well aware of the capabilities of the company to achieve its growth targets. Competition is also well known, or at least should be. In addition, internally generated growth can be more profitable and often is the least expensive alternative as well (there's no acquisition premium built into the expenses and no cost of integration). Post-merger integration issues are non-existent, as organic growth builds on the existing culture.

But organic growth has inherent problems, as noted in the box. It may be too slow if competitors are growing faster through acquisition or more aggressive internal growth or if the industry is facing imminent structural changes (such as the introduction of new production methods, new sources of raw materials, market expansion, and so on). Thus, one may be faced with the decision that a merger or acquisition is imperative. But a full acquisition is not always necessary, as partial solutions exist through the use of partial acquisitions.

Organic growth ruined by acquisition

In 1995, BHP (Broken Hill Proprietary Company) of Australia, one of the world's largest mining companies, purchased Magma Copper Company in the US. Details of this deal will be provided in the case study in the due diligence chapter, but it is also relevant here as traditionally BHP had grown organically.

After decades of principally organic growth, it had started making large overseas acquisitions in 1984 with the purchase of the mining interests of Utah International for $2.4 billion, which at the time was the largest financial deal in Australian history.

The acquisition trail began to fall apart after the Magma deal, which took place just as production costs were rising and copper prices falling. As reported by the Australian Associated Press, the deal was 'quickly exposed . . . as a failure.' The company wrote down assets by A$2.16 billion and finally closed the business in mid-1999 at a final cost of A$1.8 billion and the loss of 2630 jobs.

ALLIANCES AND JOINT VENTURES

When choosing between a merger and alliance some companies choose alliances because post-merger integrations are always a challenge. This may be short-sighted, as the alliances often have as many coordination issues as integration, yet control and decision making are frequently less clear. The proper business intelligence due diligence should uncover these issues in either form. All too often the due diligence is less rigorous in an alliance or joint venture, but it shouldn't be. Risks to the core assets of a company may be just as high as in an acquisition or merger.

Nevertheless, the decision to enter into an alliance instead of full merger may be appropriate in certain circumstances. A company might want only a specific function, product, or capability of the partner firm. Acquiring the whole unit would be tantamount to using a hatchet when a penknife would suffice.

Comments on alliances in the pharma industry

In the pharmaceutical industry, a company may want to utilize only the R&D capabilities of a biotech firm to develop a particular drug. As one pharmaceutical industry manager told us, 'Buying the whole biotech company would be an expensive way of gaining the research capability.' As said by the managing partner at another pharmaceutical company, 'Mergers require the integration of separate entities into one which is not the case in a licensing deal. Therefore, mergers are by far more complex than licensing deals.'

Another fundamental difference between an alliance and a merger is overheads. A senior officer at GlaxoSmithKline noted in an interview: 'Mergers come with a complete infrastructure, culture, and overhead. An alliance around one opportunity does not typically entail acquiring infrastructure,' and a manager at Schering AG, the German pharmaceutical company, said, 'the drug manufacturers may have a widespread marketing network that would be able to rapidly capture market share when the product is eventually developed . . . Both parties bring resources to the table and, for this one particular venture, both can gain from the other's resources. In this case, a JV might be the best choice. Later, companies might decide to pursue other joint ventures or bring their relationships to a new level.'

A JV/alliance, moreover, may be considered as a way of testing the waters, assessing how well two potential merger partners may work together. Some issues might surface, such as irreconcilable cultural differences. Should this occur, the deal can usually be unwound at comparatively lower costs in a joint venture or an alliance compared to a merger or acquisition.

In a similar vein, there is usually less regulatory scrutiny of alliances and joint ventures than acquisitions. If the antitrust authorities find a venture to be anticompetitive, it can usually be terminated at a lower cost than a merger or acquisition of a business that has been fully integrated into the parent company.

However, while alliances can create enormous wealth, they can also become black holes for management time and resources. A potential problem regarding alliances and joint ventures is that participants might lack commitment which they might have had if the activities of the venture were part of the overall business. Parties might not be willing to share intellectual property or other proprietary information. The best managers may not be assigned to the alliance as they prefer to remain in the parent where they might perceive their promotion and compensation potential to be higher.

Moreover, it needs to be remembered that partners in an alliance or joint venture can disagree on certain issues even after a deal had been signed. With an M&A, 'internal discord' is still possible but, as noted by the licensing and alliance director at one company, 'with an outright acquisition a bidder takes clear control of the target . . . and there seems to be less opportunity for conflict.' With a joint venture or alliance, each partner stays independent and has only a limited ability to control the other.

The pharmaceutical industry is an excellent example of the mix of relationships that can develop. Companies simultaneously manage a number of various deal types in their portfolios, including alliances, joint ventures, partnerships, licensing agreements, and so on. These forms of cooperation can also be seen as steps to future mergers, as noted in the box above. Some pharma companies, however, from the very beginning decide to go for a merger.

'Outsourcing is generally painful as there is no retention of rewards,' said one speaker at a pharmaceutical conference in early 2006. Once an alliance terminates, the partners inevitably lose some of the value created as the result of their joint efforts.

Once the collaboration period expires the other party might simply walk away, taking the achieved synergies with it. In this sense a merger or acquisition would allow for greater use of the developed synergistic potential and the capabilities within the business, thus growing its power. Moreover, the process of selecting, negotiating, and implementing is time and resource consuming.

In a collaboration between a large company and a smaller one, the latter runs the risk of being abandoned by the partner. Its position is vulnerable. For example, the larger company might decide to change the direction of its strategic development and cooperation with a particular partner that might no longer be needed. This will result in premature contract termination. When a smaller company is acquired, this situation seems to be more secure for the managers and employees involved. However, the smaller company might reject an opportunity to merge and choose an alliance instead as a means to remain independent. The choice will naturally depend on the particular deal.

Also, sometimes market valuations of companies may be so low that being acquired is financially less attractive than an alliance, especially if the price for the acquisition is only marginally higher than for the alliance. What is more, investors tend to interpret an acquisition as a sign of quality for the smaller company involved, especially if the smaller company is entrepreneurial or engaged in primary research and development. It proves the entrepreneur's worth and increases its chances for 'good' deals at higher valuation prices and favorable deal terms in the future.

Nevertheless, an alliance with an established pharmaceutical company sends 'a positive signal' to the investor community. Entrepreneurial companies receive substantially higher valuations from private equity investors, venture capitalists, and the public equity market after forming their first joint venture or strategic alliance.

CONCLUSION

Lastly, all the information collected from the above processes must continually feed back into the initial corporate development strategy. In this way the corporate strategy works to define the business intelligence research carried out in search of an acquisition, and in turn the information collected is used to inform the strategy. Moreover, the long-term strategic intent must at all times be kept the point of focus, albeit changing as updated by the business intelligence process.

By being comprehensive in this strategic planning process and keeping abreast of new developments, the company's M&A team will be able to make quick and informed decisions at any point in time in support of the company's overall strategy. Indeed since timing is often of the essence in M&A, an intelligence-led approach will help to maintain an active, flexible, and comprehensive knowledge base useful to the organization in other areas such as marketing, sales, product development, client support, and internal reporting systems. This will not only increase the chances of making successful and productive acquisition choices, but should also result in drastically improving the company's competitiveness. Indeed speed and flexibility are the two most important advantages that the intelligence function contributes to the process of identifying acquisition targets.

CHAPTER 6

THE BEST DEFENSE

Not all mergers are welcome. There are as many different reasons to resist a takeover as there are deals. Often resistance is a tactic to get a higher price for the target's shareholders and a better deal for management, as a strong defense will often result in a sweetening of the bidder's offer. Management of the target may actually truly believe that the company will perform better on its own. Or, cynically speaking, management may just be looking out for its own interests.

However, the shareholders – and not management – have the ultimate say in the future direction of the company. Good corporate governance, laws, and regulations require that management should act in the interest of shareholders. Directors must act in their capacity as directors of the company and not for their personal or family shareholdings. Other legal requirements may also apply to the decisions of managers and directors, depending on the jurisdiction, such as the need to consult unions or employee works councils.

Nevertheless, it is often the case that a strong defense will buy time. This additional time may bring many changes to the battle. The bidder could even become a target. The target could make a bid for the bidder or perhaps another company will enter the takeover battle and make an offer for the original bidder. Thus, a strong defense is needed by both the bidder and target. It is critical to make sure that the defense chosen is the one most likely to succeed.

Defensive preparation

As Andrew Sawers, Financial Director, said in *Accountancy Age*, 'A hostile predator can spend months analyzing your financial and competitive position, then launch a takeover bid for your company when you least expect it and you're at your most vulnerable – possibly leaving you just 14 days in which to lodge a cogent defense of your track record. But you can prepare now – and that advice might make sense even if you aren't the group FD [Financial Director] of a quoted company.'

HOSTILE BIDS

As noted earlier, it was not until the 1970s that hostile takeovers became more common, and the 1980s saw a dramatic increase in the number and sophistication of hostile attacks. A group of advisors (led by investment bank Drexel Burnham Lambert) specialized in developing more complex bidding 'weapons,' while some other investment bankers specialized in defensive tactics. Goldman Sachs, often at the top of the league tables in M&A, specialized in acquisition defense and until the late 1980s did not take on new clients who were launching hostile bids; notably, they announced in 2006 that they once again would not usually represent clients who were making unsolicited offers. Working with firms such as Goldman Sachs, by 1990, 85% of US firms had some sort of anti-takeover measures and, during the 1990s, many UK and other non-US firms also adopted such measures.

ARBITRAGEURS

An M&A deal will bring rapid changes to the mix of share-holders. When a deal is announced – and often even in advance of a takeover if some investors believe that a battle is possible or likely – a significant proportion of the shares that are available to trade in the market will be purchased by arbitrageurs ('arbs') who are not long-term investors, but rather looking to make a quick profit on the relative price movements in the shares of the bidder, the target, and perhaps other companies in the industry who could enter the battle or be affected by the changing competition.

In order to put together an effective defense (and to mount an effective offense), management and their advisors must know how the arbitrageurs operate and whether they will act as allies or adversaries, or even shift allegiance in the middle of a battle, which they can do several times. The need to act on such intelligence is great. This can be achieved either by scenario planning or by the use of 'shadow teams' role playing as the different 'arb' groups.

Arbitrageurs bet on the price movements in takeover stocks. They absorb a large percentage of available stock when a hostile deal is announced and therefore also provide liquidity to share-holders who do not want to take the risks and uncertainty of waiting out the deal. Also, since most deals are announced at a target share price premium, the arbs allow existing shareholders to take some – but not all – of their profits before the deal closing.

Given the size of their holdings, as a group the arbitrageurs often become the decision makers. Fortunately, for others involved in the deal, the arbs are extremely rational and base their de-cisions almost exclusively on short-term financial factors.

Deutsche Börse fails due to arbs

In late 2004, the Deutsche Börse launched a takeover bid for the London Stock Exchange. As the largest stock exchange on the continent, Deutsche Börse's senior management (led by Werner Seifert) and board of directors (led by the former head of Deutsche Bank, Rolf Breuer) felt that there would be significant cost savings if the exchanges were merged. This was their second pass at buying the London Stock Exchange in almost as many years.

The deal came undone when the shareholding of the Deutsche Börse changed while the deal was being negotiated. The London Stock Exchange refused to be purchased and rallied support from many of its key stakeholders, including the companies listed on the exchange, the members of the exchange who traded shares, regulators in the United Kingdom, the press and, of course, their own shareholders. At the same time, some of the shareholders of the Deutsche Börse began to exert pressure to have it drop its bid for the London Stock Exchange and instead focus on returning value to the shareholders from the core business.

During the battle, the shareholding of Deutsche Börse changed significantly, with many of their historical German long-term investors selling shares which were then purchased by the arbitrageurs, with 14 of the largest 15 shareholders by the end of the battle being arbitrageurs, as reported by the *Financial Times* and *Bloomberg*. Ultimately, led by a fund called The Children's Investment Fund and supported by a number of investment companies in the United States, the bid was called off and both CEO Seifert and board chairman Breuer were forced to resign.

To understand how the arbs will act, it is important to know what they do with their stock in takeover companies. The arbs set up positions known as 'arbitrage hedging' wherein their risk exposure is designed to be exclusively to the deal and not the market. This typically takes the form of going long on the target company and short on the bidder, because historically the share prices of bidders decline when the deal is announced and the share prices of targets increase (although often not to the level of the bid, unless the market expects additional bidders to appear to force an auction). Arbs will therefore consider the following in setting up their hedged position: the current bid and its likelihood of being completed as stated, potential bids from other companies, and any changes initiated by the target as a defense.

If it is anticipated that the arbs will play a significant role in the takeover process, then the implications for this for the bidder (or the target in determining its defense) is to think like the target company's shareholders and set a price and total bid package that will be attractive to the arbs. Intelligence on those arbs is critical, as each fund or shareholder may follow a different investment strategy. For the arb, this means that they must value the return from voting their shares with management as greater than holding the shares or voting against management.

As a bidder, therefore, this leads to two possible (and incompatible) initial bid strategies:

- Bid high (a so-called 'bear hug') to kill off all resistance. Such a bid will tend to deter competitors who will find it difficult to match the high price quickly and also pressures the target company's directors to recommend accepting the bid because it is such a good deal for the company. Initial bids with a premium of 40% or greater are usually considered as bear hugs, although non-price considerations (such as the mix of cash and equity) may also be considered. Such an offer will typically gain the support of the arbs. However, it does have the major disadvantage that the target could perhaps have been bought at a lower price and the bidder's shareholders may therefore not support the deal.

- Bid low: offer a low purchase price in order to buy the company at the lowest possible price. Although this is useful when the bidder is patient or doesn't think there will be significant competing offers, it can attract others who now see the company in play, invites the company to restructure as a defense and leads to a longer contest which is unattractive to the arbitrageurs who are very sensitive to the price and timing issues noted above.

Even without the arbitrageurs buying shares, all companies should prepare for the potential of a hostile takeover bid even if there's no current threat, just as every medieval city needed to construct protective walls to deter potential marauding princes and potentates even if no attack was imminent. And as with those city-states, a larger company can be attacked by a smaller one. Often, once a bid is launched – or a city attacked – it is too late to build up the defenses. Advance planning and intelligence are key. Such bids can come quite unexpectedly and from a direction that was not anticipated.

PRIVATE COMPANIES

The best defense is to be a private, closely held company. Hostile bids are unlikely to be launched against closely held private companies or public companies where one or several large shareholders control the company, because the likelihood of success without the support of the controlling shareholder(s) is slim. Yet even in these situations, hostile bids have been successfully launched. As the sage said, 'Everyone has his price.'

VULNERABLE COMPANIES

Certain companies are more vulnerable to unsolicited bids, most especially when their shares are publicly held. Firms that are particularly vulnerable often have the following characteristics:

- Attractive brands, market position, intellectual property (patents, copyrights, and so on).
- Steady or predictable cash flows.
- Subsidiaries or properties that could be sold without impairing the company.
- Highly liquid balance sheet with excess cash and low debt.
- Undervalued stock price.
- Little insider shareholdings.

Note that many of these characteristics also describe a well-run company. Thus it is even more important for strong companies to have a strong defense. Just as history is replete with examples of monarchs launching attacks against neighbors with important resources, so is the history of business full of examples of companies trying to take over other companies with unique market positions or talented management.

DEFENSE PREPARATION

If a company thinks it may be vulnerable – and every company is, to some degree – it should take the following steps that reflect the best use of business intelligence:

- Understand shareholders – who is friendly, who is not – so as to know where to turn for support if a hostile bid arises. Remember the British parliamentary aphorism – the opposition is in front of me; the enemy is behind me.

– Institutional shareholders who may have large blocks of shares: these large shareholders are likely be the first ones contacted by a hostile bidder as the bidder seeks to determine who will support their bid and tries to build as quickly as possible a sympathetic group of shareholders. It is therefore important for a company to be in continual close contact with these large institutional shareholders so that they can determine whether they remain supportive of management. A friendly shareholder may also alert management to any approaches from hostile bidders. On the other hand, if a significant proportion of stock is held by arbitrageurs, they will tend to support the hostile bidder (as we saw above, arbitrageurs are 'hot money' and will seek the highest return in the shortest period possible).

– Retail investors and their motivations for owning the stock: typically retail investors are not well organized and are 'passive' investors willing to take the advice of management but can be swayed by price and effective lobbying by a bidder.

– Insiders, who can be assumed to be supportive of management and in many firms are required to vote their shares with the board.

Share ownership differs in the US and the UK as compared to most of the rest of the world. Ownership of US and UK companies tends to be diverse and there is little state ownership of company shares whereas in continental Europe, for example, there are often large crossholdings of shares by companies and large government stakes in companies. These crossholder or government shareholdings may be large enough and the shareholders sufficiently supportive of management to prevent unfriendly takeovers. However, as shown in the example of the Deutsche Börse mentioned earlier, ownership can change and even a company in continental Europe can no longer depend on its shareholders to support management.

- Closely monitor share trading as an early warning sign of purchases of large positions in the company (which is often the precursor to a public bid).
- Structure the company to make itself less attractive to a bidder:
  - Increase debt to repurchase equity. This not only means that the buyer will have to assume more debt, but the repurchase of equity should result in a higher share price and therefore would make the purchase more expensive to the buyer and may mean that existing shareholders are happier with the current management.
  - Invest cash flow and excess cash in financially attractive projects to make sure that the company is growing profitably. The cash could even be used to make an acquisition.
  - Increase dividends to 'buy' the support of shareholders. Retail investors traditionally do prefer stockholdings with dividends and increased dividends may also increase the share price.
  - Divest unnecessary or unprofitable divisions and realize the true value of any undervalued assets by selling them. There may also be financial restructuring measures to achieve this revaluation without divestment. This helps avoid the problem that many older companies have where their assets are recorded at historical values that do not reflect the real worth of the company's assets.

All these steps can and should be taken before a company receives an unsolicited bid: these should be considered 'best practice' for any well-prepared company regardless of whether it believes it is vulnerable to a bid or not. If these steps have not been taken, then they are an imperative once a bid is announced, but may be more difficult to initiate for the first time after a bid has been made and management is under pressure. It is best if these activities are continually reviewed.

For these and other actions, the company will need to make sure that it is in full compliance of the laws and regulations of all the countries in which it operates as well as the stock exchanges where its shares are traded. The UK City Code is a good example of such requirements. It has four main principles:

- Shareholders should have full information and should have it in a timely fashion.
- There should be equal treatment of all shareholders within a class of stock.
- Actions by management to frustrate a target must be approved with the consent of shareholders.
- There must be disclosure of appropriate dealings.

The UK City Code limits the offer period to 60 days from posting, and the bid must remain open for at least 21 days. Of course, regulations change and there are many more details of the UK City Code, so expert advice is required when a defense is prepared.

Forte's defense against Granada's bid

In November 1995, Granada plc (a UK-based television and leisure conglomerate) launched a £3.3 billion hostile bid for Forte plc (a UK-based hotel and foods company). As reported by one of the defense team in *Accountancy Age,* as the bid arrived on November 22 and the offer document published two days later, under the UK takeover rules, Forte only had until January 2 to produce its response. It was thought that the bid was timed purposely to be disruptive to the defense team during the holiday period.

Forte was vulnerable to a bid because the share price had recently declined by 30% on poor financial results – operating profits down 11%, earnings per share down 41%, and dividends down 24%. Some expensive strategic errors had been made by Forte management (for example, it owned 69% of the prestigious Savoy Hotel in London, but controlled less than 25% of the hotel). Over 70% of senior managers in the company had been with the hotel group less than two years. Share ownership prior to the bid was as follows: 80% owned by city fund managers, with one (Mercury Asset Management) owning 14%, 12% by private investors, and 8% by the Forte family.

Granada, on the other hand, had grown through aggressively acquiring companies. It was generally a hands-off manager of the companies it acquired after it had replaced entrenched management and sold off assets. It took the classic raider approach by pursuing the line that the sum of the parts is greater than the whole. In making the bid for Forte, Granada promised increased efficiency (better management), synergies (scope and scale operations), increased market share in certain segments, and greater shareholder value. The initial bid was a 23% premium on the Forte share price. By early January, Granada had raised its shareholding in Forte to 10%.

At the time of the bid, Forte had few defensive measures in place. Forte management was quite surprised that it was the target of a hostile bid. Together with its advisors, it rapidly put together a defensive strategy that incorporated the following:

- Writing a letter to staff and shareholders.
- Disposing of £1.5 billion in assets (some core, including the Savoy Hotel stake) which generated up to 50% of revenues.

> - Share buy-back of £500 million (20% of outstanding shares).
> - Lobbying institutional shareholders.
> - Attacking the Granada bid in the press.
>
> In early January, on the last day when it could initiate such an action under the takeover regulations, Granada increased its bid from £3.2 billion to £3.9 billion. The final nail in the Forte coffin came when Mercury Asset Management indicated that it would support Granada's bid, according to the BBC and subsequent interviews. Granada successfully purchased Forte following a Forte shareholder vote in late January 1996.

PREVENTIVE DEFENSES

In addition to the preparations that a company can take, there are other more specific measures that can be implemented in advance of a takeover bid. These are called 'preventive defensive tactics,' although they are also sometimes referred to as 'passive' actions, as they just sit in the corporate charter or in other places in the organization until activated by a takeover bid. These so-called 'sleeper tactics' act just as a sleeper spy during the Cold War, waiting to be activated: many are totally innocuous until the trigger event takes place.

Some of the tactics, such as 'poison pills', that will be discussed in this section are not allowed in some jurisdictions but in an era of firms operating globally, it is important to note all of these measures, as a company seeking global leadership may run into these types of measures outside its home area.

There are a number of preventive takeover measures – some with very colorful names – which have been designed to protect a company from unwanted takeover. These measures are not mutually exclusive, and a company can utilize many of them if its shareholders approve. New measures are being continually designed by companies and their advisors. Many will require prior approval by a majority of shareholders before they can be adopted.

What is a **poison pill**? It is so called because, if the would-be acquiring company takes over the target, the acquirer will have to swallow the poisonous consequences. In the US, poison pills are actually a type of corporate charter amendment. The term 'poison pill' is used somewhat differently outside the US where it denotes any action required of the bidder that may, when taken, be prohibitively expensive. In this regard, unfunded pension plans have become very effective defensive techniques in the successful defenses of both the bookseller WH Smith and the retailer Marks & Spencer. In the latter case, the Marks & Spencer pension trustees revealed during a hostile takeover bid that additional funds on the order of £785 million would need to be contributed into the pension fund to cover the potential deficit. Along with other defenses, this was enough to cause the bidder to withdraw.

The poison pill changes the capital structure of the target and possibly even that of the acquirer in such a way that if activated ('swallowed'), the financial consequences are so drastically bad that the acquirer would walk away from the deal (or never make the offer) rather than consummate it. In practice, this means that the poison pill needs to be rescinded or resolved before a deal completes, and this typically means that the buyer needs to pay a higher price for the company than if the poison pill had not existed.

Most publicly held companies in the US have poison pills in their charter. Why don't all companies have poison pills? Usually it is because of the perception that poison pills might scare off a potential bidder and therefore would not enhance shareholder value. Our own research has shown that poison pills were one of the most effective ways to increase shareholder value in a takeover, and other studies in the US have confirmed this view. Today there is talk that poison pills, by protecting the company as it currently is run, lead to entrenched management and may be inconsistent with good corporate governance.

Misuse of poison pills

In a case that we will show again when discussing financial due diligence, Symbol Technologies in 1998 attempted to take over its smaller rival, Telxon. Both made point-of-scale scanners (such as found in retail stores) and other data-collection products. As reported in court papers, Symbol made an initial all-cash offer of around $800 million for Telxon, which was 40% higher than the market price at offering, at $38 per share and then a hybrid (cash and stock) offer at a higher price, valued around $42 per share.

In a well-publicized law suit, the shareholders sued Telxon for refusing to rescind its poison pill, and, among other items, derailed the deal. Ultimately, Telxon agreed that it would not invoke its poison pill if it received a fully financed cash offer for more than a specified premium.

In addition to poison pills, there are other preventive measures that a company can take before any bid is received:

- **'Shark repellents'** is the term used for any defensive corporate charter amendment (including poison pills). In addition to those poison pills, there are several that are now so common that they represent good corporate practice generally:

- **supermajority provisions**, whereby decisions such as the acceptance of a take-over offer requires shareholder approval well above 50% (and often as high as 75%);
- **staggered boards** so that a hostile bidder cannot replace the board in one election;
- **fair price provisions** for the protection of minority shareholders, so that all shareholders are treated equally (without such provisions, it might be possible to offer to purchase shares at a higher price for those who accept early before they would have time to analyze the deal properly);
- **dual capitalization**: two classes of stock with different voting rights (and with the assumption that there is greater power to those who might be more sympathetic to management).

- **Golden parachutes** are attractive severance agreements for top management, often for very large sums (for example, the chairman of Bankers Trust had a golden parachute reputed to be over $100 million when his company was acquired in 1999 by Deutsche Bank). Golden parachutes are not a defense by themselves, but in combination with other measures may discourage bidders by raising the price of the acquisition.
- **Managerial share ownership** refers to the fact that when management owns or controls a large portion of the company's shares, it can then vote those shares to defend against an unwanted bidder. Such managerial share ownership may come from shares issued as incentive compensation (bonuses in shares or stock options) or as part of a broader employee stock ownership plan. Since the late 1980s, companies have been encouraging current employees to have larger share ownership, not just to prevent unwanted takeovers but also to give the employees a stake in the company's future and therefore to align their motivations closer to the firm.
- Lastly, it is possible for a company to **reincorporate** in a jurisdiction where it may be more difficult for a bidder to be

successful in a hostile takeover situation. Some countries and other legal jurisdictions (such as individual states in the US) have laws that protect companies from unsolicited bids or that offer greater protections for shareholders than other jurisdictions. For example, in the US most large public companies are incorporated in Delaware where there is significant legal experience and case history developed in corporate law and where the requirements regarding hostile bids are well documented. Other states with less developed corporate law may be less clear as to the required actions of both the bidder and the target. In Europe, France is known to protect its companies from foreign takeovers.

ACTIVE DEFENSES

As with the passive defenses, there are a number of sometimes very colorful terms used to describe the variety of active anti-takeover measures. Given the frequency with which a number of these measures have been used, it is useful to discuss some of them in more detail.

Four major groupings of active takeover defenses

- Direct approach to bidder:
  - greenmail: payment of a premium to buy shares of a bidder threatening hostile action;
  - standstill agreements: payment to an existing shareholder not to purchase any more shares, usually just for a specific period of time;
  - Pac-Man defense: turn the tables and make an offer for the hostile bidder.

- Spoiling tactics: forging arrangements with allies:
    - white knight: friendly buyer preferred to the hostile buyer ('black knight');
    - white squire: friendly buyer of a block of stock that is put in safe hands until the battle is over;
    - lock-up transactions: sale of assets that makes target less desirable, especially an asset that a particular hostile bidder may be seeking;
    - lock-up options: an option that gives a potential buyer the right to buy certain assets at an attractive price; a lock-up transaction can be structured in this way;
    - powerful stakeholder allies: blocking/delaying measures by stakeholders (e.g. unions, governments, and so on).
- Financial actions:
    - capital structure change: through recapitalization or other changes, target assumes more debt or pays out a sizeable special dividend;
    - asset revaluation: revalue balance sheet items (such as real estate) to raise the share price;
    - declare dividend: sell core or highly valued assets (or even better, unwanted assets) to return cash to shareholders.
- Communications:
    - just say 'no': publicly state that the offer is resoundingly rejected;
    - throw mud: personal attacks on opposition management;
    - appeal to shareholders: publicize a convincing strategic plan and financial forecast showing how the company can independently increase its share price;
    - identify conflicts of interest and mistakes: careful scrutiny of advisor roles;
    - litigation: tie up the bidder in the courts to distract them.

The use of **greenmail** virtually disappeared in the 1990s because of tax law changes in the US and the fear of litigation. Prior to this, greenmail could be 'demanded' by raiders and paid by targets to prevent takeovers. Before those legal changes, in the mid-1980s, a number of companies adopted corporate charter amendments that prevented the payment of greenmail.

Standstill agreements were most common in the 1980s. For example, Drexel Burnham Lambert accepted $1.75 million not to help another bidder make a bid for Gillette. Later, in a June 1998 lawsuit by shareholders following a takeover attempt of Coniston, it was revealed that at least 10 other companies accepted greenmail from Gillette, including well-known firms such as Colgate-Palmolive, Ralston Purina, Anheuser-Busch, PepsiCo, Citicorp, Kohlberg Kravis, and Forstmann Little.

As third-party companies riding to the rescue of the target of an unwelcome bid, **white knights** may represent an attractive defense. However, most studies have shown that the white knights tend to incur losses because the acquisitions are put together in haste in the midst of active takeover bids. The acquisition may therefore not be part of a long-term strategic plan and may not be as advisable as other deals that are more thought out. In addition, the white knights are attempting to take over companies that already have one bidder. With the appearance of the white knight, an auction is created, which tends to result in higher values as well. However, if the white knight had anyway been contemplating such an acquisition (and particularly if the white knight had already considered that particular target company) or if acquisition of the target by a competitor would allow that competitor to become unacceptably stronger when compared to the unchanged position of the white knight, then such an acquisition by a white knight might be advisable.

Capital structure changes can take a number of forms. These include issuing more shares (a general issue or for a **white squire**), buying back shares (using a self tender, targeted share repurchases, or open market purchases), assuming more debt (by issuing bonds or taking out a bank loan), or recapitalizing. Recapitalizations generally mean that the capital structure is changed either through a leveraged recapitalization (changing the capital structure through the increased use of debt) or even more significant recapitalizations such as taking a company private in a leveraged buy-out, selling off valued assets or at least assets of great value to the hostile bidder (also known as a **lock–up transaction**), liquidating the company (which actually may result in a higher value for shareholders in some instances), or acquiring other companies. In a takeover context, when debt is increased, it may include using proceeds to finance a counterbid for the company that is trying to take the target over (a **Pac-Man defense** named after the popular early video game of the same name).

Some companies have found that they can marshal the support of **powerful allies** to their cause of preventing a hostile takeover. These allies can be organizations already affiliated with the target company which have a vested interest in the deal (such as unions, who may seek to preserve jobs, as unions know that most mergers are quickly followed by at least one wave of redundancies). In some jurisdictions, the government may even act as an ally, such as a national government trying to preserve for prestige reasons the local ownership of a leading company in a critical industry (especially companies in the defense industry, utilities and public services, banking and insurance, and some major manufacturers such as automobiles).

UK government rides to the rescue

In early 2006, Russia's Gazprom, the world's biggest gas company, proposed an acquisition of Centrica, Britain's largest supplier of gas and electricity. As reported on the BBC, the UK government was concerned about this deal as it raised strategic issues such as the future security of the supply of natural gas to the UK. In the end, the British government said it would not stand in the way of a purchase. However, before that statement, this issue raised concerns among Russian investors and significantly delayed the whole process. Even though the deal never took place, the Russians also were unenthusiastic about letting third parties gain access to Gazprom's export pipelines as had been proposed.

Another famous example cited frequently was the French government's resistance to the purchase of Danone, the yoghurt company, on national security grounds.

Another measure is the **just say 'no' defense**. Courts have ruled (in the US and UK) that it is legal for a board simply to reject an offer if it believes it to be inadequate. Boards must be able to show that they have acted with due diligence and in good faith, or they open themselves up to shareholder suits.

Organizations may also use business intelligence as a bid defense mechanism against unwanted interest from third parties. Many companies use the 'court of public opinion' to appeal to shareholders in order to derail a bid attempt. Whether using business intelligence techniques to 'dig dirt' on potential acquirers (such as irregularities and acts of fraud, regulatory violations and conflicts of interest among stakeholders), **throw mud** or attempt simply to shoot down a bid, it is evident that business intelligence has a pivotal role to play in enabling parties to a transaction to gain the upper hand. One of the most crucial, and least discussed, elements of intelligence is *dis*information. Remember, when informants provide information, they may not be working for you.

Throwing dirt

The £1.6 billion attempted hostile takeover by Elders IXL (now Fosters Group) of Scottish and Newcastle (S&N) in 1988 not only witnessed the referral of the bid to the Monopolies and Mergers Commission (MMC), but also led to the sponsorship of a full-page hostile advert by S&N in the *Melbourne Age* newspaper in Australia on the eve of Elders' annual general meeting (entitled 'Ten things Elders IXL's shareholders may wish to ask their board'), an investigation into allegations that Elders bought a significant stake in S&N through 'short selling' by City professionals, and the publication of a wide-ranging report examining Elders' past takeover tactics and its level of debt, alleging that the company was unfit to be a worthy owner of Britain's (then) fifth-biggest brewer.

Similarly, in early 2005, Marks & Spencer used litigation to stall Sir Philip Green's attempted takeover of Marks & Spencer. As noted in court documents, Marks & Spencer lawyers argued successfully before the judge that Green's legal advisor, Freshfields Bruckhaus Deringer, was in possession of sensitive information that was related directly to the bid and therefore had a conflict of interest. They claimed that Freshfields had previously advised Marks & Spencer on the employment contract for the designer of one of Marks & Spencer's key clothing brands and had also worked on behalf of Marks & Spencer in a legal battle with one of its suppliers. Ultimately, Green was forced to change law firms, giving a temporary advantage to Marks and Spencer. As Stuart Rose said, 'It wasn't a big deal, but for two or three days, Green was without a lawyer. That gave us some breathing space.'

Litigation can be used quite effectively as a defense. One goal of such litigation is to choose a more favorable forum for the target's defense (usually a 'home' court where a friendly ruling is more likely), precluding the raider from taking the initiative and suing first, delaying the bidder to allow time to adopt other defensive tactics and simultaneously providing a psychological lift to the target's management. The litigation can be based on antitrust concerns (especially effective in horizontal mergers) or charges of inadequate disclosure or fraud. Our analysis has shown that companies willing to use the courts are more successful in their defenses against unwanted takeovers.

'Just say no' and litigate

In early 2006, Mirant Corporation sent a $7.8 billion unsolicited proposal to the larger NRG Energy, Inc. to purchase 100% of its competitor. Both companies operated in the energy market. Mirant had been in bankruptcy for three years and had only emerged from bankruptcy four months before the offer. NRG had itself been in talks to acquire Mirant six months earlier.

Nevertheless, NRG's board 'unanimously rejected' the bid immediately. In its press release, the chairman and CEO of NRG said that they had 'concluded that Mirant is a company and stock with flat earnings, little to no growth opportunity beyond 2007, substantial and imminent environmental capital expenditures, and significant [earnings] exposure to developing country risk.' He went on to say that the earlier discussions had ended for reasons 'which neither [Mirant] nor Goldman Sachs [Mirant's financial advisor] has ever attempted to refute.' He concluded by stating that Mirant's 'proposal is simply the wrong deal at the wrong time.'

According to press reports and as reported by *The New York Times*, the two companies had been in secret negotiations for at least two years. They also reported that Mirant had even filed a lawsuit against NRG in which it said that Goldman Sachs may have been conflicted because they had inside information about both companies. Not unexpectedly, Goldman Sachs resigned from working with NRG on the deal.

CONCLUSION

It is often difficult if not impossible to know exactly what defense will work. Each merger or acquisition is different. There may be many merger arbitrageurs taking positions and each with different motivations as well. Empirical evidence shows that among those firms targeted in a hostile bid, only approximately one third were able to remain independent (the raider only succeeded less than 50% of the time, and the remaining companies were acquired by a third party). Therefore, most defending companies and their advisors put together a complex combination of passive and active defenses – not knowing which will ultimately be the measure (or measures) that enable shareholders to maximize the value of the company or that will cause the hostile bidder to withdraw.

Defensive measures taken by a target (or potential target) are designed to make it difficult, but not impossible, for a hostile bid to succeed. These measures should exact a higher price and buy time to mount a more effective active defense. Research shows that defensive tactics are beneficial to shareholders and that companies with either or both preventive and active defenses provide up to 30% higher returns to shareholders than companies without such defenses. It is impossible to overemphasize the significance of comprehensive knowledge about targets and bidders. A failure to resource the intelligence machinery that would provide such knowledge is an unnecessarily risky decision.

CHAPTER 7

DUE DILIGENCE

*I*n M&A, due diligence is the process of investigating the details of a potential target and the industry within which it operates. Buyers must understand what they are buying. Targets must understand who is pursuing them and whether they should accept an offer.

This due diligence process includes the verification of material facts and an examination of the external relationships of the company and the internal finances, operations, and management. Due diligence is often seen as the bidder's responsibility. This is wrong. It is just as important for the target to conduct due diligence on the bidder in order to determine whether the offer is bona fide and legitimate – specifically and most importantly to ascertain whether the bidder has the financial capacity to complete the transaction. In such situations the target is conducting due diligence in order to provide its board with the ability to make an informed recommendation to shareholders as to whether to accept the offer. In a merger situation where the parties are 'equals,' both companies should do due full diligence on each other.

Target due diligence on the bidder

In late April 1991, James Hanson and Gordon White of Hanson plc (at the time, a large multi-national conglomerate) purchased a 2.8% stake in ICI, the UK-based giant global chemicals firm. The stake was reported to be a lead-up to a possible £10 billion acquisition of the company.

Little more than a month later, it was reported that Lord White had been using the company's money to purchase racing horses, but losing nearly £8 million over the prior four years. Eighty percent of the company owning the horses was in the hands of Hanson, but corporate officers personally owned the remaining portion. As reported by the *Independent on Sunday*, 'This sort of mixing of personal and public company interests is bad form even when it is disclosed and profitable, but in this case it was neither. It must be on the edges of acceptable public company behavior to indulge the pleasures and hobbies of executives in this manner. Let's hope for Hanson's sake that there are no other nasties of this type lurking in its cupboard.'

The Sunday Times reported the same day that ICI 'suspects Hanson wants to take it over [and] cannot believe its luck. Last week's revelation about Hanson's unsuccessful investments in horseflesh has raised all sorts of issues on corporate governance; the kind of issues that ICI will drag up as a defence if Hanson does produce a blockbusting cash bid.'

Yet, in reality business intelligence is also often ignored for a variety of reasons, some unfortunately driven by the personal agendas of those involved in the deal. Indeed, as one mining industry executive expressed to us, with '. . . individuals' personal credibility or job promotions riding on a deal, they are often encouraged by their own egos to ensure that a deal doesn't fail as a result of "uncomfortable" information. . . .' Alternatively, mistakenly presuming facts to be irrelevant (when they are not) can also result in catastrophic intelligence and commercial failures for companies involved in deficient M&A deals. As Marco Boschetti, Principal in M&A at Towers Perrin, told us, 'Due diligence is about analyzing data the vendor provides in response to detailed requests. Business intelligence ensures you ask – and focus – on the *right* questions.'

However, an often neglected reason that due diligence is poorly conducted is not that the personnel are unfocused or biased or, indeed, incompetent; rather the real reason is that due diligence is seen as a project-based activity. Strategy, due diligence, and post-merger management are seen as separate activities. In one of the case studies that follow we look at how a venture capitalist, Alchemy, incorporates business intelligence in the entire acquisition process and as part of its normal operational procedures. That is the lesson for other corporates – integrate the intelligence function in the day-to-day business routine.

Even in organizations that nominally have a business intelligence function, the M&A group rarely engage the intelligence staff other than as a provider, and usually at the last minute. Our interviews with business intelligence staff confirm this and also confirm that they feel undervalued and peripheral. As such they become disengaged and can even become obstructive. The integration of the intelligence function into the normal operating routine will speed the due diligence because most of the intelligence will be available on demand and may actually be able to be accessed directly from an in-house database. Finally, such a function will often generate ideas for potential M&A targets.

Irrespective of the existence of an internal or external intelligence function, there are rules that can increase the likelihood of competitive advantage. To be successfully conducted, due diligence must have senior management involvement and control, often assisted by outside experts such as management consulting firms, accountants, or investment banks (who may not be disinterested parties, as noted in the chapter on advisors).

Ideally, the due diligence should start during the deal conception phase and use available public information. It should then continue throughout the merger process as further information becomes available. It is easier to achieve high quality data if the deal is friendly; in unfriendly deals the due diligence may never progress further than publicly available data until after the deal is approved. This is where the intelligence function of the bidding organization is most needed. Due diligence also identifies contingent issues for the deal, that is, issues that cannot be resolved at the time of the negotiation or where further information is needed to reach an agreement.

Intelligence failure in due diligence: VeriSign's purchase of Jamba

On June 3, 2004, VeriSign acquired privately held Berlin-based Jamba AG for $273 million. The initial market reaction was positive, as VeriSign's stock closed up 3.4% on the day.

VeriSign Inc. was an internet infrastructure services company founded in the US in 1995 as a spin-off from another internet company. At the time of the Jamba purchase, VeriSign was processing up to 18 billion internet interactions daily and supported over 100 million phone calls. They provided the services that enabled over 3000 enterprises and 500 000 websites to operate. Through its domain name registry, it managed over 50 million digital identities in over 350 languages. Revenues were over $1 billion in 2003 although the company operated at a loss, losing almost $260 million in that year. VeriSign had extensive experience with acquisitions, having made 17 acquisitions prior to Jamba, including four that were valued more than the Jamba purchase.

Jamba AG was started in August 2000 by two brothers in Germany. With millions of subscribers, Jamba was the leading provider of mobile content delivery services in Europe and operated in 18 countries worldwide. Jamba was best known for the Crazy Frog character used in the marketing of the ring tone which was the most successful ring tone of all time and made Jamba $14 million.

VeriSign's press release on the Jamba acquisition described it as 'an extension of their Communications Services Intelligent Communication, Commerce, and Content (IC3) strategy, which provides carriers with the intelligent infrastructure services they need to help their customers find, connect, secure, and transact over any network, anywhere.' Jamba gave VeriSign relationships with 13 European telecommunications carriers, 180 content providers, and a growing European customer base.

The purchase was initially highly praised. In October 2005, Frost & Sullivan, a global consulting company, awarded VeriSign with its 2005 Premium Mobile Content Acquisition of the Year Award for the Jamba acquisition. But at the same time, VeriSign was announcing that it would miss its third quarter earnings target due to European regulations on mobile content. The next day, the press was reporting that this was due to the Jamba acquisition.

Complaints to regulators had noted that Jamster, the UK and US rebranding of Jamba, was targeting children despite the fact that Jamster's mobile content services were intended for adult customers only. New UK regulations in September

2005 required that Jamster television advertisements appear only after 9:00 pm. Perhaps more disturbingly, only days before the acquisition, VeriSign discovered that a significant portion of Jamba's profits came from the distribution of adult content in Germany – despite a VeriSign policy of not supporting adult or pornographic companies where possible. There were backlashes in Germany over other issues and Jamba was forced to make a declaration of discontinuance regarding many of its contracts. Also in Germany, a society of German music authors submitted an application to an arbitration board for copyright matters. Suits had also been filed in the US where parents formed a class-action suit against Jamster and VeriSign regarding unwanted subscriptions, unsolicited texts, and misleading advertising. Lastly, another US company, Jamdat Mobile, sued for trademark infringement over the Jamster brand.

These are all issues that could have been identified in the due diligence process preceding purchase. Notably, Jamba's revenues peaked in the June 2005 quarter and subsequently declined.

The growth of 'enhanced' due diligence – driven in part by compliance with American legislation such as Sarbanes-Oxley, the Patriot Act, and the Foreign Corrupt Practices Act to ensure that targets are not involved in illegal practices – has in many ways become one of the defining features of the latest wave of M&A deals, which in turn has (hopefully) led to companies paying a more accurate price for their targets. In fact, our most recent research (as discussed in Chapter 1) has discovered that the average M&A deal in the current merger wave is finally making money for the acquirer's shareholders. This is in distinct contrast to the merger waves before the new millennium when shareholder value was lost on average for the acquiring company.

Faced with the combined risks that an acquisition may fail to achieve its set objectives for the buyer, that it may be unable to continue to carry on its business after the acquisition, or that it may prove difficult to integrate and then manage or control within the framework of a new owner, many prospective acquirers now tend towards a comprehensive due diligence process in order to mitigate the plethora of risks that surround an M&A deal.

Furthermore, given the potential to rush into deals without adequate analysis or planning, companies need to perform adequate and comprehensive due diligence to ensure that acquisition targets are carefully selected and priced appropriately. Given managements' often overconfidence in their abilities to manage the assets being acquired, so due diligence needs to serve as a brake of sorts in the M&A process to ensure that shareholders do not suffer the consequences of irrational premiums being paid for targets – the so-called 'winner's curse.'

Dire impact of not uncovering critical issues

The acquisition of International Signal and Control (ISC) by Ferranti, a British defense electronics company in 1987, clearly highlights the consequences of inadequate financial due diligence.

Having paid £215 million for the company, unknown to Ferranti, ISC's business primarily consisted of illegal arms sales started at the behest of various US clandestine organizations. While on paper the firm looked to be extremely profitable off the back of sales of high margin 'above-board' goods and services, in reality, however, the company's financial buoyancy was driven instead by £200 million worth of illegal contracts which ceased with the sale to Ferranti.

> With no obvious legal cash flow to support the business, Ferranti had to write off the entire investment in ISC, with the ensuing massive financial and legal difficulties forcing the combined company into bankruptcy in December 1993.
>
> Most interesting was that Ferranti's chairman, Sir Derek Alun-Jones, was reported by *The Economist* in September 1989 as having said, 'We were an early investor in ISC . . . so we probably know them better than anyone in the world.' *The Economist* then wrote: 'That boast now sounds horribly hollow . . . It is hard to imagine how Ferranti's management overlooked such danger signals, particularly Sir Derek, a lawyer who was brought into Ferranti after a government rescue in 1975 to bring hard-nosed business expertise to a company thought too dominated by technologists.'

ORGANIZING FOR DUE DILIGENCE

At its most obvious, business intelligence within a deal is about collecting as much information as possible at every level and around each facet of the takeover. It makes perfect sense that the more information there is the more likely the right measures can be taken to increase success. To quote from a Pricewaterhouse-Coopers report issued in late 2002: 'We always have to make decisions based on imperfect information. But the more information you have and the more you transform that into what we call knowledge, the more likely you are to be successful.'

That said, simply gaining more and more information is not enough, since there is only a certain amount that can be handled by the number of people involved, the time restrictions under which they are working, the quality and variety of resources available to them, as well as the perspectives and intentions of those who are imparting the information to them. Moreover there is the danger of being overloaded by too much information if those involved do not have good management methods. The absorption capacity can be expanded with special intelligence training; however, this can in large part be achieved by a focus on improvements in deal management and approach. Recalling the integration of intelligence mentioned earlier in the chapter, having that information already to hand and already analyzed will speed the process and that may give the bidder the crucial edge.

By and large it is not the quantity of information that matters so much as the quality and how it is used. The questions that must therefore be posed here are: how do we identify important issues, how do we access them as efficiently as possible, and how do we effectively manage the flow of information such that we can inform our decision making processes as effectively as possible.

While diligence may not be cheap (as a result of fees charged for often highly complex work by professional services firms), the alternative of litigation or the destruction of shareholder value on the other hand (as a consequence of having been 'penny wise and pound foolish' in the execution of the due diligence process) may prove far more costly in the long run as the direct result of failing to make proper enquiries. Thus, as a way of mitigating the potential failure of a warranty claim or to enable a buyer to avoid leaving itself open to criticism if an acquisition fails or if the price paid is judged to have been excessive when facts come to light 'post ante,' the effective due diligence process will help to reduce the probability that problems will surface later in the transaction or after the deal has closed.

It is important to manage the outflow of information as well during the due diligence and, in fact, during the entire deal process. There is a notoriously bad track record of confidentiality in the market. The defensive aspects of business intelligence are especially significant here. Again, if these are not second nature and normal procedure and are only enacted during a deal, they will not be effective. Highly confidential or sensitive information, such as the details that go into the valuation and pricing of a deal, for example, must be kept under strict control of the absolute few who require it. However, all other degrees of confidential information, from the least to the middle levels, can be used as bargaining chips or negotiation pieces that provide varying degrees of leverage, especially during the negotiation of a deal.

Since it is near impossible to stop leakage of information, it makes sense to use the power of the information being given out of the company as a means to negotiating a level of trust or in exchange for other information. However, in order to establish and really maximize this, the company must have formal and explicit principles and procedures designed to control, manage and reap the benefits of this approach. Towards that end, the last few years have seen an increase in in-house M&A teams in order to limit information leakage. This development also enables them to promote and benefit directly from their own expertise which then becomes the substance of their unique competitive advantage. As one of our interviewees succinctly phrased it 'having people who have done it time and time again really improves your productivity.'

THE DUE DILIGENCE PROCESS

While due diligence may only be one part of an acquisition or investment exercise, in many ways it is by far the most significant aspect of the M&A process, enabling companies to control risk while contributing to the effective management of the target and the realization of the goals of the acquisition.

Bridging the strategic review and completion phases of any merger or acquisition exercise, the due diligence process allows prospective acquirers to understand as much as possible about the target company and make sure that what it believes is being purchased is actually what is being purchased. It therefore identifies both the 'knowns' as well as the issues that cannot be resolved prior to the purchase. It identifies negotiating issues and provides information of relevance to the ongoing post-deal integration planning. Having utilized business intelligence techniques to search and gather detailed information on potential strong contenders for purchase (or merger), the due diligence process digs deeper *before* the point of no return in consummating a deal.

Although there is no discretionary or legal definition of 'due diligence' *per se*, the process – encompassing the enquiry, investigation and review of a plethora of different elements of a business – allows firms to understand more about their target and the uncertainties surrounding a deal. Thus, by helping acquirers to identify issues and concerns, the due diligence process can feed into price negotiations between firms while enabling companies to 'de-risk' a deal by pinpointing aspects against which legal and contractual protection should be sought via indemnities or warranties. As an instrument through which to reveal and remedy potential sources of risk, due diligence – by confirming the expectations of the buyer – enables firms to formulate remedies and solutions to any 'uncovered' problems, so enabling a deal to proceed. In many ways, therefore, due diligence as an activity lends comfort to an acquirer's senior management, the board, and ultimately the shareholders, who should all insist on a rigorous due diligence process that provides them with relative (though not absolute) assurance that their bid is both sensible and that they have uncovered any risks and problems pertaining to a deal that may derail matters in the future.

The key factors in conducting informative and timely due diligence are the following:

- Identifying the most important items to collect, as in most deals there is not enough time to look at everything in as much detail as desired.

- Identifying the right sources for the desired information within the required time frame.
- Identifying the right people to review the data: this should naturally include the people who know most about that area and should also include people who are expected to be managing the business post-acquisition and therefore who will use that information.

The target company is not required to provide to a bidder (or vice versa) any confidential or non-public information unless in a situation where compelled by the courts (as in a bankruptcy) for example if an auction process has been initiated by the target so that there are multiple bidders (in which case the target does not need to disclose anything but if it does, it must disclose information equally to all parties when requested by those parties) or if the management of the target determines that it is in the best interests of their shareholders that such information be disclosed. The target is also not required to disclose information to any party that the party has not requested. Of course, withholding information is not necessarily recommended, especially if it is necessary to keep the deal friendly and to get a higher price (assuming that the information is positive, or else the inverse would be true).

If non-public information is disclosed during due diligence, then the company providing that information may want to protect it through a confidentiality agreement. Such an agreement may include other restrictions on the requesting party, such as limiting share purchases or prohibiting the initiation of or participation in tender offers without the target's permission. Such agreements must be applied equally to all parties requesting information. The target may not play favorites, even if one potential buyer is friendly and another hostile. Legal advice should always be sought when deciding whether to withhold information requested formally.

Borrowing from Irving Janis' groundbreaking work on 'Groupthink', the M&A decision making process – shaped and framed by time restrictions, tensions, and anxiety – often results in a reduction of tolerance to non-conformist views as a group becomes overcoherent and overly confident, sharing expectations and norms. Indeed, according to Janis, such are the potential defects in the decision making process (applicable to M&A deals) that the initial strategic objectives – to be fulfilled by transactions – are often neither reviewed nor challenged, while newly discovered risks (arising as a result of due diligence and information searches) are not used to challenge the preferred course of action. Instead, by emphasizing and prioritizing information that backs its original hypothesis, the group ignores newly discovered intelligence that may have dissuaded them from pursuing an M&A deal.

TYPES OF DUE DILIGENCE INFORMATION

Due diligence can be divided into external and internal information. As noted above, external due diligence should, if possible, be conducted *before* the deal is under way when the time pressures may not be as extreme as the period after the deal is announced and in order to determine as best as possible if the deal is viable. Internal due diligence is conducted throughout the deal. Both need to be continually updated as conditions change.

While a buyer needs to be sensitive to the stress that the disruption of a due diligence assignment can place on its own personnel and on its relationship with the vendor, the process nevertheless needs to provide a comprehensive view of a target firm through the amalgamation of a variety of different types of due diligence. Even though there may be limitations placed on the amount of investigative work that can be performed (due to time restrictions, vendor constraints, or as a result of restricted access in the case of a hostile bid), due diligence assignments nonetheless still necessitate the gathering and sharing of a wide range of different types of data and information to enable companies to make a definite commitment to acquire all or part of another entity.

Although traditionally 'due diligence' referred to legal and accounting issues only, and some practitioners still may make this assumption, today it has been expanded to include the other business areas and activities of the target (as noted in Table 7.1).

Table 7.1 Due Diligence Topics.

External due diligence topics

Economic analysis
- Macroeconomic analysis
- Regional economic analysis

Industry analysis and trends
- Historical and forecasted growth
- Competition
- Regulation and deregulation
- Innovation and other changes in the industry

Internal due diligence topics

- Strategic and operational (such as business descriptions, business plans, customers, competition, marketing, sales, suppliers)
- Financial: profitability, cash flow, funding/capitalization, financial statements, tax, inventories and receivables, and so on
- Technology (including all IT systems)
- Product/Intellectual property
- Legal issues, including corporate structure, divisions, contracts, and active or pending litigation
- Human resources, including employment contracts, compensation structure, benefit plans, pensions, labor agreements, management, culture
- Miscellaneous: fixed assets (land, buildings, and factories), leases, insurance, trademarks, licenses, environmental issues, and so on

---

Each industry will have its own special due diligence requirements as well. For example, a retailer may need to have its shop floor and warehoused inventory reviewed and an analysis of its store leases conducted, while a bank being purchased would require a review of its securities trading positions and cash management systems.

While due diligence does enable prospective acquirers to look for potential 'black holes,' the aim of due diligence should be this and more, including looking for opportunities to realize future prospects for the enlarged corporation via the leveraging of the acquirer and acquired firm's resources and capabilities, the identification of synergistic benefits, and the post-merger integration planning. As an effective process that should originate at the earliest stages of the acquisition process, due diligence should not only assist a firm to select a target to help it achieve a long-term competitive advantage and increase shareholder wealth but also help the acquirer to determine an appropriate bid price for the target. Thus, structured to serve today's fast paced and perilous commercial environment, a well-managed due diligence assignment − varied in each specific case by scope and scale to reflect the unique issues in each deal − will help firms to improve their financial performance, strengthen their competitive positioning, develop internal 'know-how', and be better able to grow through M&A. It is no wonder that Cervantes referred to diligence as 'the mother of good fortune.'

Business intelligence is at the heart of due diligence. When derived from the right information sources, it provides company executives with the kind of insight that enables them to make appropriate commercial decisions and plan for the future. At whatever stage in the M&A process, the significance and importance of information can never be overstated − permitting companies to strategize, formulate acquisitions plans, devise tactics for bidding and negotiating, and implement post-merger integration plans. Yet, while nearly 90% or more of information required for merger or acquisition activity is widely available, the key skill in this entire process is the ability to identify what information is needed, where it is most likely to be found and then determining a way to extract that information. Split between 'desk' research, the buyer's own organization, a target's management, and primary interviews with people, different information sources enable companies to distill, define, and analyze the most important issues and intelligence, thereby allowing them to recommend the most appropriate course(s) of action to be taken in the field of M&A.

Holding your nerve and getting it right – Alchemy, Rover, and BMW

An example of best practice was that carried out by Alchemy, the private equity turnaround experts, when they attempted to buy MG Rover from BMW. With BMW so desperate to exit from their disastrous British adventure, Alchemy held its nerve and continued with genuine due diligence in the face of enormous pressure, political and economic, to complete.

In total, including advisors, Alchemy had nearly 100 people working on the deal. In many respects, they were starting from scratch: 'At the time the deal was announced, we had never met anyone from Rover, we had not been to the Longbridge [factory] site, and had never had anything to do with the finance department, apart from very fragmentary contact,' said Jon Moulton, head of the company.

According to Moulton and Eric Walters, one of his partners, the Alchemy team soon discovered that many facts contained in their letter of intent were wrong. BMW executives had simply been unaware of the real situation at Rover. 'They were shocked by things our investigation found out,' said

Moulton. 'The due diligence process was a mutual voyage of discovery.'

But while most outsiders now took it for granted that the Alchemy deal would go through, Moulton and Walters were making no such assumptions. For them, signing the letter of intent was only base camp. And the deeper they delved, the less they liked what they saw. 'There were distribution issues, warranty issues, tax issues, and pension issues,' said Moulton. 'This was a business turning over £3 billion a year. Transactions don't get any more complicated.' Distribution, he said, 'was a total nightmare.' In France, where the three franchises – BMW, Land Rover, and Rover – had been merged into one, the process of separating out Rover would be complex in the extreme. Alchemy believed it would also create employment and contractual law problems. Similar difficulties cropped up around the world. In Australia, the dealers had five separate franchise arrangements; apart from the big three, there were also discrete Mini and MG franchises.

Another issue was the value of Rover's unsold cars. New Zealand, one of the few right-hand-drive markets in the world, was the last refuge for vehicles that were surplus to British and Japanese demand. The number of MGFs (two-seater Rover cars) in New Zealand, according to Alchemy, was equivalent at prevailing rates of sale to 25 years' stock. One of the main reasons for the overhang, Moulton said, was that dealers there had been told to price BMW's Z3 sports coupé at £3000 less than the MGF – another sign of how the BMW side of the group had competed against Rover instead of working with it. The worldwide stocks – but particularly those in Britain, where thousands of unsold cars were scattered across disused airfields – also formed by far the biggest element in Rover's asset base.

'We were going to get a £500 million dowry and a balance sheet with a lot of assets that could be converted into cash,' said Moulton. But during the due diligence period,

BMW sold many of the stockpiled cars at reduced prices, effectively liquidating many of the assets Alchemy had expected to acquire. By the first week of April, with the halfway point in the exclusivity period approaching, Alchemy already knew that the deal was going sour.

Eventually, Alchemy withdrew and in 2006 MG Rover, under its new owners, finally collapsed. By carrying out genuine due diligence, which they insisted BMW fund, Alchemy walked away unscathed. Ultimately, their reputation was actually enhanced.

SECONDARY SOURCES OF INFORMATION

The first area is the use of external sources where business intelligence techniques are most useful. While rarely covering specific niches in enough detail – and certainly not providing sufficient overview of organizations at the level required to obtain a proper understanding for due diligence purposes – secondary sources nonetheless equip a company's senior management with valuable information about an industry, allowing them to strategize and develop honed and more focused questions for their due diligence on the prospective acquisition.

Painting a broad (and often colorful) picture of what is happening in the wider world of business, secondary source material acquired through desk research can furnish not only useful information, but also will normally identify the general availability of information and how it will need to be accessed. Across a spectrum of publicly available evidence – including the internet, trade journals, brokers' reports, and published market reports – desk research can be a major asset. But these same publicly available sources can be dangerous if the due diligence stops with them.

They need confirmation and often need updating. They also represent the same information that would be available to a competitor, so just having that data is not sufficient in creating a competitive edge. In short, companies in the 21st century have the ability to amass a wealth of information about their competitive environment, which while varying in usefulness, timeliness, and accuracy, constitutes a good starting point in the search for acquisition or merger candidates.

External information sources may even already reside within the company. Items such as corporate library files and trade association reports often carry both a breadth and depth of material related to specific industries or companies that can aid senior managements' search for trends, patterns, and insights. Over and above this, any proprietary market research reports retained by an organization should also contain useful data for managers at any stage in the M&A process – providing an awareness of a range of facts (such as market share, customer satisfaction, and key customer bases) to aid their quest.

From an external perspective, the proliferation of the internet has served to augment the amount – if not necessarily the quality – of publicly available information. Ranging from annual reports and accounts, stock exchange (and, if relevant, regulators such as the US Securities and Exchange Commission, the UK Financial Services Authority, and the Japanese Ministry of Finance) filings, company prospectuses, brochures, and PR material to glossy product catalogs, company newsletters, brokers' reports, credit agency reports, national and local press reports, business journals, academic publications, industry newsletters, internet 'chat-rooms' and blogs, and government statistics, the array of desk-based research and reports that analysts can 'tap' to feed the information search as part of the M&A process can often be endless, allowing managers a degree of depth and insight into a company's inner workings that hitherto were either not available or simply too difficult to collate before the genesis of the internet in the mid-1990s. Lastly, the use of the court system to undertake searches to ensure that no steps have been taken to place the target in receivership or check that there is no (undisclosed) litigation pending provide additional credible sources of business intelligence as part of the M&A process.

Secondary information can help in almost every area of planning and due diligence, not just in identifying potential takeover targets but also to aid in understanding which opportunities in the marketplace others may be considering, and therefore enable the company to act quickly and take 'first-mover advantage' against direct rivals and indirect competitors. It can also be used to determine the value of the company and the potential fit. The secondary information need not even be from the obvious sources and a competitive edge can be gained by using information from unexpected places or in ways not intended by those who collected or first analyzed the data, as shown in the example below when KPMG represented a grocery company.

Use of animal rights activists' websites

During the 2003–2004 acquisition process of a large grocery chain, the target employed KPMG to help them identify potential supply chain synergies between themselves and the major supermarkets that were bidding to acquire them, in an effort to drive up the acquisition price. Using a series of animal rights activists' websites that provided details of each bidder's store and warehouse network, the professional services firm was able to liaise with their client to provide a robust vendor's commercial due diligence report that illustrated the potential synergies and cost savings for each company, nudging up the purchase price.

However, primary face-to-face meetings with a broad range of people across various fields of expertise more often than not prove the most valuable seam of information in which to mine for data, insight, and intelligence. While there is never one proven source of information and companies need to cross-check material in order to eliminate bias and find a consistent message, primary sources nevertheless remain the most viable way to obtain the required information about a target and its markets.

The range of information sources that can be tapped into is vast – reflecting the multitude of stakeholders in a business – each offering a unique and different perspective from which a prospective acquirer's management can judge the feasibility or desire to execute an M&A deal. While there is no limit to the number of people that can be questioned for intelligence (provided they can be identified and contacted in time), in the first instance, a company's customers are possibly the most important group of people to talk to, offering a relatively good cut of a target's strengths, weaknesses, and plans, having had direct experience of a target's operations. Thus, combining a mix of interviews with a potential acquisition's past and present customers allows managers a high degree of insight into a target's current performance and key performance indicators.

Over and above this, a target's competitors are often the second most important source of primary information, providing informed opinions about the target and the competitive landscape of the industry. Likewise, former employees – not just those found in your own company – can also prove to be a very valuable source of information during the course of a commercial due diligence exercise. Ex-members of staff of a prospective acquisition often provide a unique perspective on intangible elements of a business (such as corporate culture) that aid the acquisition process and help management decide on whether or how to proceed with an acquisition or merger.

Yet, beyond a company's direct stakeholders (employees, customers, and competitors), a raft of other players in the field – including industry observers, journalists, distributors, suppliers, and regulators – can provide access to a tremendous amount of knowledge of a particular sector, potentially having followed developments closely in an industry over a significant period of time. Providing a good introductory briefing to an industry – ranging from market structure and customer needs and opinions through to prescriptive laws and regulations affecting entire industries – 'second tier' primary sources can offer welcome insights and perspectives for potential deal makers.

For those sources not bound by confidentiality agreements, the opportunity to talk when approached by companies considering an M&A deal often presents prospective acquirers with a vast amount of tacit knowledge. By going into 'sales mode' and if prompted by people with robust interviewing skills, primary source candidates – feeling wanted, keen to be seen to help others, and willing to talk about themselves – allow companies to gather first-hand information that otherwise would prove inaccessible.

Lastly, endowed with a tremendous wealth of industry knowledge are the advisors to the industry, such as the accountants, bankers, lawyers, and specialized consultants. They continually update their perspective on the industry while pitching potential transactions and working on existing contracts. They can often determine what is true and what is not true in the rumor mill that exists in every industry and know that any rumors would be ignored at a company's own risk.

Drawing on a wide range of information to generate deal-related intelligence, corporate investigation firms have the capability and wherewithal to tap into public sources and high level contacts in a broad spectrum of sectors and industries to provide the necessary facts to enable acquirers to make relevant decisions. Providing strategic insight into operational risk issues, integrity due diligence work enables firms to execute – or abandon – transactions with confidence, having confirmed the reputations, associations, activities, and ethics of potential merger partners or the management of a prospective investment. In short, since due diligence has grown in importance in M&A deals, so firms increasingly tap the business intelligence resources of intelligence specialist firms like Kroll and Control Risks to gain assurance regarding the integrity and ethics of their partners in a transaction.

> **Tax surprise for MCI**
>
> In August 1998, MCI purchased a controlling 51.79% voting share (but only a 19.26% economic share) of Embratel, a state-owned long-distance telephone company in Brazil, for $2.3 billion – only to receive a demand for payment two months later from the Brazilian authorities for back taxes of $650 million owing from a period when the company was a state-owned enterprise, according to *Business Week*. Almost six years later in April 2004, they sold it to Telmex, Mexico's leading telecommunications company, for $400 million.

While most companies are loath to reveal the hand of corporate investigative firms in M&A deals, the enlisting of private investigators on M&A transactions by companies and private equity firms – while potentially embarrassing if revealed – is in reality quite commonplace, with even investment banks hiring corporate sleuths to conduct due diligence on well-known businessmen before agreeing to act on their behalf in a deal. Yet, beyond an investigation into the reputation and background of individuals, companies are also now inclined to guard against an array of wider commercial dangers that could wreck a company as a result of an acquisition, such as MCI found in the case above.

Utilizing a wide range of intelligence sources, companies involved in M&A transactions need to undertake the necessary investigation work to ensure that their acquired subsidiaries are not involved in unethical or improper activities (given the legal issues as well as press and consumer response to issues such as the use of child labor, sweatshop workers, the environment, or bribing officials), or harboring large unprovisioned tax or environmental liabilities. Operating within the law (both to protect their own reputations and ensure that the evidence is admissible in a court room), companies – either directly or outsourced to third parties – use a mixture of databases and public record searches, independent source interviews, and legitimate surveillance techniques to gather the necessary information as part of the deal process.

Use of investigative firms in M&A

Control Risks acted on behalf of the Co-operative Wholesale Society (CWS) to reveal that Andrew Regan's Larnica Trust (which was attempting a hostile takeover of CWS' non-food business in 1997) had persuaded certain Co-op senior executives to provide confidential information about their company's business prospects to him, including copies of management accounts, draft accounts for the financial year, lists of stores and their market value, details of membership, and documents showing voting rights of corporate members. According to *Reuters* and *The Times*, CWS also asked its lawyers, Linklaters & Paines, and its accountants, KPMG, to investigate Andrew Regan's business dealings.

There are other examples as well, such as the discovery during the 1980s £1.9 billion hostile takeover battle for Distillers, the drinks group, that James 'Jimmy' Gulliver, Chairman of Argyll, the food producer, had a misleading CV in which he exaggerated his attendance at Harvard Business School as he had only attended a course for a few days. Distillers was ultimately purchased by Guinness in what a former Safeway chairman and former colleague of Gulliver's called 'the dirtiest, ugliest takeover battle of all time.'

INTERNAL DUE DILIGENCE INFORMATION AVAILABLE IN THE BIDDER

The easiest is often forgotten, which is certainly true of many of the existing internal sources of business intelligence, most expecially the client-facing teams. Salespeople should be one of the best sources of information about the market and in many M&A deals the acquisition target is close enough to the bidder as a customer, supplier, or competitor that the salespeople should have some relevant knowledge on that target company (although they will most likely not know why they are being asked!). On a day-to-day basis while selling to customers, these salespeople will find out a wealth of information about the competition, clients, and changes to the industry. Rarely tapped, these individuals should meet with the business intelligence team frequently. In a similar light, one of the first steps in a deal should be to find out from human resources if there are any employees in the company who have worked for the target recently. Think of what they can tell, although increasingly employees are required to sign confidentiality agreements when leaving a company that prohibit them from disclosing non-public information.

From the inside of their own organization, company management are also able to source a wealth of information needed at various points in the M&A process. Whether taken from staff files (covering areas of interest such as competitors' R&D, production capabilities, patents, and technologies) or sales representatives' reports as discussed above, internal information sources can provide numerous opportunities for obtaining invaluable and hard-won information that aids companies' selections of potential M&A targets.

Indeed, more often than not, it is the 'tacit' (and unwritten) information residing with members of staff that proves the most valuable. Providing trade gossip about competitors, their sales and technical staff, new product developments, service problems, and corporate culture, company staff (as representatives in the field) act as invaluable commercial scouts, reporting back rumor, gossip, and office grapevine information about competitors from their informal networks developed at events such as trade shows, exhibitions, and conferences – all of which may build up a pattern of behavior that proves invaluable to those members of a corporate development team looking for potential merger partners or acquisition candidates.

FINANCIAL DUE DILIGENCE

Interviews with a target's management also allow acquirers to open a line of communication with potential acquirees and so collect basic information. As such, if an approach is friendly and management is amenable, prospective acquirers can often glean a huge amount of insider information on a business and its markets – together with an agreed way to approach customers and contacts.

Accounting issues uncovered in financial due diligence

The $22 billion merger of CUC International (a membership-based consumer services company selling merchandise and travel packages) and 'HFS Incorporated' (a leading franchiser of Avis and Ramada Inn in the USA and several real estate firms) in 1997 to form 'Cendant Corporation' was also marked by what was then the biggest accounting scandal in corporate history.

Having fraudulently overstated its income by more than $500 million over a period of 10 years or more, CUC International's 'widespread and systematic' practice of inflating or possibly fabricating results caused Cendant's share price to plummet from $39 to $20 in one day, costing shareholders about $14 billion and leading to considerable turmoil within the firm.

Cendant Chairman, President and CEO Henry Silverman later stated the problem he faced to Daniel Kadlec who wrote the following in his book *Masters of the Universe*: 'Due diligence, like the rest of our financial system, is based on trust. You have a duty to ask a lot of questions. In acquiring CUC, I talked to some of America's most respected managers and investors and with CUC's business partners – their bankers, lawyers, auditors, major shareholders, customers, suppliers – as well as many sell-side analysts. But even that may not protect you. Fraud, outright lies, and deliberate attempts to conceal are very difficult to detect, especially when they are not subject to external verification.'

Silverman was then asked what he would do differently in the due diligence process in future acquisitions. 'That's a question I have asked myself and our staff. What you do normally when you do an acquisition is you quiz management, you quiz the inside and outside auditors and review the auditors' work papers, you talk to customers and vendors and suppliers, you talk to some major managers and investors about the character of the people you are merging with. We did all this, so I'm not sure what we would do differently seeing as we've done the same thing on 28 very successful acquisitions and this was our 29th transaction . . . This was a merger. CUC was putting its stock in a pot and we were putting our stock in a pot. We were going to be partners going forward. So the last thing frankly which ever would have crossed my mind was that they were defrauding us as well as their prior investors.'

Financial due diligence, often the mainstay of the whole process, enables companies to obtain a view of an organization's underlying historical profits, which can then be used as a canvas on which to paint a picture of the company's financial future. Scrutinizing a prospective target's financial statements (sourced initially through Companies House in the UK or via the SEC in the US if the company is listed) may allow acquirers (by paying attention to trends and recent developments in a company's operating and financial history) to identify reasons why a company wishes either to merge or sell out. Developed around an array of building blocks – including auditing and verifying financial results on which an offer is based, identifying deal breakers, providing ammunition for negotiators, pinpointing areas where warranties or indemnities may be needed and providing confidence in the underlying performance (and therefore future profits) of a corporation – financial due diligence, by concentrating on revenue and cost forecasts, prospective earnings and future cash flows, helps acquirers to identify and realize value from M&A acquisition opportunities. Proper financial due diligence will allow the bidder to make the proper offer for the target or perhaps it will uncover reasons not to proceed with the deal.

By way of quick examples, in financial due diligence the assets and liabilities of the balance sheet and the items on the income statements must be probed, even when they come with auditor assurances. In this context, speaking to the accountants responsible would be important in order to understand whether there have been recent changes in approach and what issues have arisen in the production of the accounts. As another example, when carrying out operational due diligence, if trading updates are being used to assess the current performance of managers, it is important to validate that the value chain has not been overloaded in the short term (known as 'channel stuffing') since this would give misleading operational or growth figures. Lastly, from the target's perspective it might wish to monitor the information usage patterns in order to assess how serious the buyer is and what its standpoint might be.

Financial due diligence lowers the offer price

In a case study discussed earlier in relation to poison pills, Symbol Technologies first attempted to acquire Telxon Corporation in 1998. It is a case in point to illustrate the fundamental importance of proper and rigorous financial investigations into acquisition targets.

In court papers it was revealed that Telxon had told Symbol that it would accept an offer at a certain level 'if the deal were closed quickly and without an examination of the books.' As was then reported in the *Wall Street Journal*, Symbol insisted on looking at the financial books and 'what they found not only helped derail a $900 million takeover, but also was followed within a single week by a restatement of Telxon's earnings. . . .'

Having undertaken that full financial due diligence, Symbol Technologies found that Telxon had made $14 million in improperly recognized revenue at the close of the second quarter of its most recent fiscal year. In court papers filed in the subsequent law suits, it was claimed that this overstated profits by 47%. Once discovered, Telxon was forced to restate its accounts, resulting in its share price falling by 45% – with the upshot that Symbol eventually acquired Telxon (two years later) for less than half what it initially offered to pay for the company.

Yet, in spite of the centrality of financial due diligence, examples abound of transactions that were either completed without sufficient time to perform due diligence work effectively or as a result of management hubris, resulting in devastating losses of shareholder value.

LEGAL DUE DILIGENCE

Alongside financial due diligence, legal investigative work performed by an acquirer on a target must constitute a core component of the due diligence process. While most of the information for legal due diligence work comes from the vendor by way of a series of disclosure letters or from its lawyers in response to questionnaires, for the acquirer, the process of obtaining information and reviewing documentation carries on right until it is satisfied that it has received sufficient comfort in respect of any legal matters. This must be supplemented by building up a profile of the target from various other sources as well. Thus, legal due diligence is central to the entire process simply because it forms the basis for the sale and purchase agreement between the various parties to the M&A transaction. The externally sourced information, because of its independent nature, may be of greater strategic use because it may represent information that the target does not have.

As companies expand to hitherto commercially less experienced parts of the world in search of new markets and products (such as the People's Republic of China), the requirement to conduct effective and sufficient legal due diligence work can prove more trying and in certain cases, near impossible, depending on the level and quality of legal records kept by the relevant authorities. Nevertheless, the need to check 'title' over assets that are being sold and to ensure that the entity being acquired is legitimate and is free of any contractual or legal obstacles that might derail the M&A process will undoubtedly remain pivotal to the due diligence process no matter where the target resides.

COMMERCIAL DUE DILIGENCE

As referred to previously, the due diligence process is there to provide a comprehensive overview of the target firm – one that goes beyond the narrow and prescriptive confines of financial and legal due diligence. Concerned not just with managing risk but the achievement of the goals of the acquisition as well, corporations regularly undertake a host of other types of due diligence, using a variety of other sources of business intelligence. It is clear that effective due diligence goes beyond the 'numbers' and legal documentation, using a variety of sources of information to help acquirers clarify whether in reality the target will actually enable it to execute its strategic vision for the future.

Given that companies are bought, not for their past performance, but for their ability to generate profits in the future, acquirers use commercial due diligence to obtain an objective perspective on a company's markets, future prospects, and competitive position. As a complement to other types of due diligence, commercial information is specifically obtained by organizations from outside their target, using published sources or talking to knowledgeable people who are in the same marketplace as the target. This information can then be compared to the data sourced from the target itself and often shows how effective the target company has been in using such information in its own planning.

Whether obtained to reduce risk around the transaction, to help with the company valuation, or to plan for post-merger integration, commercial due diligence enables acquirers to examine a target's markets and commercial performance, identifying strengths, weaknesses, opportunities, and threats (SWOT) that can aid with the bid and subsequent negotiations. Focused on the likely strategic position of the combined entity, commercial due diligence – by reviewing the 'drivers' that underpin forecasts and business plans – concentrates on the ability of the target's businesses to achieve the projected sales and profitability growth post-acquisition.

In short, the use of business intelligence techniques in the commercial due diligence process allows acquirers to obtain a qualitative insight that is otherwise unlikely to be uncovered, while the verification of the future outlook for the business enables prospective acquirers to determine whether an acquisition matches their expectations. By aiding the establishment of the 'merged entity' with an eye towards future market potential and the longer-term prospects for the business, commercial due diligence provides a counterbalance to the 'short-termism' of financial and legal due diligence, helping acquirers to understand how markets and competitive environments will affect their purchase while confirming that the opportunity is sensible to undertake from a commercial and strategic perspective.

In order to obtain the required information for this type of due diligence work, firms (or their professional advisors) can turn to a number of different sources. As such, if the deal is friendly and welcomed by the board, then by interviewing management and key members of staff at an organization, a potential acquirer can often collect detailed information on the business together with an overview of its markets, while obtaining an agreed way to approach a target's customers, suppliers, and other stakeholders. But as noted above, this should only be a starting point, and reliance on the target's own information (and interpretation of that information) is dangerous.

It is therefore necessary to seek other sources of commercial intelligence. There is always a huge amount of knowledge residing with internal contacts (such as from former target employees now working for the acquirer, salesmen, and others in day-to-day contact with the company) and these organizations are able to utilize these invaluable sources of detailed information. This type of business intelligence source can also be complemented by published or publicly available information or by first-hand contact with individuals who are in a position to share valuable background information about the industry and sector that the target resides in, including specialized consultants. Either way, the wealth of information sources available should enable the company to paint a relatively comprehensive picture of the target that will assist their decision making process regarding whether (or not) to proceed with an M&A transaction and how to structure the deal and plan its aftermath.

Rising importance of looking at foreign corrupt practices

In the US and increasingly in other countries, it is critical to look at whether a target has engaged in unethical or illegal activities – illegal not just in the country where the activities have taken place, but in other countries where the company operates. In the US, these have been set into law in the Foreign Corrupt Practices Act (FCPA), initially enacted in 1977 to halt bribery as a means of obtaining foreign contracts.

As reported in *Mergers & Acquisitions: The Dealmaker's Journal* in 2005, there were at least three major transactions that ran foul of the FCPA. In all three cases, the deal was significantly delayed and in one case ultimately resulted in a termination of the deal.

In 2003, Lockheed Martin, the world's largest defense contractor, wished to purchase Titan, another defense technology company, for around $1.8 billion. During the due diligence, it was uncovered that Titan had made payments in Africa, Asia, and the Middle East to foreign consultants related to the sale of the company's radio systems to foreign military agencies. After Titan failed to resolve the issues with the US Department of Justice, Lockheed dropped its planned acquisition.

The other two deals went through, but after long delays and with the acquirer requiring the target to make assurances that the practices had been resolved in terms of both the acceptability of the bribery payments and the legal resolution with the US government. One was the 2004 sale (originally scheduled for 2003) of the US subsidiaries of Swiss-based ABB, a provider of power and automation technologies. The other was the 2004 purchase by General Electric of InVision Technologies, a California-based manufacturer of airport bomb detection equipment, for $900 million.

In all three cases, not only were there large fines levied by the US authorities on the companies involved, but their reputations were significantly affected.

Despite the seemingly obvious pivotal benefits that commercial due diligence can lend to acquiring organizations, *Competitive Intelligence Magazine* reported in 2003 that '. . . only 10% of respondents to an Accenture survey of M&A practitioners said that their due diligence process included four or more sources from outside the company. . . .' Therefore, in the vast majority of deals conducted, a target's competitors, customers, suppliers, joint venture partners, and former employees are simply ignored as sources of data, information, and insight. Whether or not a dearth of commercial oversight provides substantive reasons for the high M&A failure rate, nevertheless by neglecting systematically to gather and analyze information in relation to the general business trends of an industry or sector, acquirers run the risk of buying companies that lack operational or strategic fit with the bidder, or worse will fail to meet the purchasers' revenue and profit targets. Ignoring the obvious sources of commercial data is often due to the overconfidence of the bidder that it already understands the target's markets and business models, or a similar overconfidence in its ability to manage the business post-deal no matter what it has purchased.

Given what must be assumed is the centrality of commercial due diligence to the M&A process, it should come as no surprise therefore that examples abound of deals that have either been 'called off' or amended as a result of commercial due diligence work being undertaken in one form or another – or worse, of acquirers who failed to perform such reviews and ended up destroying shareholder value in the long run. One such example was shown earlier: the acquisition of Snapple Beverage Company by Quaker Oats for $1.7 billion in 1994. That deal clearly illustrates a failure to conduct arguably the most basic commercial due diligence, resulting in the company subsequently being divested three years later at a loss of $1.4 billion to Quaker Oats. Having failed to anticipate broad differences between Snapple and its existing Gatorade brand in areas such as pricing strategy, distribution, and advertising, or having received substantive responses to questions about the Snapple business as part of its due diligence work, the Quaker board nevertheless proceeded to acquire its target in spite of market sentiment that it had overpaid for a company and brand that had yet to prove itself worth the asking price.

Lack of commercial due diligence

AT&T's 1991 acquisition of NCR, BHP's purchase of Magma in 1996 (shown as a case study in Chapter 5) and AMP's decision to buy National Provident Institution (NPI) in 1999 all proceeded without (arguably) substantive commercial due diligence having been performed on the targets and their marketplace.

Having acquired NCR for $7.4 billion in an effort to break into the market offering IT solutions for retail and financial companies, AT&T subsequently found itself in the unenviable position of having to inject a further $2 billion of cash – before deciding to eject the company from the group five years later in 1996 at a loss on disposal to AT&T of over $5 billion. Citing '. . . changes in customer needs . . .' and the '. . . need for focused management time and attention . . .' in an information statement sent to shareholders in 1996, the failure of the NCR acquisition clearly indicates a lack of substantive commercial due diligence on the part of AT&T – leading to the supposed '. . . advantages of vertical integration [being] outweighed by its costs and disadvantages . . . [on account] of the reluctance of AT&T's competitors to make purchases from an AT&T subsidiary. . . .'

Likewise, Australia's BHP's A$3.2 billion purchase of US-based Magma Copper in 1996 to produce the world's second largest copper producer also provides an indication of the acquirer's failure to understand either the business itself or the global copper market *per se*. Without a local supply of concentrates, no port, and poor transport links, Magma's copper operations in the US effectively became economically unviable within three years, on account of rising costs and lower copper prices, exposing the deal as a failure for BHP. Through failure to understand the quality of the assets acquired and tending to manage the acquisition aggressively, Magma's assets fell short in providing substantive synergies for BHP, resulting, as noted earlier, in BHP '. . . gradually writing down the assets by A$2.16 billion with the bleeding finally ending in June 1999 with [the company] mothballing the assets at a final cost of A$1.8 billion and 2630 jobs,' according to the Australian Associated Press.

The acquisition of NPI, a British life insurer, for £2.7 billion by AMP Limited also provides a case in point of failed or inadequate commercial due diligence on behalf of an acquirer, according to *The Sunday Telegraph* in December 2000. Having been sold to AMP, plummeting stock markets wreaked havoc on NPI's highly exposed insurance business, resulting in a further £500 million cash injection from its parent to prevent NPI from breaching its UK regulatory solvency requirements. Having realized by June 2003 – merely four years later – that its quest was hopeless, AMP closed its doors to new business in the UK, withdrawing via a demerger and flotation of NPI (having been merged with Pearl UK, another AMP acquisition) in order to achieve a clean and efficient way to exit the UK market.

MANAGEMENT DUE DILIGENCE

Turning our attentions now to 'integrity' or management due diligence, it has also become common practice (especially in the US and UK) for acquirers to perform discrete investigations in order to evaluate both the competence of the target's management and the quality of their past performances and to ensure that the management of the target and acquirer are personally compatible. Since often it will be management who will be carrying it all forward, it is crucial that adequate time is spent on making sure the best people are in place with all the support they might need.

Oracle's management lists

In the lead-up to an acquisition in early 2006, Oracle was given the names of 53 key people that could not be poached during the merger discussions or afterwards for a period in case the deal fell through.

If one is given such a list, as noted by the Senior HR Director for Europe, the acquirer has the beginnings of a tool to check with customers and former employees as much as it can about those 53 people – as they are presumably the best of the best in that target company. This process can identify possible problems and issues with those individuals and with the organization.

In addition, it turns something meant to be defensive on the part of the target (as it was requested to prevent poaching of staff) into something of even greater value to the bidder in the due diligence process.

Focused on the individuals themselves, this type of intelligence work can range from very simple background checks to exhaustive interviews with the senior management team. In some instances there will be investigative reports and detective agencies involved, especially in hostile deals or where questions have been raised by the earlier background checks and interviews. These management audits allow acquirers to manage business risk by ensuring that their potential business partners or target are not tainted by the stains of money laundering, potential terrorist links, fraudulent activity, illegally acquired wealth, or undisclosed directorships (especially those of companies that no longer exist). Often using corporate investigation firms to identify the integrity and reputation of the target's management, acquirers will seek out and contact third parties who have had business dealings with senior individuals at the target to ensure that they know the quality of management, whether they can be trusted in transactions and wider corporate activities and ultimately whether to retain those managers or make them redundant as part of the acquisition process.

Given the rocky state of the financial markets since 2001, companies are increasingly using corporate investigation firms as an automatic part of the deal process – if only to assure shareholders that they have carried out the necessary checks before undertaking a deal. While companies may indicate reluctance to spend money with firms such as Kroll, Control Risks and Risk Advisory Group (for fear of the target responding badly to being investigated), nevertheless, 'off balance sheet' due diligence – involving a thorough investigation of a company's executives and past practices – is increasingly necessary. Those investigative companies can also be retained confidentially, of course. Whether checking business records, searching for criminal convictions or investigating possible personal problems or drug abuse, acquirers need to be seen to have dug deeper to find out about companies and their executives. In short, this so-called 'integrity due diligence' is all about looking between the lines for information that would not othewise be revealed. In many cases, it includes looking at the personal lives of key senior executives as well.

But even though these sources of information have been available for years, the most basic investigative due diligence on management is still not being carried out by many firms in many deals. One mid-sized private equity firm interviewed recently said that its senior management felt confident enough in its own ability to conduct its management due diligence that it could do this 'over a cup of tea,' eyeing the management team from across the table.

CULTURAL DUE DILIGENCE

Although 'cultural' due diligence may not appear to have the same degree of significance as other (more prescriptive) types of review work as part of an M&A assignment, nevertheless if carried out, this type of due diligence can – and does – play an important role in planning for the post-acquisition aftermath. As such, since one of the more difficult areas for integrating two companies concerns combining their corporate cultures, so due care and attention needs to be applied to ensure cultural fit. Indeed, cultural fit is so important, that 85% of underperforming acquisitions blame different management attitudes and culture for poor performance of the combined entity. Thus, by assessing 'soft' factors such as a company's leadership style, corporate behavior, and even areas such as dress code, an acquirer may be able to build an accurate picture of a target's values, attitudes, and beliefs, and so determine if there will be a good cultural fit with their own organizational structure.

Yet, in reality cultural due diligence is rarely conducted properly and as such little is pre-emptively done to bring down the barriers to integration at a cultural level, often resulting in the loss of shareholder value.

No cultural fit for Sony in the movie industry

One example that illustrates how important culture can be within an M&A environment is that of the failed acquisition of Columbia Pictures (an American moviemaker) by Sony (a Japanese electronics manufacturer) for $3.4 billion in 1988. With cultures that could scarcely have been more different, the acquisition – having involved little consideration of cultural fit between the two entities – failed to live up to commercial expectations, with Sony famously writing down $2.7 billion on the deal by 1994, as reported in its annual report.

While gathering hard cultural evidence can be a fairly uncertain task, nevertheless, by getting out, kicking the tires, and talking to people, it is possible to gain some pretty good impressions of a prospective acquisition's cultural framework, thereby enabling acquirers to make more informed decisions within an M&A environment. This is also an area where personnel consultants can play a useful role in assessing the cultural fit with an independent view uncluttered by focus on their own culture.

ETHICAL DUE DILIGENCE

There is an emerging area of due diligence best described as 'ethical due diligence' that overlaps in many ways with management and cultural due diligence.

The most obvious requirement of ethical due diligence is to determine if management have engaged in unethical professional acts (as defined, usually, by the ethical standard of the acquiring company and which therefore may not even be considered unethical by the management, employees, regulators, customers, or supplier of the target). Such acts may include issues considered illegal (such as age discrimination or giving bribes to customers or governments officials which are illegal for American or Western European firms) or just inappropriate (such as circulating jokes that are not explicitly illegal but that might offend some people – for example, about animal cruelty).

Management acting unethically usually sets the tone or standard for the company as a whole, and this can be uncovered by looking at the actions of employees at all levels of the firm. This can also take the form of management condoning unethical acts but doing nothing to stop them, or even purposefully ignoring or even knowingly tolerating such practices in those beneath them in the organization even if they would not engage in such acts themselves.

As we will show later in the chapter on post-merger integration, it is critical that the two companies be able to merge rapidly and smoothly after the deal is completed. Major differences in ethical standards can cause problems with that integration and should therefore be identified early in the due diligence process.

CONCLUSIONS

In all of this, business intelligence plays a pivotal role, injecting valuable insight into acquisition decisions across a broad range of company issues while validating the strategic, commercial, operational, financial, legal, and cultural assumptions underpinning a deal. Akin to power in the M&A environment, due diligence –

by arming a buyer with knowledge – allows them not only to be better prepared for the negotiations ahead but also enables them to assess risk effectively and determine whether or not to proceed with a transaction. Subsequent to the '9/11' attacks on the US and the accounting scandals endured by the shareholders of Enron, WorldCom, Parmalat, and Tyco, companies – devoid of trust and confidence in 'the system' – simply want to go beyond the realm of normal (that is, financial and legal) due diligence to avoid being penalized as a result of being a participant in an M&A transaction. Given managers' desperation to obtain as much information and insight as possible into a deal, so business intelligence adds invaluable credence to the pre-deal analysis and formal deal phases of the M&A process.

Indeed the statistics collected by Accenture and the Economist Intelligence Unit in 2005 are fully supportive of the need to improve due diligence. According to their conclusions, only 18% of executives were highly confident that their company had carried out satisfactory due diligence.

In summary, the importance of collecting, analyzing, and utilizing information in its plethora of forms to drive the M&A process cannot be overstated. This is of course the very role that a permanent intelligence function would perform; indeed, the entire breadth of the M&A process not only requires but demands the involvement of accurate and timely information to ensure that insightful business intelligence drives a shareholder value-enhancing transaction process. To this end, the next chapter highlights the importance of the use of intelligence in the pricing and financing of M&A deals.

CHAPTER 8

VALUATION, PRICING, AND FINANCING

*P*roper valuation is critical to the success of any merger or acquisition. Without it, a company might pay too much for the target or the target might accept a price that is lower than the value shareholders should accept.

Each company and deal is different and there is no single best way to value a company – no 'one size fits all.' In many ways, valuation in M&A is an art and not a science. Proper valuation comes with experience. Each valuation includes myriad assumptions which need to be made and small changes in any of the assumptions can have large impacts on the valuation.

CONTROL PREMIUMS

One of the most important factors in an M&A valuation is the control premium. In order to take a company over – to buy 100%

of the company – the current owners need to be 'bribed' to sell their shares to the new owner. This control premium averages approximately 20–40%, and has remained remarkably consistent within this range over the past several merger waves.

Normally, day-to-day share prices quoted on the stock exchange typically do not include a control premium, as most trades are minority stakes. The control premium will differ by industry, market, and so on, and is best determined by looking at recent previous acquisition transactions. Some industries may experience periods when the industry is 'in play' as one or a number of acquisitions and mergers are taking place. In this case, part or the entire control premium may be reflected in the current stock price as there is an expectation that the independent companies in the industry will also be acquired at a premium.

ALTERNATIVE METHODS OF VALUATION

Significant time pressures force short-cuts to be made, especially in hostile, unsolicited bids. Traditional corporate finance and venture capital methods of valuation are not typically applicable on their own, as M&A valuation is driven by more unknowns.

For example, when valuing a company for an initial public offering (IPO), there is usually a discount applied to the ultimate price in order to give the initial investors some upside potential in share price and to improve market liquidity by making sure that the volume of shares that will trade is adequate. While an M&A deal is typically transacted at a premium to market price as noted above, most IPOs have a target discount of 5–15%. Stock prices for the target in the middle of being acquired may therefore be as much as 50% higher than if the company were going public.

M&A deals must look at the synergies and changes brought about through the combination of two previously unrelated companies, while IPO, venture capital, and other typical corporate finance methodologies consider a company to be a standalone entity.

EXPERTS

In order to conduct the financial analyses that will lead to the valuation, most companies employ outside experts such as investment bankers or accountants to complement their own internal financial team. Nevertheless, even with such experienced experts, the bidder is always at an information disadvantage because the bidder (and the bidder's advisors) will never know as much about the company as the insiders of the target (and their advisors). This problem is exacerbated in hostile deals, where often, especially in the early stages of the deal, the bidder has no access to non-public information. This is an area where business intelligence techniques *must* be used to fill the gap with the best information available. Also, recall our warning in Chapter 6 to be wary of disinformation and the motivations of those providing non-public information.

M&A valuation also differs from valuation techniques used in the venture capital and private equity world. Most private equity firms look for an exit from their investment in a five to seven year time frame (on average) with an internal rate of return (IRR) for the entire investment period of anywhere from 20 to 35% (depending on the market: IRR return expectations were very high in the late 1990s but declined soon after 2000). The exit multiple is usually based on the entry multiple and then the cash flows are computed to determine the total return. This is a very narrow method of valuation when compared to the typical M&A valuation as discussed in this chapter, although this private equity method should be considered by acquisition bidders as one of the many ways of looking at the value of the business. One or more of the bidders or potential bidders could be a venture capital firm, so their method of valuation should be considered carefully.

There exist a number of common myths about valuations in mergers and acquisitions, perpetuated by those who either are considered 'valuation experts' or those who do not get involved in the valuations at all. Some of the common myths are noted in Table 8.1.

ADJUSTMENTS TO FINANCIAL STATEMENTS

Specialist M&A analysts look at financial statements differently from analysts considering a company as a going concern (accountants and equity research analysts, for example). In a merger situation, not only is it important to determine the financial health of the target company, but the balance sheet and income statement of the target itself may be used to finance the deal.

For the balance sheet, consideration must be made of the following items. Some assets, such as cash and marketable securities, can be used to finance the offer as that cash will be available to the bidder when they take over the company. In the same way, accounts receivable and inventories can be used, although for each of these other categories, a discount must be made because they cannot be exchanged into cash for 100% of the book value. Property, factories, and equipment must be revalued to their current market level, as these otherwise are usually shown on the balance sheet at historical cost which may even have a depreciation account attached. Other items of value are the intangibles, which notably are often valued on the balance sheet at a figure

Table 8.1 Myths and Realities about M&A Valuations.

Myth	Reality
The experts (accountants and investment bankers) know how to produce valuations	It is impossible to know the future accurately. Experts have more experience, but it is dangerous to assume that their experience gives them complete knowledge about a particular company or deal.
Valuations are accurate	Even with the most rigorous application of business intelligence, valuation is biased in subtle and not so subtle ways, such as in the assumptions used and in the motivations of those producing the valuation.
	A valuation is never precise and is never quite finished. Which methods of valuation to use and the weight given to each is based more on the experience of the people producing the valuation than any financial model of what is 'accurate.'
You need many complex models to produce an accurate valuation	Complexity comes with a cost, especially in taking more time to produce and the likelihood that the number of possible errors introduced into the models will increase with the models' size and complexity. More information is not necessarily better than less information. Simplicity is often the best answer. Also, complex spreadsheet models are inherently difficult for others to audit.

Table 8.1 (*Continued*)

Myth	Reality
	What is important is finding a price that both the bidder and target will find acceptable. This 'market clearing price' is often more based on recent comparable transactions than the very complex valuation models, although the models are often (incorrectly) needed to provide justification for the valuation of the company.
You do not need to change good valuations or good valuation models	During the deal negotiation stage, the valuations are often updated daily. Each input should change as new information becomes available. Internal and external markets change: stock markets, interest rates, risk premiums, economic growth, political risk, industry information such as legal or tax changes, new technology, and company-specific information such as new financial data, management changes, and competitive actions. Even the methods of valuation used may need to change during a deal.
You cannot value start-up companies with no earnings history	Valuation is admittedly difficult when a company is at the start-up phase when it likely has negative earnings and low revenues, little or no sales history, and perhaps even with very few direct competitors offering comparables (and even if similar competitors do exist, they are not likely to all be at the same stage of their life cycle as the firm being valued). Difficult doesn't mean impossible, but sometimes creative methods need to be used.

that is far different – usually below – from the value of those assets to the bidder.

The liability side of the balance sheet will also require adjustment. This is certainly true of any debt that is fully repayable to the bank or bond holder upon a change of control such as an acquisition or merger. Hidden liabilities must be included, such as potential legal settlements and redundancy payments, which were discussed in the due diligence chapter.

Likewise, the income statement needs recasting. Depreciation has a large impact on cash flow and the accounting method used for depreciation can affect the income statement (especially if the target uses different depreciation and amortization methods than the bidder). This is true of inventories as well, as some companies use the FIFO (first in, first out) method while others use the LIFO (last in, first out) method.

All of these considerations drive the production of cash flow statements. Cash flow statements are preferred over income statements for M&A valuation as typically they are subject to fewer possible manipulations yet the above adjustments still need to be made. They are also particularly important when looking at the new company's ability to service the debt that it may take on to finance the acquisition.

TOTAL DEAL COST

In assessing the economics of a deal, the shareholders and other analysts will assess whether the gains from the merger will exceed the costs. In an M&A deal, the costs can be significant. Naturally, there is the expense of the target company: how much the target shareholders will need to be paid to part with their holdings, which includes the acquisition premium. Then, there are the 'known' and relatively easily calculated expenses such as the fees paid to the investment bankers, lawyers, accountants, and other professional advisors and the expenses of taking over the new company, including debt borrowed. Opportunity costs and post-merger integration costs (see box below) are almost impossible to quantify accurately even with the best use of business intelligence. Nevertheless, a complete financial analysis should include an attempt to bracket these costs, perhaps by providing a range of possible values.

Formula for calculating whether an M&A deal makes financial sense

$$V_{A+B} > [V_A + V_B] + P + E + OC + IC$$

where:

V_{A+B} = value of the newly combined company

V_A = value of the bidder

V_B = value of the target before the bid was announced

P = premium to existing market value of the target (on average, around 20–40%)

E = 'cash' costs, or the expenses of the acquisition process (investment banking fees, legal fees, accountant's fees, other fees (such as printing), and interest payments on debt)

OC = 'opportunity costs' (management distraction, loss of sales force focus and the resulting negative reaction of customers, competitive responses both on the product side and in poaching staff)

IC = cost of post-merger integration (redundancy payments, training, system integration costs, rebranding costs, communication expenses, and so on)

PUBLIC COMPANY VALUATIONS

It is much easier to value public companies, because in the public market there exists at all times a simple value for the company: the market capitalization which is the stock price multiplied by the number of shares outstanding. In an M&A transaction, the easiest method may appear to be the public value of the company (the stock market value of the outstanding shares) plus the control premium.

Unfortunately, this valuation method is not as simple as it may seem. For example, which stock price should be chosen to value the company? Future stock price projections from analyst reports? Most recent share price such as the price on the day of first negotiation? Historical average? And if historical, over what period? If the historical period chosen is recent, then a takeover premium may already be reflected in the stock price, especially if there has been takeover activity in a competitor's stock or rumors of the company being targeted. This again shows the reason why M&A valuation is an art and not a science.

PRIVATE COMPANY VALUATIONS

The valuation of private companies is much more difficult, for a number of reasons. First, pre-analysis is normally not possible because private companies' financial information is not usually publicly available. No data will therefore be available when negotiations start, and even then may be limited. The financial statements may not have been audited and therefore may not be as reliable as for public companies. Financial statements may contain many expenses of doing business that are not really costs but rather a way to compensate the owners. Also, private companies may have greater flexibility in showing higher costs in order to lower taxes; for most private companies, keeping taxes low is a primary concern and showing high 'paper' profits is less important as they don't have to please the stock market. Since private companies cannot be purchased except as a friendly deal, it is usually easy to gain access to the company accounts and to senior management in order to get the information to make the adjustments to the accounts.

VALUATIONS AND BUSINESS INTELLIGENCE

In order to get around these problems, the income and cash flow statements must be recast by adjusting for the items that are most commonly accounted for differently between public and private companies:

- Owners' compensation, as high compensation is often the most tax-effective way for earnings to be distributed to the owners of a private company.
- Travel and entertainment expenses are often higher than they would be in a publicly held firm and represent another form of owners' compensation; these may include spousal/family travel and trips linked with holiday which wouldn't be allowed in a corporate travel policy.
- Pension contributions as a future form of owners' compensation.
- Automobile expenses, used for personal trips as well as business.
- Insurance, which covers both personal and business areas.
- High office rent payments if offices are more 'prestigious' and costly than necessary (although the inverse can also be true).

In valuing a private company being purchased by a publicly held company, these extra expenses will typically be deducted from expenses and therefore earnings will be higher. However, there may be other expenses which offset these 'savings.' Once the private company is part of a large corporate, it may be internally 'taxed' with head office and overhead management charges. Be careful in using these extras to value the target as they usually do not represent increased incremental expenses to the newly combined organization, but rather a mere reallocation of expenses which will remain whether the acquisition is made or not.

ALTERNATIVE PRICING METHODS

There are many ways to calculate the appropriate price for companies in an M&A situation. Some of these methods overlap, and in some transactions certain methods may not even apply. The most common methods are listed, and discussed briefly, below.

- **Liquidation value** is the value that the owner realizes when the business is terminated and the assets are sold off, including all the costs of liquidation (commissions, legal, and accounting):
  - orderly liquidation: assets are sold over a reasonable time period so as to get the best price;
  - forced liquidation: assets are sold quickly, such as through an auction sale, usually because of bankruptcy.
  Liquidation value is often a reasonable floor price for some focused firms; for others (particularly conglomerates), it may actually be higher than the current market price.
- **Book value** (an accounting term: Book Value = Assets − Liabilities) has associated with it a number of concerns that limit its value for M&A transactions. Assets are usually valued on the balance sheet at historical costs minus depreciation (which understates in many situations the current value) and intangible assets are not generally included on a balance sheet and therefore also contribute to the understatement of the true value of the firm if this method is used. However, as with liquidation value, it may set a reasonable floor for a

transaction. Also, for some firms (principally financial firms where the substantial assets are marked-to-market each accounting period), it is a useful value.

- **Comparable market multiples** (otherwise known as 'market ratios') are commonly used where comparable public companies and similar deals exist. Depending on the company and the industry within which the bidder and target operate, the following can be used:
  - price/earnings (P/E) multiples;
  - liquidity ratios (such as current ratio, quick ratio);
  - activity ratios (for instance, average collection period, inventory turns);
  - financial leverage ratios (for example, debt ratio, debt/equity);
  - profitability ratios (such as return on investment (ROI), return on equity (ROE)).

  The best market ratios to use would be those for recent similar M&A deals, as these would already incorporate the premiums paid.
- **Net asset value** is used for some businesses (for example, real estate companies) but for most companies there is potential for inaccuracy, as the net assets may not reflect the earning power of the business and assets may be kept on the books at values that are not current. The greater the deviation from current market values, the less useful this method is.
- **Discounted cash flows** (DCF) are used when there is sufficient information available to forecast future earnings and cash flows for an accurate projection of the potential of the company. Because it uses the concept of net present value (NPV), it is also known as the 'NPV method.' Best is to use future free cash flows (FCF), which accounts for anticipated future capital expenditures; typically a five year period is selected. The cash flows in future periods are discounted back to today as is a terminal value of the company which repre-

sents the value of the company as an ongoing concern. As noted above, the cash flows should reflect the incremental cash to the newly combined company, not the acquisition as a standalone entity or with corporate overheads allocated to it. Synergies with the existing business should also be included.

For completeness, an analyst should run different scenarios regarding the expected future performance of the company (typically three scenarios are produced: optimistic, most likely, and pessimistic, although sometimes more scenarios are used), and the projected outcome would be a weighted average or a simple average of these scenarios. Note that the probabilities assigned to the different scenarios can be different; there is no need for the probability to be the same for the high and low cases.

Weighting scheme for discounted cash flow scenarios

Weights may reflect the probability of occurrence of the scenarios used

Example:

High growth earnings (X_1) with a 20% probability (p_1) of occurrence

Moderate growth earnings (X_2) with a 55% probability (p_2) of occurrence

Low or negative growth earnings (X_3) with a 25% probability (p_3) of occurrence

Therefore, the expected value can be calculated as follows:

Expected value $= \Sigma p_i X_i$
Expected value $= (0.20 * X_1) + (0.55 * X_2) + (0.25 * X_3)$

- **Payback method** is the amount of time it takes until incremental new earnings equal purchase price. For example, with a company where the purchase price was $1 000 000 and annual incremental earnings are $200 000, this means that the payback is five years.

- **Capitalization of earnings** is used when there is a relatively constant rate of growth in the company and when its post-acquisition structure will be similar to the pre-merger structure (that is, when the acquired company will operate as a semi-autonomous or independent division of the new parent). The capitalization rate is the reciprocal of the P/E ratio and the payback method: thus if the P/E ratio is 5 or the payback period is five years, then the capitalization rate is 1/5 or 20%.

  This method therefore becomes an easy method to do on the back of an envelope if discussions about a deal start (as often happens!) in a restaurant or airport lounge and both parties want a ballpark figure to determine if discussions can or should continue. One needs only to know the industry's price/earnings ratio (which a senior manager may already know from his or her own company) and then to divide the most recent earnings for the current year projection by the reciprocal of that figure. The resulting number is not the final valuation of course, but may be a starting point for negotiations to continue.

Capitalization of earnings

Method:

Step 1: Select an appropriate earnings base
Step 2: Select an appropriate capitalization rate

- Select a discount rate, select a growth rate and subtract the growth rate from the discount rate, or
- Take the inverse of payback or the price/earnings ratio

Step 3: Divide the earnings base by the capitalization rate

Example:

- Company X's earnings are expected to be $20 million
- Earnings have been growing at 5% per year; 15% discount rate has been selected; therefore the capitalization rate = 15% − 5% = 10%, or the Price/Earnings ratio was 10 (the capitalization rate would be the inverse: 1/10 = 10%)
- Value = $20 million/0.10 = $200 million

Sensitivity:

Note that small changes in growth rate can lead to significantly different values. In the example below, there is a change of just one percentage point in the projected growth rate of the company from 5 to 6%:

- $E_1/(r - g)$ = $20 million/(0.15 − 0.05) = $200 million
- $E_1/(r - g)$ = $20 million/(0.15 − 0.06) = $222 million

Thus over $22 million difference (11%) in value due to the one percentage point change in the growth rate assumption.

Other methods can be used as well, including real options, dividend discount models, and a number of proprietary valuation techniques developed by the investment banks, accountancies, and valuation firms. These are beyond the scope of this book to discuss, but the Bibliography contains some excellent resources on valuation.

ASSUMPTIONS

All industries, companies, and deals are different. One must therefore be especially careful about the assumptions used, as small changes can make large differences (see box above). Different practitioners will have very different approaches to valuation.

- In using industry ratios, the target firm's P/E may be different from industry P/E because:
  - the target's expected earnings growth may be different from the industry's average earnings growth;
  - the firm's risk factors may be different from the industry's because of geography, management, marketing plan, or other factors;
  - the company may be a mix of businesses; in this case, an attempt should be made to use a P/E for each division separately – multiple P/E ratios would then be used and applied against each line of business and then reaggregated to determine a hybrid P/E for the combined businesses.
- Buyers will value assets differently from sellers. For example, the company's assets may be worth more to its buyer than its seller due to synergies with the new business. The buyer may also plan to use assets differently, including selling some assets upon change of control.
- The impact of non-operating assets (assets not used in the operations of the business) needs to be taken into account. These should be valued separately and added to the earnings valuation. An example of this is high value real estate not involved in the business.
- Minority discount: if valuing a minority share and not a controlling position, then a minority discount needs to be applied to the market multiples. The value of a minority interest is less than the proportionate share of the fair market

value of 100% of the company because the minority interest lacks control. A single minority stockholder can, at best, only elect a minority of the board of directors and will otherwise have little ability to determine management, strategy, or finances of the company.

- When an investment lacks marketability (as with a privately held company), it is often more difficult to sell to buyers. Also because of the differences in accounts noted earlier in this chapter, a discount should therefore be taken when market multiples are used from public companies to value a private company.

- The impact of risk arbitrageurs must also be considered as discussed in Chapter 6. These traders will purchase minority positions in stocks where they believe a merger or acquisition will take place. These positions are considered 'hot money' and the arbitrageur will sell the position strictly for financial return. If a company has a substantial portion of its shares in the hands of arbitrageurs, this may make an acquisition faster and easier, although not necessarily less expensive.

- It is important to be explicit about exactly what is being included and excluded in a deal, especially when acquiring only a part of a company. Some participants will refer to enterprise value (the value of the whole company: from an asset valuation perspective, it is the value of the assets, which also equals the debt plus equity) whereas others will refer to the equity value (which is the value of the company excluding outstanding debt). Without clarity as to what terminology is being used, very different assumptions on price will be made.

MERGERS vs ACQUISITIONS

Another issue in valuation is determining whether the deal is in fact a merger or an acquisition. If it is an acquisition, then there should be an acquisition premium because the target's management and shareholders give up control and therefore require a premium to be compensated for this loss of control. If the deal is structured instead as a merger, the two companies are equals and therefore future control is shared and no premium is required as neither side loses control – or perhaps both sides equally do!

Is it a merger or acquisition: J.P. Morgan/Bank One

In 2004, J.P. Morgan, one of the oldest banks in the United States, proposed a friendly combination with Bank One, another large US bank. At the time of the announcement, Bill Harrison was the CEO of J.P. Morgan and Jamie Dimon the CEO of Bank One.

According to the *Financial Times*, Dimon said that J.P. Morgan could purchase Bank One at its current market price without premium if he was given the top job in the newly combined bank immediately. He argued that if it was a merger there should be no premium but that the two senior managers must then be co-CEOs.

However, Bill Harrison decided to remain as the sole CEO and therefore J.P. Morgan ended up paying a 14% premium for Bank One (over $7 billion more than the current market price of Bank One).

By paying the 14% premium to keep the top job and not cede it to Jamie Dimon, Bill Harrison demonstrated that the deal was in fact a takeover, not a merger.

MULTIPLE VALUATION METHODS

It is important to use as many valuation methods as possible in each transaction. There will rarely be a situation where only one method should be used and even each individual method may have several scenarios as noted earlier in this chapter.

Since not all methods are equal in terms of certainty or reliability of data or relevancy to the deal, when using multiple methods they must be weighted to come up with a single figure. Most external advisors will show a wide variety of methods of valuation in their fairness opinions and pricing recommendations; however, it is ultimately the board's responsibility to determine which figure(s) to use.

How do you determine the relative weightings between the different valuation methods and their scenarios? Think about what aspects of the business tend to give rise to its value:

- Is the balance sheet liquid? The book value may be most relevant.
- Is it its assets? Then net asset value should get greater weight than otherwise.
- Is it its earning power? Used most often in private equity and venture capital valuation models that depend on the development of a profitable earnings stream, then give future cash flow methods more weight than the other methods.
- Are there recent similar transactions? Then give more weight to the market multiples using recent deals.

Table 8.2 gives an example of a transaction using such weightings. The actual valuation recommendation in a real M&A deal should

Table 8.2 Weighted Earnings Calculation.

Method	Value	Weight	Adjusted Value
Discounted Cash Flow	£20 million	50%	£10.0 million
DCF high	*£24 million*	*30%*	*£7.2 million*
DCF medium	*£21 million*	*50%*	*£10.5 million*
DCF low	*£11 million*	*20%*	*£2.2 million*
P/E method	£17 million	30%	£5.1 million
Book value	£15 million	10%	£1.5 million
Net assets	£5 million	10%	£0.5 million
Weighted total		**100%**	**£17.1 million**

incorporate many more methods and would incorporate a suggested negotiation range as well.

Ultimately even a 'final' figure determined through the above methodology will serve only as a starting point. Other factors will have to be considered as noted earlier, such as the costs of the deal discussed (fees billed by the bankers, brokers, accountants, lawyers, and so on), the opportunity costs, and the integration costs. The negotiating strategy will also have to be considered: will the first bid be very low with an expectation that the final price will be higher, or will a bear-hug strategy (see next chapter) be employed where a high price is presented first?

ROLE OF BUSINESS INTELLIGENCE

Naturally, no matter how good the analysis, there is no deal unless both the buyer and the target agree on a price. Not all buyers and sellers are rational. Determining what is likely to be acceptable to the other side requires the use of business intelligence.

A key area where business intelligence is critical is to determine how to pay for the deal. Knowing the needs of the principal target shareholders is an imperative. The issue of payment is of interest not just to the bidder (who will need to know whether it can afford to make the purchase), but also to the target who will need to know whether the bidder has the ability to pay for the company being sold. In addition, the issue of how the payment is structured – whether cash, debt, stock, hybrid instruments, or some combination of these – is often an important part of the negotiations.

If there is uncertainty about key aspects of the deal – often uncovered because of the effective use of business intelligence techniques – then the payment of the purchase price and even the closing can be structured to reduce the risk to the purchaser.

This is very common in the private equity and venture capital industries where 'earn-outs' are used both to retain key senior managers, keep clients, and to make the final price dependent on the performance of the company or division. 'Earn-outs' also reduce the upfront payment by the acquirer and in many instances maximize the price received by the target if they achieve the robust earnings growth that they expect but that would otherwise have been discounted by the purchaser. Other partial payment deals or staged acquisitions can be dependent on additional factors, such as regulatory approvals and R&D risk, as shown in the box.

Managing regulatory risk: a staged acquisition in biotech

In early 1997, Genzyme announced a planned joint venture with GelTex, an early stage biotech research company with only two drugs in development, one of which, Renagel, a treatment for end-stage renal disease, was the primary focus of the deal. GelTex was looking for a partner to contribute resources and expertise toward the marketing of the new drug for a share of the profit.

According to Reuters and Dow Jones, the deal consisted of a $27.5 million payment for a 50% interest in GelTex. The issue for Genzyme was the uncertainty of FDA approval of Renagel, as it was still in Stage III clinical trials. To address this regulatory risk, Genzyme negotiated a staged investment strategy and thereby hedged the FDA approval risk. A $2.5 million investment was made initially. Genzyme would wait to see if the drug garnered FDA approval, giving Genzyme the option to continue with the investment or decline further investment. This 'wait and see' flexibility intrinsically added value to the company while hedging potential regulatory risk. Use of staged investment deals has been more commonplace in research-heavy industries like biotech for this reason.

By late 2000, studies showed improvement in morbidity and improved trends in mortality among patients treated with Renagel versus other drugs designed to treat end-stage renal disease. Sales in 2000 for Renagel almost tripled to $56 million compared to $19.5 million in 1999 – well above expectations. Then, in the 3rd quarter of 2000, in an effort to capitalize on this success and augment its short-term pipeline, Genzyme announced its intention to acquire GelTex in a $1 billion stock and cash transaction. The deal was at a 27% premium on GelTex's stock price – the sale closed on December 15, 2000. Sales of Renagel in 2005 were approximately $415 million.

FINANCING THE DEAL

When an acquisition is to include an element of cash paid to the target shareholders, the purchaser is faced with the issue of where to get the cash (unless the company is fortunate enough to have the cash already at hand which may often be the case for acquisitions of companies much smaller than the bidder). Broadly, the choices for obtaining new cash are either to issue new equity (issued as rights to existing shareholders or placed out to new shareholders) or to take on new debt. Some of the payment can also be deferred (typically subject to performance criteria).

Financing issues drive the takeover of Manchester United

In March 2003, Malcolm Glazer quietly bought his first shares of Manchester United, one of the most successful soccer teams in Europe and arguably the most popular sports franchise in the world with an estimated 23 million supporters in China alone. Glazer was already the owner of an American football team, the Tampa Bay Buccaneers. The Buccaneers under his ownership went from being the least profitable team in the National Football League to one of the most profitable – as well as winning the Super Bowl.

It was not until September 2003, when he added to his stake in the company, that it became public that Glazer was a significant shareholder of the football team. By year-end he held over 14% and in February 2004, Manchester United was formally put into play when Glazer announced that he was considering a bid for the company. No formal bid developed.

By October 2004, there were two major shareholders of the football team: Glazer with over 28% and Cubic Expression (an investment vehicle of two Irish financiers, J.P. McManus and John Magnier) with over 24%.

When Glazer finally did decide to launch a bid, Manchester United's board fought hard to reject his offers. They were supported by a group of fans called 'Shareholders United' who had been instrumental in fighting off a takeover by Rupert Murdoch several years earlier. The board and Shareholders United argued that the highly leveraged nature of Glazer's bid would be detrimental to the future of the football club, as Glazer would be forced to raise ticket prices to pay the interest on his debt. They also said that the high level of bank loans would make it impossible for him to invest in the club, including the purchase of player contracts necessary to keep Manchester United at the top of the Premier League. Some fans recommended boycotts of the club's main sponsors, Nike and Vodafone, and there were numerous protests, including some chants from Manchester United's rivals. Glazer reportedly asked the police to keep his address secret and even Glazer's advisors were targeted.

Ultimately, Glazer was successful in first getting over 75% of the shares which allowed him to take the company private and eventually achieving a share ownership of 98% which gave him complete control of the football team in late June 2005. As reported in the *Financial Times,* the total cost of his purchase was £790 million, although the transaction fees raised the total cost to £812 million.

Glazer did put together a complex financing package to pay for his purchase. This included £265 million in debt secured against Manchester United's assets (including Old Trafford stadium) and £275 million in pay-in-kind loans that had a very high yield payable at maturity in 2015. The remainder of the financing came from the Glazer family equity in Manchester United.

Over a year later, in July 2006, Glazer had been able to refinance much of high cost debt and reduce his annual interest payments from £90 million to £62 million despite increasing the debt to £660 million (to be used, among other things, to expand the capacity of Old Trafford stadium). The positive financial results also triggered other deals in English football such as the August 2006 buy-out of another football club, Aston Villa, and later deals at West Ham United and Liverpool.

It is not only the target's needs that drive the financing structure. The buyer must also know its own financial situation well enough to make sure that it can afford the deal in both the short and long term. In putting together the financing package, the acquirer must therefore balance business risk and financial risk (see Figure 8.1).

- Business risk is the inherent risk associated with the operating profits and the cash flows of the company. It is composed of strategic risk and transaction risk:

– strategic risk is the long-term risk of operating in a particular economy, a specific industry (at a stage of its cycle) and with a specific competitive strategy;

– transaction risk is the risk of an interruption of the firm's short-term asset conversion cycle ('business cycle'), that is, the conversion of cash into products/services and back into cash.

• Financial risk is the risk associated with the type of funding used to finance the business (that is, the capital structure of the deal). Financial risk is the risk to the company of defaulting on its debt obligations. It is measured and assessed by both gearing and interest cover:

– level of debt to equity ('gearing');

– ability of the company to service the interest on its debt ('interest cover ratio').

High business risk should be matched by low financial risk, and vice versa. Of the two 'risks,' it is a great deal easier for management to adjust or change the financial risk of a company than its business risk.

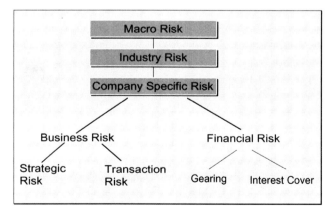

Figure 8.1 Financing Risk Factors.

There are three major areas that will be considered by the acquirer and its advisors in arriving at the financing decision:

- Transaction details, including short-term dilution (earnings per share and impact on existing shareholders), balance sheet gearing, and interest coverage ratios.
- Balance sheet management, such as the expected long-term cost of the financing instrument and the flexibility to restructure the balance sheet.
- Getting the deal done: issues of confidentiality, speed, and other factors unique to the company or transaction such as knowing well what the other side wants.

CONCLUSION

To many who have participated in M&A deals or analyzed them, valuation and other financial issues (such as identifying the appropriate financing mix) are the most important factor in determining the success of any M&A deal. However, 'valuation' is actually only one of many important areas and often not the most critical: we have seen earlier how the wrong merger strategy can cause a deal to fail and we will later discuss the other principal factor in determining success, post-merger integration and human resource issues. Ultimately, the most important factor in valuation is finding a narrow range of company value which allows both sides to negotiate all the other non-financial details of the transaction. Only then will a final value be determined.

CHAPTER 9

NEGOTIATION AND BIDDING

With the satisfactory due diligence work and pricing performed (although still being updated throughout the deal), a company will know, as much as is possible, the strengths and weaknesses of the target. Then, if it continues to make strategic sense, the parties progress rapidly towards the stage of finalizing the details of the deal and signing the sale and purchase agreement. Feeding their due diligence work into the closing negotiations, the various parties to the deal process should typically employ business intelligence techniques to identify those risks which can be mitigated by way of some sort of 'protection,' such as a price reduction or warranty which would be conditional as part of the deal closure. Excellent intelligence will also enhance the negotiating strength, fulfilling the aphorism: 'Knowledge is power.'

BUSINESS INTELLIGENCE IN EFFECTIVE NEGOTIATIONS

For the participants in a deal, the final stage of the negotiations – replete with posturing, horse-trading, and wrangling – is best conducted with Sun Tsu's 'foreknowledge.' Any information about the other parties to a deal is useful, not simply of opponents but also more about your own company, business partners, and providers. Such information can aid the conclusion of a deal with a greater degree of value to whosoever secures it. Whether employing considerable ingenuity to obtain information or doing so with little trouble, either way, business intelligence can play a pivotal role for the various constituents in an M&A deal allowing each side to unearth their opponents' real motivations and imperatives, their attitudes to risk and uncertainty, their speed of change and decision making, and their focus on the big picture versus the detailed minutiae of the deal.

Conducted in an atmosphere that is more often than not enveloped in intrigue and maneuvering, the final stages of a deal involve the various players obtaining and evaluating as much intelligence and private information as possible about the target or bidder in order to gain favorable positions during negotiations. Used to determine a range of negotiation parameters and develop an appropriate set of bid and defense strategies and tactics, parties to an M&A transaction employ intelligence techniques to their advantage in order to gain the upper hand against their rivals. Thus, employed to negotiate a better deal for themselves, good negotiators try to uncover damaging information at this stage, allowing management a better negotiating position. This hopefully leads to more realistic pricing and thus reduces the risk of overbidding.

Playing hard ball, or was it for show?

One such example of the use of business intelligence in the negotiating process involves a client of KPMG's Corporate Intelligence Division in the UK who, while in the process of acquiring a target, found that the vendor party was playing 'hard ball' during deal negotiations. Using the professional services firm to covertly uncover that the vendor was in fact on the verge of bankruptcy and actually desperate to sell – albeit at the highest price and with terms in their favor – such intelligence and 'private' information helped KPMG's client to adjust their negotiation tactics appropriately and in their favor.

In light of the hostile environment in which M&A deals are sometimes conducted and the anxiousness and determination of parties to put one over the opposition, it should come as no surprise that professional advisors such as George Magan (formerly of Morgan Grenfell), if advising a client on a bid, would, as reported in the *Evening Standard* in 2004, 'ask a corporate investigation agency to look at the client, to shake out the skeletons from their cupboard [in order] to see what the other side might throw at them. . . .' In short, by enabling parties to a transaction to maintain either a strong competitive bid or defense position for as long as possible, business information keeps the tension in the deal right to the point at which the deal closes. It is no wonder therefore that M&A transactions grab the business headlines in the way that they do.

Yet, the M&A process also carries with it vast potential commercial risks for either the buyer or a target company itself by exposing various forms of business intelligence to an existing or potential competitor. Whether disclosing trade secrets or confidential information, due diligence (and the wider M&A

process *per se*) may ultimately weaken a seller by divulging the problems of a target business to a prospective buyer. Thus, from this standpoint, the whole deal process becomes a double-edged sword simultaneously necessitating companies to lower their guard and impart confidential information to competitors, yet without a guarantee that the deal will ultimately be consummated. This is why the use of clean teams have been increasing.

Clean teams

There is an increasing trend to use third-party 'clean teams' at the early stages of negotiation when one or both parties are concerned about disclosing confidential information to the other side. A clean team is typically a management consulting firm and sits between the two companies. All information is initially passed through the clean team.

In the initial stages of the negotiation, the data analysis regarding the potential for the deal is also conducted by the clean team, which reports to both sides. Ultimately the clean team can support the formal negotiation process as well, although it is more common for the team to be less active as each side conducts its own negotiation (only being involved on particularly contentious issues) or even disband at the time.

If a clean team is used, very clear terms of engagement must be determined at the outset and reviewed throughout the process. It must be remembered as well that although the information given to the clean team will be kept confidential from the other side, the information is still being disclosed to a third party outside the company and is therefore now part of their intellectual database. As with all use of advisors, if the clean team is part of a reputable firm, one can be confident that it will not be used or disclosed explicitly; but the knowledge of the people on the advisory team involved will not disappear as they move to the next assignment or client.

As much as in other elements of the M&A cycle, there is conceivably no end to the use of business intelligence in the latter stages of any M&A deal process. Once detailed due diligence has begun, the multitude of actors in any deal get down to the real business. The chips are on the table, the face cards have been revealed, but the hole cards remain unknown. If that final piece of information can be acquired, the deal can be concluded precisely to the acquirer's (or target's) satisfaction. They interact with one another, swapping and leaking valuable information and disinformation in order to drive the deal towards a conclusion – one way or another.

Each of the participants uses different levels of intelligence gathering to gain a sustainable competitive advantage in the M&A game. It is of no consequence whether they are corporate organizations using investment bankers to build a profile of shareholders (and so draw conclusions regarding the price at which they would be likely to sell), event-driven hedge funds (acting as arbitrageurs) betting on short-term price movements in companies' share prices, or private investigation firms sifting through professional advisors' rubbish bags in order to glean nuggets of information for their clients. Like poker, the game will be won by the player with the most resources and most information. While the accepted wisdom is that friendly bids can be completed without much of the business intelligence needed for hostile or unfriendly takeovers, it must be understood that friendly bids can turn unfriendly. Therefore, it is sensible always to gather as much information in all situations.

The nature of friendly bids with unlimited access to the target can lead managers to assume that less rigorous due diligence is needed than for hostile deals where access to the company is limited or non-existent. This attitude should be avoided. Sometimes the target won't know itself as well as the bidder would wish. More often there are things that are not known or even deliberately hidden from management.

TAKEOVER STRATEGIES

Since the advent in the 1970s and 1980s of stronger target defense mechanisms, hostile mergers have focused on three major tactics: 'bear hugs,' tender offers, and proxy fights. But even before initiating one or more of these mechanisms, a bidder should consider whether it should try two other tactics: toehold share purchases and a 'casual pass.' Each of these is discussed in greater detail in this section. Of course, as covered in the earlier chapters, any action taken as part of the merger and acquisition process should be part of a grand strategy, and the tactics covered in this chapter would be part of that overall process.

TOEHOLDS

Toeholds are purchases of stakes in a target's stock, usually below the regulatory disclosure threshold (5% in the US; 3% in the UK). Multiple toeholds may also be purchased in alternative targets, in case the bidder later discovers that the first-choice target either has defense mechanisms that are too strong to overcome or because the due diligence process uncovers reasons not to pursue that particular target. Here again, the value of timely intelligence cannot be understated. There may be a point at which the negotiation has been allowed to proceed so far that it is impossible to exit. Consequently, the earlier intelligence is gathered the more value it adds to the negotiation.

If the number of shares purchased is above a certain threshold, stock exchange regulations in most countries require that the purchase be made public, and other restrictions may also then come into effect. For example, in the UK, once holdings reach more than 3% of outstanding stock, this must not only be disclosed within two days of purchase, but all future purchases must also be disclosed. This has the effect of announcing to the market that a potential bid is under way.

Establishing a toehold may allow for less expensive purchases of a target's stock, because the toehold is typically purchased before any announced bid for the company and therefore before any acquisition premium is added to the stock price. This toehold may therefore lower the average cost of the takeover (the opposite can also occur, depending on market conditions). In some jurisdictions (for instance, the UK), there are rules governing the price of the offer if a toehold has been taken (that is, the offer must be at least as high as the highest price paid for shares in the prior three months). Another advantage to the toehold is that it may give the bidder leverage with target management, as the acquiring company is now both a bidder and a shareholder. Should there be any decisions put to a shareholder vote, the bidder now controls some of the stock. Similarly, the bidder may gain access to information otherwise not available if it were not a large shareholder.

Although it would seem axiomatic that any hostile bidder would want to have a toehold in the target before launching a public bid, a study by Arturo Bris at Yale University found that only 15% of his sample of hostile deals in the US and UK had toehold initial purchases and the authors of another study published in early 2006 by the European Corporate Governance Institute were puzzled that they found only 11% of initial bidders in more than 12000 contests had toeholds. This is especially surprising as research also shows that deals that included a toehold were more likely to succeed and at a lower cost to the bidder than deals where no toehold had been taken, despite the fact that the toehold held the risk of signaling a potential bid to the market.

Many times a toehold is purchased from one or just a few shareholders. This has the advantage of keeping the purchases quiet until such time as the bidder wishes to disclose its purchases (assuming that the amount purchased is below the disclosure threshold). Another variation is to carry out open market purchases, typically using multiple brokers in order to disguise the bidder's intentions.

One further variation is known as a 'street sweep' (so called first in the US because the bidder is trying to sweep up all the shares it can on Wall Street, the location of the New York Stock Exchange and the traditional headquarters of many of the US brokers). Street sweeps are purchases of as many shares as possible in the public market in as short a time as possible, very often done overnight or within a few hours. In essence, this is a toehold taken immediately to its logical conclusion – control of the company or as close as possible. It is difficult to keep such purchases secret. When word gets out, the price of the stock rises. At this stage disinformation techniques can be used to deflect attention away from the street sweep for a sufficient amount of time to allow the requisite number of shares to be purchased.

Street sweeps can be done as an alternative to a tender offer (see Hanson Trust plc case study later). But as noted above, after crossing the 5% threshold (US) or 3% threshold (UK), the bidder has to disclose its purchases to the regulators. In the UK, purchases in excess of 10% of the shares within a seven day period may constitute a takeover bid and have other implications; purchases above 30% require a bid for all shares.

CASUAL PASS

The 'casual pass' is when a bidder attempts a friendly overture prior to initiating a hostile bid, giving the opportunity to the target to avoid the difficulties of a public hostile bid. Sometimes the casual pass is done when the bidder is unsure what the target's response will be. Of course, it may backfire, as it does give advance warning to the target that a hostile bid may be forthcoming, thus giving time to the target to hire a defense team and possibly even enough time to erect new defenses. There are two other major disadvantages to the casual pass:

- It may start the clock ticking where there are regulations regarding the timing of offers to remain open, sending documents to shareholders, and so on.
- Advisors also often tell the management of the target not to enter into any 'casual pass' discussions with the bidder under any circumstances, so in fact the bidder may not get any new information and could therefore misinterpret the target's actual intentions. Of course, the correct level of intelligence should already have provided sufficient data. The casual pass is primarily to 'feel' the mood of the target which is best done face to face. This can be done by 'pretexting' (which has now been ruled illegal in the Hewlett-Packard case referred to in Chapter 2).

BEAR HUGS

'Bear hugs' are situations where the bidder brings the offer directly to the target company's board of directors, bypassing the shareholders (although, of course, the shareholders will eventually need to approve the deal; often this approval is more likely if the directors recommend acceptance to the shareholders). The bear hug appears friendly, but carries the real threat that a hostile bid will be forthcoming if the directors do not accept the bid (hence the name: a hug from a bear may seem warm, fuzzy, and friendly, but if the bear chooses to squeeze harder and then eat you, it can).

The bear hug is designed to take advantage of the legal duties of directors to consider any offer that they receive carefully and diligently. But directors do not have a legal duty to sell the corporation, so they do not have to succumb to the bear hug offer if they feel that it is inadequate or if they believe they have a viable alternative (including continuing the current strategy).

Bear hugs were popular in the mid- to late 1990s, when several large deals used the technique (for example, the large telecommunications and technology merger of 1999, Vodafone/ Mannesmann).

TENDER OFFERS

Tender offers are the most common tactic used in hostile take-overs. In a tender offer, the bidder directly approaches the share-holders of the target and offers to buy their shares at a specified price (in which case the shareholders would 'tender' their shares to the bidder). The terms of the offer specify a time limit within which the shareholders need to tender their shares and whether the offer is for cash or securities, which depends on a variety of factors including time (cash is faster), availability in cross-border deals (share deals may not be possible or practical in a cross-border transaction), tax issues, regulations, and so on.

What constitutes a tender offer? In the UK, after acquiring 30% of a company's stock, a bidder must make an offer for all remaining shares at the highest price it paid to acquire its stock position within the prior three months, or higher. This renders partial bids and two-tiered offers (see below) impracticable.

The success rate of tender offers for publicly traded companies is very high (83.4% according to Mergerstat Review) and, when uncontested, even higher (91.6%). The contested success rate is 52.4%. Why is the success rate so high? Because shareholders are often quite happy to tender their shares in order to benefit from the financial windfall arising from the offer price being higher than the recent share price (due to the control premium which we saw in an earlier chapter averages around 20–40%).

A tactic that had been used during some of the earlier merger waves was the two-tiered tender offer (also called a front-end loaded offer). This is where shareholders who tender their stock quickly in response to an offer receive a higher price than share-holders who delay. However, in the 1980s and 1990s, most courts found them to be illegal as they are coercive; the best price rule renders the tactic unworkable, as would fair price provisions in laws and company charters.

By their very nature, tender offers are considered hostile. They are more expensive than a friendly deal, because of the time it takes to complete and because the tender offer team can be very large – investment bankers, legal advisors, accountants, information agents, depository banks, forwarding agents, and so on. Therefore a tender offer should be used only when a friendly approach is not viable.

Combination of takeover tactics (Hanson Trust plc)

It is possible to combine negotiating tactics. An example of this was the hostile bid for SCM by Hanson Trust.

In 1985, Hanson Trust plc made a tender offer for SCM Corp. This bid was strongly resisted by SCM and its team of advisors. Hanson therefore cancelled its tender offer and immediately initiated a street sweep, in which it bought 25% of SCM in six separate transactions.

SCM sued Hanson in the US courts and contended that these purchases violated securities laws. However, the court ruled that Hanson's tactics were legal. This ruling now forms the legal basis for street sweeps in the US and has henceforth made targets there vulnerable to such street sweeps.

PROXY FIGHTS

There are two types of proxy fights: contests for seats on the board of directors (possibly including an insurgent group trying to replace management) and contests about management proposals such as mergers, acquisitions, or anti-takeover amendments. These can certainly take place at the same time for the same M&A deal, as a bidder may seek to pack the board with friendly directors prior to launching a formal bid for the company.

There are a number of characteristics of a target company that increase the likelihood of a proxy fight being successful:

- Management has insufficient voting support (in situations where management does not hold many votes, such as in the Forte situation described in the case study in Chapter 6, where the Forte family controlled only 8% of outstanding shares at the time that Granada launched its hostile bid).
- Poor operating performance (the worse the operating performance, the more likely that shareholders are unhappy with management).
- Sound alternative operating plan (insurgents must have a good plan to improve shareholder returns, and if such a plan appears to shareholders to be likely to provide a better return, then management is disadvantaged).

Since it is critical in a hostile takeover to get the support of as many shares as possible, it is necessary to use business intelligence to understand the motivations of each major shareholder or group of shareholders. What an acquiring company's intelligence function would seek to ascertain would be:

- Insurgents and groups unfriendly to management (presumably friendly to the bidder).
- Directors, officers, and employees owning stock (including retirement plans), who are likely to vote against the insurgents.
- Brokerage firms: shares are often held 'in street name' which means that the stock owners have instructed their brokers to retain their shares and keep the shares in the name of the broker so the shareowners are not publicly identifiable; these can often be very large blocks of shares although they are composed of many individual shareholders. Stock held in street name can often represent the majority of shares.
- Institutional shareholdings (pension funds, mutual funds, and so on); the most intense lobbying typically takes place with

these influential shareholders as they are likely to hold large blocks of shares.

- Individuals, who are more difficult to contact and who are also more difficult to judge how they will respond.

Some of this information can be gathered using open source electronic intelligence gathering techniques (elint) but most would need to be gathered by human beings (humint). This is at the individual company's discretion because subterfuge and deception lie in a gray ethical and legal zone.

Three-way suitors were increasingly common in the 1990s. This is when two companies agree to merge or where one company makes a bid for another, and then a third company comes on the scene and makes a bid for the target or even for both companies. For example, in 1999, two copper companies, Asarco Inc. and Cyprus Amax Minerals, agreed to merge on a friendly basis, as each felt that the combined company would be a stronger competitor in an increasingly consolidating market. Phelps Dodge, one of the world's largest mining companies, then came on the scene and made a bid for both companies. This is yet another example of the dangers of companies entering into M&A situations even on a friendly basis; once they have started the process, it is difficult to control the outcome.

FREEZE-OUTS

Minority shareholders are required to sell their shares to the bidder once a deal is approved by the requisite majority or super-majority of the shareholders. This is called a 'freeze-out' (or, less commonly, a 'squeeze-out') as it prevents the minority share-holders from exercising their minority voting rights and forces the dissident shareholders to sell their shares at the same price as the other shareholders have accepted. Regulators and courts have designed this to prevent a hold-out problem where a small group of shareholders prevents a deal from being consummated when the majority of the shareholders have already approved the deal. In most countries, this level is set by the regulators at 5 or 10% – that is, if 90 or 95% of the shareholders have approved the deal, the remaining shareholders must also sell.

In a freeze-out situation, if minority shareholders disagree on the value or treatment they received, they can then initiate shareholder appraisal rights to get the difference between the value they contend and the value they receive. In order to do this, they have to follow certain procedures exactly, which include raising the issue in the courts. If a suit is filed, a court may also appoint an independent appraiser.

Dissident shareholders and 'freeze-outs'

In April 2005, as reported in *The Times* and *Dow Jones*, Shire Pharmaceuticals attempted an all-cash friendly takeover of Transkaryotic Therapies (TKT) for $1.6 billion, a premium of 44% over its pre-bid share price. The bid was subject to, among other things, government clearance (as both companies were engaged in the pharmaceutical industry, which is heavily regulated) and the approval of shareholders. It was the third bid that Shire had made for TKT, with the TKT board rejecting the previous two bids. The current bid was supported by the TKT board who recommended that shareholders support the takeover. Shire believed that it could save over $200 million in costs from the combination of the two companies.

The acquisition agreement included break fees in case the deal did not proceed, including penalties if the shareholders did not approve the deal. TKT's penalty fee was to be $40 million.

In June, a group of TKT shareholders holding almost 16% of the outstanding shares said it opposed the deal as the sale price was too low because of the pending results from the clinical trials of one of TKT's drugs at the time of the bid that many claimed could now yield over $200 million annually in sales. A month later, the billionaire investor, Carl Icahn, joined the opposition and brought the opposition to over 21%.

In late July, Shire won the support of the TKT shareholders, but with only 52.6% of the outstanding shares. Almost 28% of the shareholders rejected the takeover, which was enough to exercise its freeze-out rights. The dissidents then asked a judge to value their shares in a process that could take years. In the meanwhile, Shire must still purchase the outstanding shares at the offer price at any time.

FAIRNESS OPINIONS

To avoid this potential problem, most bidders include in their bid a fairness opinion on the value of the company being acquired, issued by an expert. Such valuations are often conducted by investment bankers. This can create a conflict of interest, as the investment banks may have a stake in the success of the deal (bankers are often paid more for deals where the deal is successful, as we saw in Chapter 4). Also, the fees paid to some advisors (at least including the investment banks) are the same amount whether the deal closes in three weeks or nine months, so the motivation for the advisory bankers is to close the deal quickly once it is under way. This conflict of interest is not totally avoidable, but to prevent it from being an issue, a firm may also hire an independent valuation firm.

NEGOTIATION PROCESS

Negotiation is communication and decision making between two parties that have different interests and/or agendas. In M&A, this clearly relates to a situation where two firms are negotiating their very existence.

There are as many negotiating styles as there are negotiators (and perhaps even more, as most good negotiators have developed skills in several ways of negotiating, changing their methods to suit the particular situation). However, in almost any negotiation, it is recommended that at least the following points be considered as part of the process.

- Clarify the starting point.
- Identify the resistance points.
- Find the 'agreement zone'.
- Determine the best possible solution(s) for both parties.

Several factors in the process can significantly affect the result:

- Involvement of specialists and analysts with independent goals (such as advisors who are paid for the success of the deal).
- The need for secrecy, limiting the number of people who can participate.
- The requirement for a substantial and uninterrupted time commitment, especially by the most senior managers in the company.
- Increasing momentum to close the deal.
- Managers who see that closing the deal will be a promotion and compensation stepping-stone forward.
- Investment bankers and other advisors who may be motivated to close quickly.
- Inability to resolve important areas of ambiguity before closing – or the deliberate postponement of these issues to a later point.

There are many ways to improve the negotiation process. Each company should focus throughout the process on the end result – not the deal closing – while being clear about key objectives and remaining flexible on non-essential issues (although recognizing that each side may differ on what is key and what is non-essential). One way to avoid some of the potential pitfalls is to create two teams – one that supports the deal and one opposing – to ensure that the acquisition itself is challenged internally. These two teams should each include specialists/experts and operating managers, but no matter who participates, it is important to understand the motivations of each of the team members. Additional value would be provided by a more embedded intelligence function with shadow teams operating on a permanent basis. Lastly, the management and board of the bidder should be willing to walk away from a deal if major issues remain unresolved. They need to resist the temptation to let the momentum move a bad or questionable deal to closing.

HARD vs SOFT NEGOTIATIONS

There are two basic negotiation styles. The first is called 'soft' and is typical of situations where the two (or more) parties are acting as partners (as with a merger or a friendly acquisition). The aim is to reach agreement, with both parties being flexible, willing to make offers, avoiding confrontation, and basing their negotiations on trust. The other style is 'hard,' and is characteristic of situations where the parties negotiating are enemies or have conflicting agendas or goals. Here, the aim of each party is to win, often at any cost. Each party distrusts the other and engages in trench warfare, including the possible use of threats; one party will ultimately lose.

For those knowingly entering into a hostile bid situation (using the 'hard' negotiating style), a number of different tactics have been used: deliberately misguiding (introducing ambiguity in facts, implying false goals and interests, misleading through the decision process and decision authority), psychological warfare (for instance, creating stress, making personal attacks, 'throwing mud,' playing 'good cop/bad cop,' playing 'chicken'), and finally, deliberately pressurizing the situation (refusing to negotiate, taking extreme starting positions, reopening already closed positions, burning bridges, being late on purpose, being impersonal, providing 'take it or leave it' offers). Even for those who find such tactics unethical or immoral, it is important to know that there may be others on the opposing side who may use them.

Aggressive ('dirty'?) tactics in the battle for Marks & Spencer

In Sir Philip Green's attempted hostile takeover in 2004 of the leading British retailer Marks & Spencer, a number of very aggressive – and to some people, questionable – tactics were used on both sides. Sir Philip Green was the billionaire businessman who owned some of the UK's largest retailers, including Bhs and Arcadia Group. Marks & Spencer was one of the UK's best known retailers, led during the takeover battle by a former employee of Green, Stuart Rose.

Green attempted to discredit Rose through accusations that Rose had illegally profited from material non-public information relating to the bid. Sir Philip Green's team was reported to have accessed the Marks & Spencer CEO's mobile phone records in an attempt to prove that.

Sir Philip Green also initiated a heated encounter with Stuart Rose on the street in public (and with reporters around) near to Marks & Spencer's headquarters. He reportedly seized Rose by the jacket and uttered some unprintable expletives. In response, Rose was quoted in the *Financial Times* as saying, 'I'm walking around now with a pair of dark glasses and a moustache on.'

Marks & Spencer also refused to provide Green with information that he requested as part of the due diligence process. The board refused to give Green access to company financials, presumably causing him greater difficulty to fine tune his bid. The pension fund also refused to provide Green access to their accounts.

RESISTANCE STRATEGIES

To combat these 'hard' lines of attack, there are five strategies that have been found to be particularly effective:

- 'Take a deep breath and count to ten . . . ,' because the natural reaction is to fight back, so pause; be careful not to become part of the problem.
- 'Walk in their shoes.' Look at the problem from the other side's perspective while trying to listen actively to and show respect for the other party's views; agree when possible.
- 'Change the game' by asking problem-solving questions such as 'why?,' 'why not?,' 'what if?'; don't reject without careful consideration.
- 'Build bridges,' don't burn them by, among other things, issuing threats; look for the win/win result and work towards that result slowly and step by step; uncover the other side's requirements and incorporate those into the result.
- 'Learn judo philosophy' by recognizing and neutralizing negative negotiation tactics on the other side; don't force the other side to surrender; point out the consequences of not reaching an agreement and look for viable alternatives.

Note that all of these strategies can also be used in friendly transactions as well to expedite the ultimate result.

CONCLUSION

The topic of effective negotiation could be a book in and of itself and, indeed, there are a plethora of books telling us how to do it. One of the better ones is Eric Evans' *Mastering Negotiation*. Evans provides the following checklist:

- Identify the balance of power.
- Empathize with the other player.
- Identify your genuine interests rather than your negotiating position.
- Identify any common ground.
- Is a long-term relationship important to you? If so, don't win too heavily.
- Is there a radical solution you could propose?
- Have you considered the mechanics of the negotiation, such as venue, seating arrangements, attendees, time, temperature?
- Rehearse.

To this list could be added some other summary recommendations:

- Never start with your best offer.
- Don't negotiate against yourself – if the other side has not responded to an offer, don't lower (or raise) your offer unilaterally.
- Don't change your offer in small steps or too frequently.
- Be alert and read all the signs (body language, voice inflections, pauses, and timing), including the tendency to rely too much on one single source or piece of information.
- Document all of the steps taken so that they can be justified later.

Finally, never forget the mantra from the play and later movie, *Glengarry Glenross* – ABC: Always Be Closing. Time wasted on an unsuccessful bid limits time available for winnable bids.

In many deals (the unsuccessful ones!), the process and negotiation focus almost exclusively on strategic fit, personnel (especially senior management), and financial issues – and not post-merger integration issues. However, as we will see in the next chapter, the success of the deal is ultimately determined more by the post-merger integration process than any other factor and therefore the negotiations should also provide adequate focus on the post-merger issues.

CHAPTER 10

POST-MERGER INTEGRATION

An M&A deal does not end with the completion of the transaction at closing, although very often that is when the public attention to the deal from outside the company largely disappears. It may therefore seem to outsiders that the deal is complete, but in most cases the closing of the deal is only the start of the truly hard work of making the newly formed company work. The success of the previous phases (strategic planning, financial analysis, deal structuring, negotiation) will typically depend upon a robust and dynamic post-merger integration plan and the successful implementation of that plan.

M&A is a means to an end – not just an end in itself. Unfortunately, in many deals the focus is exclusively on completing the deal and not enough attention has been paid to the various organizational and people issues that will be faced after the closing. This contributes to the high failure rate of M&A deals.

Post-merger integration is the 'quiet' phase of the typical merger, as to the outside world there is usually very little discussion about the deal in this phase unless, of course, it is falling apart and was a high profile deal. It may be headline-grabbing 'news' when two large firms decide to merge and this is especially true when the transaction is a hostile one and competing bidders enter the fray, but once the deal is completed, the focus usually shifts internally. As post-merger integration is the most important phase of the deal, the lower level of public attention should not be considered a proxy for how significant this phase actually is.

Success of the deal actually depends more upon the post-merger integration than any other single step in the M&A process. This is often misunderstood by many M&A practitioners and advisors who believe that success will naturally follow when there has been proper selection of target combined with best price/ valuation.

A merger will likely fail if it has the right strategic rationale but that strategy is implemented poorly; likewise, failure will follow a merger carried out at the best price but with bad post-merger integration. On the other hand, if a deal has no sound strategic rationale or if the strategy was based on circumstances that have now changed, and even if the deal was done for far too high a price, the newly combined firm can still be successful if there is effective and creative management of the new organization after the merger.

As we saw at the beginning of Chapter 1, most mergers have been failures: the simplest way to improve that track record is to focus on the post-merger integration.

CHANGE MANAGEMENT

The post-merger integration period is very similar to any strategic change management process for a company. As such, it must continually assess the speed of the changes being made (fast or slow, incremental or discontinuous), establish clear leadership, communicate effectively, maintain customer focus throughout the process, deal with resistance both internal and external, make tough decisions and take initiatives focused on the end result. It must be dynamic, adapting to the ever-changing circumstances.

As acquisitions occur for different reasons, the post-merger planning should reflect the desired change from the deal (see Figure 10.1). If the strategy behind the deal is unclear, then there is no reason to expect successful post-merger integration. Different types of acquisitions bring with them different post-merger problems. For example, a company dealing with overcapacity in a mature market will need to reduce costs quickly and will typically impose its own systems on the target (although willing to look for 'best of breed' as the target may have some better systems). If a company is using acquisitions as a substitute for in-house R&D as is common with many technology and pharmaceutical companies, then it will typically keep the research functions separate after the acquisition for a period but rapidly integrate other areas. Each situation is unique.

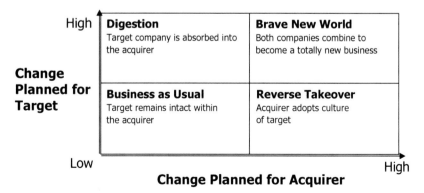

Figure 10.1 Post-merger changes.

INTEGRATION COSTS

The costs of doing the integration poorly can be immense. These costs are not just limited to the visible out-of-pocket quantifiable expenses of the deal such as the rebranding of products and branches, printing new brochures and business cards, marketing campaigns, redundancy packages, and systems integration costs. As discussed in the valuation chapter, the overall cost also includes items that are very difficult to quantify but that will have a major impact on the newly merged company's bottom line. Some of these items include the following:

- Hiring and training new employees and existing employees in new positions.
- Time-consuming and distracting meetings and activities during integration (diverting focus from marketing, new product development, and other non-merger activities).
- Dysfunctional politicking and power fights.
- Decrease in employee efficiency during the period of uncertainty.
- Customer confusion and competitors' attempts to poach clients during this period.

INTEGRATION PLANNING

Integration planning should begin at the deal idea-generation stage and continue throughout the merger process. Where sound strategic and financial strategies have been followed that have combined to bring the merger or acquisition to fruition, they become the basis of the post-merger integration.

Unfortunately, there are often very large disconnects between the various deal teams: those which developed the strategy, the financial team valuing the firms, the negotiation team, and then the team – the whole new organization – that must implement the integration. Many of the external advisors to the deal are also gone once the deal is completed and even the internal planners may now be focused on the next deal. It is often left to the 'new' managers itself to implement what others have planned.

There are five major stages in the post-merger integration process, each with distinctive characteristics that must be handled differently.

1. High level merger planning: discussion at the senior executive level which should be kept confidential; those discussions should include talks about how the companies can or will combine. The advisors for the post-merger period may be selected at this time and some deals will have been initiated with the advisors.

2. Formal (or leaked) announcement: employees and management will have mixed emotions, expectations rise in many cases due to the external discussion about the deal's potential; for some organizations, there can be relief due to knowledge of a deal having been announced, especially if the company had been in trouble and there had been rumors of a merger or a previous attempt at one that had fallen through; excitement by some, especially those who were engaged in the merger planning. Due to the natural uncertainty by most about the deal, it is important to be able to announce some integration plans at the same time or within days of the deal announcement.

3. Initial organizational merger planning: the organization is unstable and although many employees have the best intentions to cooperate, goodwill quickly erodes; post-merger planning is now out in the open with a need for effective use of business intelligence. A large number of people both internal and external will be engaged in these planning efforts.

4. Initial post-deal integration: often intense during this period (typically 100 days) but with a high level of organizational instability including 'us–them' mentality and intra- and interdepartmental hostility; with a well-developed

post-merger plan combined with the business intelligence techniques noted earlier, these problems can be anticipated, but flexibility around the changing organization is important despite a few major decisions being 'cast in concrete' so that employees and others have some indication of future stability.

5. Psychological integration: roles and systems are by this point clarified and there are successes demonstrating the power of the new organization; this is a long-term, gradual process which may take years to finalize.

Note that formal post-merger integration does not start until the deal is completed (stage 4 above), but the planning for that post-merger period should be discussed from the very start in stage 1.

These stages can take a varying amount of time to complete, and the last phase can remain still unfinished as long as a decade after the deal is completed. For example, in a case we also saw in Chapter 1, Morgan Stanley took eleven years following its 1997 merger with Dean Witter finally to consolidate its two broker dealers into one, only dropping the Dean Witter name in April 2007. Even following a successful integration, many companies still have employees who will identify themselves many years later as being from either one or the other original company.

Integration process during the Hewlett-Packard/ Compaq merger

The merger in 2002 of Hewlett-Packard (HP) and Compaq is an example of how a process can be designed for rapid and effective integration across two very large and successful companies, both with a very strong market presence and culture.

At the outset, a strategic goal and rationale for the HP/ Compaq merger was announced: reduce costs by $2.5 billion by making 15 000 staff redundant (out of a combined total of 145 000) and eliminating other expenses. The integration teams quickly identified 163 overlapping product lines that could be consolidated to help achieve the cost savings.

However, as could be expected, there was disagreement – often quite emotional – about which product lines to retain among each of the former HP or Compaq groups that developed, produced, or marketed these products. It was therefore decided that a formal structure needed to be developed that could be used by the entire organization in making these decisions.

The resulting structure was as follows, as described by an HP executive at a public lecture at Cass Business School in London shortly after the merger:

Step 1: The decision factory:

> Appointment of two integration managers (one from each company, one of whom had been with HP for 31 years), and appointment of an integration group ('clean team') that had 1000 members at its peak.

Step 2: 'Adopt-and-go':

> Selection of product lines to be retained and identification of staff and management for redundancy.

Step 3: Feed the fast track:

> Introduction of new products on schedule: dozens of new product launches.

Step 4: Enforce cost deadlines:

> Integration managers with the authority to enforce savings.

Ultimately, the above cost goal was achieved 18 months ahead of schedule, with an additional $500 million savings eventually achieved (but with 18 000 redundancies).

KEYS TO INTEGRATION SUCCESS

In order to achieve a successful post-merger integration – and thus the success of the whole deal – there are eight areas that require attention which will be discussed in more detail below:

- **L**eadership
- **E**ngineer successes
- **A**ct quickly
- **R**etain key employees
- **N**urture clients

- **C**ommunicate
- **I**ntegrate the two cultures
- **A**djust, plan, and monitor

These can be remembered by a simple mnemonic related to the intelligence community: LEARN CIA for short.

LEADERSHIP

It is important to set up the appropriate structure and organization for the post-merger integration, starting with the **Leadership**. The top of the company needs to be seen internally and externally as being focused on the success of the deal and with managers and employees internally. It is the senior management of the company that must challenge decisions and assess the progress of the integration.

Leading by example

David Mellor, a former managing director in private equity at Deutsche Bank and currently an advisor to many firms on M&A deals, tells a story from before his first direct experience with M&A at Midland Bank, now part of HSBC Bank.

He was having lunch with the head of the UK branch of a Swiss bank, which had recently merged its commercial and investment banking businesses. Mellor asked him: if he was able to do the deal over again, what would he have done differently. He replied that the key issue to which he would have devoted even more time and attention the second time around would be to make sure that the leadership team (a) led by example and (b) transparently worked as a team to make the merger work. If this did not happen, then you could not expect the 'footsoldiers' to perform efficiently and effectively. The end result invariably was unexploitation of in-house talent due to leadership mismanagement and client defection and alienation due to in-house squabbling and competition.

Mellor recalled as well in another merger where three business units within the same bank were bidding for the same piece of business, much to the client's confusion and amusement, and yet another deal where seven different salesmen from one newly merged company introduced themselves in a meeting to a client as the client's primary relationship manager!

The CEO needs to appoint an integration manager who comes from a high level in the organization, ensures middle management buy-in and involvement through the use of integration planning committees and task forces, and makes quick decisions on compensation where necessary (such as retention contracts). The CEO should be meeting with clients, suppliers, and analysts perhaps even more frequently than usual.

A single integration manager will need to be appointed. (Some mergers have co-managers, with a senior individual from both companies who together have responsibility for the integration, although it is rare that this structure can work as efficiently as one manager.) These integration managers are needed to speed up the integration process, create a structure, forge social connections between the two organizations, and help engineer short-term successes. The integration manager should be identified and should start the post-merger planning at the very outset of the merger process, even when it is not yet certain that a deal will be consummated. The earlier that the post-merger planning can start, the easier and more effective the post-merger integration will be. In fact, the integration manager should ideally be present at all of the major pre-merger planning meetings. This continuity of planning and implementation should be present in all deals.

Who would make the ideal integration manager? It is best if such an individual has deep knowledge of the acquiring company, is successful in his/her own career to date, does not need to take credit for the success of the deal, is comfortable with chaos, is willing to put in the long hours typically required, is trusted by senior management in the acquirer, has emotional and cultural intelligence, and has an ability to delegate. It would also be ideal to have someone familiar with the acquired company, its products, and culture. Even when two integration managers are selected (one from each company), it is important that one of the managers has the ultimate authority to make the final tough decisions.

One of the original companies in any merger or acquisition will be the leader in the new organization (and it often may be the smaller of the two companies), and it is dangerous to pretend that the two companies are equals. This is especially important where the deal is obviously an acquisition − unfortunately, there are many examples where the acquirer has been improperly advised to refer to the deal as a 'merger' in order to mollify the staff of the acquired company (for example, the acquisition of Bankers Trust by Deutsche Bank in 1999 when Deutsche Bank was sensitive about the cultural issues involved in being the first European bank to acquire a major US bank with a long and proud history).

Deutsche Bank's ideal integration manager

John Ross was appointed by the Board of Deutsche Bank to oversee the integration of US-based Bankers Trust following its acquisition in 1999. This was a very complex merger as noted above. Deutsche Bank recognized the importance of having a powerful and effective head of the post-merger integration.

Ross had been Treasurer of Deutsche Bank (based at its headquarters in Frankfurt, Germany), but also had been Chief Executive for the Asia-Pacific region. Importantly for the integration of Bankers Trust, Ross was an American and had previously had a 21-year career with Bank of New York where he had held senior positions in both London and New York. He therefore had a unique combination of being able to understand Deutsche Bank as well as anyone plus knowing the business, management, and cultural issues involved in the acquisition of an American bank.

In an interview with his alma mater, Wharton, he later said, 'Deutsche Bank . . . recognized that it is absolutely critical in a merger to quickly establish unambiguous lines of responsibility and make senior executive decisions as rapidly as possible. Such decisions should also be implemented as soon as possible. We did that with Bankers Trust, so that there was no confusion about who was running what, who was responsible

> for what, and what was the game-plan and strategy going forward.'
>
> 'We had a period of almost six months from the date of the merger agreement to the change of control date. Therefore, on the actual day when the change of control occurred, June 4, 1999, it wasn't a sudden change. It was the continuation of a strategy and chain of command that had already been well communicated during the prior four months.'

The integration should also be facilitated by a number of task forces. The precise number will be dependent on the size and complexity (product and geography) of the combined organization. These task forces will exist at different levels in the organization, although best practice would suggest the need for one overall 'integration steering committee' to manage the whole process. They should also be managed by and composed of full-time employees, with external assistance where required. This process cannot be effectively outsourced, and companies that have tried to use consultants and others to manage the integration process have typically done so less successfully than those who recognize the importance of the tasks and therefore allocate adequate internal senior resources to management and coordination of the following key tasks:

- Key manager decisions
- Aligning strategies
- Aligning structures, systems, processes
- Identifying key business risks
- Corporate identity, brands, names
- Communications
- Resolving conflicts

All of these areas are critical, whether obvious from the outset (such as culture or product overlaps) or whether seemingly superficial but actually very important to some individuals (such as brand and company name). It is important to identify all of these issues early in the post-merger integration process or even before the acquisition closes.

There will be a number of 'outsiders' who will play various roles in the post-merger integration, just as many of these individuals and organizations assisted the pre-merger process. In fact, some external advisors are needed for their requisite skills (for example, certain human resource issues such as pension fund planning and key manager appointments, legal advice regarding redundancies, outplacement services, and accounting issues), as these skills typically do not exist in most companies that only make an occasional acquisition. Some outsiders will be 'controlled,' such as the consultants working for the integration task forces, lawyers completing various aspects of the deal, and ac-countants who will continue to assist in the financial consolidation of the two companies. Of more concern will be the 'uncontrollable' outsiders (such as regulators, the press, financial analysts, and competitors) who will also need managing to the greatest degree possible. The integration manager and the task forces need to be leading this effort.

ENGINEER SUCCESSES

One way to maintain the client base and even to grow it is through the **engineering of successes**, even if these are not 'real.' This can be used to demonstrate the power of the new organization and should be done as soon as possible after the deal is announced (and planned well before that time). Some organizations bring salespeople from the target to meetings in order to be able to announce that the deal was won by the new organization (even if the deal was already in the bag with the old sales force). These wins, when communicated properly, can be an effective morale booster internally as well. It is important that these pre-closing 'successes' – as with all the interactions between the two companies before the closing – are monitored by those familiar with the appropriate laws and regulations, especially in mergers of competitors where regulatory approvals are required.

ACT QUICKLY

When talking to almost anyone involved in a successful integration, the need for **speed** is usually mentioned in the first sentence. Not necessarily speed of integration as that will depend on the type of deal and there may be reasons to keep the newly acquired company separate due to cultural or other business reasons. But it is critically important to make the key decisions very quickly. Uncertainty is the virus of successful post-merger integration, as this will lead to customers, managers, and employees leaving. It is not critical that every decision is made correctly; in fact, those same CEOs and senior managers have said that they do not require 100% certainty. The first decisions should be about the key managers at the top of the newly combined organization as noted by the integration manager in the case study on Deutsche Bank earlier in this chapter.

RETAIN KEY EMPLOYEES

All of the above factors are closely linked to the ability to **retain key employees** in both the acquiring and acquired companies. Each employee will be most concerned about 'me.' If those concerns are not addressed, no other business will get done properly as managers and employees will be distracted. The intelligence function should help the acquirer identify their key personnel.

Human resource management issues during integration will include changing the board of directors, choosing the right people for the right positions at all levels in the organization, management and workforce redundancies, aligning performance evaluation and reward systems, developing employment packages and strategies to retain key people, and generally managing conflicting expectations of staff throughout the new company. All of this takes a high degree of coordination and sensitivity.

An organization going through a merger or acquisition is similar to an individual going through a marriage or divorce: it is a significant event and there are certain emotional responses that the organization or individual will pass through in becoming comfortable with the new situation, just as people going through a divorce will work through the psychological phases from denial and anger, through sadness and relief to the end result where there is enjoyment or at least acceptance of the situation and a feeling that 'it's actually working out well.'

People-related issues typically represent much of the hidden post-merger integration cost to the new organization. These hidden costs, noted earlier in this chapter are often difficult to quantify. Organizations that anticipate these issues will be best positioned to deal with them effectively and to minimize the negative financial impact they represent.

As with the stages of combination noted above, it is important to provide assistance to the organization and individuals to move them through these stages as rapidly as possible. Individuals within the acquirer and individuals within the target will behave differently. Often managers in the buyer will act with an air of superiority combined with a drive to dominate all the meetings and move as rapidly as possible to full integration. This may be at odds with the speed of integration needed to realize the benefits that the target brings to the new organization.

The target managers – those that have been chosen or who have decided to remain – may still be recovering from the shock of being taken over and will tend to be defensive about the strengths they bring (including the strengths of their systems and culture). They may have a sense of fatalism about them as they realize their lack of power to determine the outcome of meetings and may therefore consciously or unconsciously resist the changes.

Integration process at Cisco Systems Inc.

Cisco is a serial acquirer and has been through periods where it will acquire up to 50 companies in a year. As a result, it has developed a standardized model for integration that has proven to be very effective.

A team drawn from all the major departments of Cisco determines if and how the upper management and line level employees fit into Cisco's structure. Engineers from Cisco examine the technology and the finance department vets accounts.

As soon as the deal is completed, they send in their post-merger integration SWAT team. This is a team that exists permanently (or, in times of less frequent acquisitions, can be assembled rapidly). As an information technology (IT) company, the IT team has particular relevance. For example, Cisco's IT team has a strict methodology for integrating all electronic mail, websites, product order systems and telephone numbers into Cisco's systems. That and the other integration teams gave each target pre-specified company information about Cisco, according to *ECCH Bulletin*.

The acquired company often becomes a discrete subdivision of Cisco so that unique and valuable processes are not lost. Nevertheless, personnel were integrated into Cisco immediately. The CEO of the acquired company was always appointed as a vice-president of Cisco Systems Inc. and most staff continued to report to their former CEO. All staff were offered stock options which acted as 'golden handcuffs' to discourage them from leaving for competitors. The employees were immediately told their new positions, titles, and compensation packages. Importantly, no staff could be dismissed without the agreement of their vice-president (that is, their former CEO) and the Cisco CEO, but those who were made redundant usually found out very soon after the deal closed.

The entire process was designed to take 100 days for the acquired company to be presented as part of Cisco, regardless of the size of the acquired company.

During a merger, it is critical to monitor employees closely to determine how they feel and therefore whether anything can be done by the organization to assist employees in adapting to the new company. Certain warning signs that things may not be going as well as anticipated could include any of the following:

- Key employee departures to competitors.
- Increasing absenteeism and poor time-keeping.
- More customer complaints.
- Increasing union activity.
- Low level of employee participation at social events, training, or management courses.

- More legal claims.
- Deteriorating accident and safety record.
- Declining product quality.
- Increase in health insurance claims, especially stress related.

All are evident from tracking employees, encouraging two-way communication, and the intelligence function. Often independent organizations will be used to survey employees, but management need to be trained and encouraged to watch themselves for the warning signs as well to act to retain key employees.

NURTURE CLIENTS

With all the above principally internal problems of integrating two different companies, it is easy to lose sight of the revenue side of the business, the **focus on clients**. While the company is worrying about integration, the outside world will not be so distracted: customers can be poached if not nurtured, and the uncertainty caused by a merger is often used by competitors to their advantage while the attention of the new company is focused elsewhere. Likewise, supplier relationships are at risk as well. It is therefore important to encourage the sales force and relationship managers to be alert to signs that there are problems. This can be done through effective use of business intelligence. For example, Maersk Lines, in its 2005 acquisition of Royal P&O Nedlloyd to create the largest shipping carrier in the world, focused much of its post-merger integration effort on the retention of customers from both the Maersk Line side of the business and also the target's side. From their experience with earlier acquisitions, they had developed good post-merger communication processes with customers linked to a monitoring program to track revenues. This acquisition will be discussed further in the next chapter.

COMMUNICATE

The integration team will also need to make sure that there is adequate focus on **communication**. The communications must emanate from the very top of both organizations or else they run the risk of lacking credibility. Managers must 'walk the talk' and show that they have recognized the changes to the organization and their impact on individual employees. The very senior managers can best communicate the vision of the deal and the related business logic.

There is no best way to provide this communication, as each organization will have its own culture and existing communications tools. These can be in the form of hotlines, newsletters, presentations, and workshops. The informal lines of communication are potentially of greater importance, and although differing in each organization, ways should be found to exploit them.

No matter what methods are used to communicate, they must demonstrate transparency and openness at all times; a lack of candor or honesty will be immediately sensed by most employees, and the goodwill that is critical to have in place for the successful implementation of the deal will be destroyed. It is best to tell employees, communities, and other stakeholders everything that you can as early as you can, especially when the news is negative. Positive messages should be repeated. Management should recognize that their actions speak louder than words.

One way to achieve success is to avoid some of the communications pitfalls that companies have fallen into in the past when merging or acquiring. The temptation to communicate in a way that placates staff is intense, yet can often backfire as reality appears. This is especially true if senior managers begin to believe the hype and spin of their own public communication statements: the press releases that they've issued through their public relations agencies, the presentations to investment banking industry analysts, and the memos sent by their internal communication teams.

Avoid communication 'temptations' during post-merger integration

- 'We'll tell you when there's something to tell'

There should be continual communication using many ways of communicating, as noted above. A period of no formal communication is a time when gossip and rumor will prevail . . . and gossip is difficult if not impossible for management to control. During the integration period, there is *always* something to communicate, and repetition is not necessarily bad. You can decide when the formal integration period is over (sometimes considered to be the first 100 days), but still communication should continue and the integration messages continually reinforced.

- 'This is a merger of equals, not an acquisition'

It is also often heard: 'This is not an acquisition, it's the merger of two excellent organizations.' But there is never a merger of equals even when the two companies are the same size based on *some* factors. This misconception of equality creates the impression and perhaps even the expectation that decisions will be made in some democratic or egalitarian fashion (decisions such as whom to make redundant, which systems to adopt and brands to retain, how to rationalize overlapping products, and so on). There needs to be someone senior in the organization who will ultimately resolve the inevitable conflicts and make the final decisions – the really difficult decisions cannot be made by committee as group decisions in these situations are inefficient at best and at worst merely satisfice.

- 'We will pick the best of both organizations'

Although this is often the instruction from senior management, there is often a lot of ambiguity and therefore so much gray area in decisions about systems, processes, brands, products, suppliers, distributors, internal staff and so on. Politics will play a role. A related statement is: 'We will keep only the best, regardless from which organization.'

* 'The right decisions about the new organization will take time'

There will always be resistance to change: avoid the tendency to let the organization dictate the integration pace. Rarely will speed of decision making be anything but an imperative, especially when making the tough decisions. People usually prefer certainty to uncertainty, even if they are negatively affected as it will allow them to move on. There is no way to sugar-coat these painful decisions. The best route forward is usually to let people know both the good and bad news as quickly as possible. Decisions during merger integration can be fast and painful or slow and painful; the former is preferred. Therefore make decisions on 80% knowledge – don't wait for 100% certainty. Remember that implementation of the decision will depend upon the integration strategy most appropriate to the acquisition as discussed in the first section of this chapter and therefore some integrations will be planned to take time but the decisions about those slow integrations should still be made quickly.

* 'There will be no more redundancies'

There are always reasons to make changes in the workforce, even if driven by external changes in the market and not the acquisition. If job losses occur anywhere near the time of the integration, employees will blame the merger/acquisition. This may be true even one or two years after deal closing. Yet it is very important to try to announce *all* the redundancies at one time early in the integration, even if somewhat more than necessary; avoid if possible more than one round of redundancies.

- 'Decisions about who will retain each job will be made on merit'

As with all human resources decisions – and despite the best of intentions – there must be some subjectivity. Politics play an important role in the jockeying for power in the new organization. Employees will not believe statements that do not acknowledge this and, by stating it, the credibility of other important statements is called into doubt.

- 'No further acquisitions will be required'

This is also not credible either to employees or external analysts. One cannot anticipate how the markets will change and whether further acquisitions will be necessary.

INTEGRATE THE TWO CULTURES

Employees embody and embrace their company's culture, and culture will differ between the two organizations. These cultures will necessarily change during the integration even in the acquirer. **Cultural integration** is paramount and ignoring the 'soft' cultural issues of the two companies is a recipe for failure (recall the case study of Quaker Oats shown in Chapter 1 where the entrepreneurial and quirky culture of Snapple could not be effectively integrated into the old-line, conservative culture of Quaker Oats, despite the fact that management of Quaker Oats had intended that the acquisition would help to revitalize its company with new ideas).

From the cultural side, it is important to make the social connections in terms of communication, identification of common core values and recognizing the importance of 'superficial' issues such as titles and company and division names. It is an issue not just for senior managers but at all levels of the organization, as both companies will have had unique cultures that may not instantly or naturally mesh. As noted above, there is no merger of equals and this illusion should also not be applied to the cultures either.

Cultural integration in a cross-border acquisition – BASF/Knoll acquisition of Boots Pharmaceuticals

In 1998, Knoll, a division of BASF (a German chemicals and pharmaceuticals company) acquired the pharmaceuticals divisions from Boots (a diversified British company). This acquisition was driven by Knoll's desire to exploit synergies and achieve significant cost reductions primarily in R&D and production, as well as to widen their product portfolio and accelerate time to market of several new products including a new drug designed to reduce obesity (Sibutramine).

As outlined in a Manchester Business School case study of the merger, there were significant opportunities to achieve superior economies of scale through global restructuring. This would be particularly concentrated on the consolidation of manufacturing and research and development sites on a continent-by-continent basis, and a reduction of headcount designed ultimately to achieve cost reductions across the new company. In addition, Knoll intended to consolidate its sales forces to increase the sales of existing products through a more thorough, comprehensive and region-wide market exposure.

What were the cultural issues in the deal? Knoll wanted to create a more culturally diverse company, better able to compete on a global scale. This was important because they recognized the need for cultural harmony to bring about synergies. The significant differences between British and German cultures had to be addressed. Knoll also hoped to change its own culture by incorporating Boots' widely acknowledged 'value-based management' practices.

Strategies used by Knoll to facilitate the cultural integration were:

- Seminars and workshops established to enhance cross-cultural/cross-company relations.
- English- and German-language courses provided to both sets of employees to encourage greater communication and exchange of information.
- Customized workshops for personnel involved in international project teams.
- General manager appointments, coupled with an initial launch message, particularly in the UK, staged to appease a potentially disaffected workforce.
- Delayering of the 'hierarchical structure' from seven to four layers in line with the rest of the company.
- Increased employee consultation/involvement (greater levels of autonomy and employee empowerment).
- Rationalization of employment terms and benefits, pension scheme, and discontinuation of bonus scheme.

These steps had the following positive benefits:

- The corporate video and the managerial presentations and 'terms/benefits' packages were well received, and helped to create initial excitement and energy.
- Empowerment helped to defuse the 'acquisition' scenario and increased motivation in the Boots Pharmaceutical

workforce, though this may have caused some confusion within BASF/Knoll ranks.

- According to the company, delayering led to the eradication of 'complexity that causes lethargy and inertia [making] companies unresponsive and inflexible'; also there was an increase in workforce motivation and actualization of cost synergies.

- Reasonable selection of key retained personnel coupled with an increasing workforce led to a belief in job safety with BASF/Knoll as opposed to the expected job cuts/ morale loss at Boots Pharmaceutical before the merger.

Yet despite these tools, too much emphasis was placed on linguistic barriers, as opposed to creating actual 'connective tissue' to bridge the cultural gap. There was a lack of role models to inspire the workforce. The redundancy news was also delayed and there were subsequently job cuts and other 'creeping changes,' again leading to uncertainty and a 'debilitating drain of value from the acquisition' as noted by authors Ashkenas, DeMonaco, and Francis. In essence, too many people were left in the dark and although this may have been intentional, it created an adverse effect. This then resulted in a loss of key staff from Boots Pharmaceutical and especially increased R&D staff turnover. Further cuts led to rumors that the German side of the business was not affected and this therefore severely affected relationships between the two companies.

All the above ensured that the Boots Pharmaceutical workforce felt misled or even 'sold out,' despite all of the appropriate actions noted above having been taken.

The management expert Peter Drucker posited 'Five Commandments' for successful mergers, which mostly point to the importance of getting the culture right:

- Acquirer must contribute something to the acquired company.
- A common core of unity is required.
- Acquirer must respect the business of the acquired company.
- Within a year or so, the acquiring company must be able to provide top management to the acquired company.
- Within the first year of merger, management in both companies should receive promotions across the entities.

Similarly, the acquisition will be a catalyst for other changes, such as management board responsibilities and risk management, and even the acquirer needs to be prepared to give up its identity.

Oracle's acquisition of PeopleSoft

When Oracle made a hostile acquisition of PeopleSoft, it was assumed by many that there would be much bloodshed in terms of both lost customers and employees. However, according to their public statements, Oracle was able to retain 95% of its customers after the merger by taking active measures to listen to its customers. And by retaining employees in the R&D department, Oracle was able to understand the pulse of the newly acquired business.

The takeover was publicly hostile with both companies taking out full page advertisements in the *Financial Times* and other newspapers, but Oracle early in the process recognized the importance of the combined customer bases and clearly focused on developing a strategy to retain PeopleSoft's customer base and targeted them directly. Moreover by valuing the creative know-how of the target, especially the client support teams that were their main revenue producers, they were able to listen to the needs of the key target client-facing employees and support them through the merger.

ADJUST, PLAN, AND MONITOR

Adjustment, planning, and monitoring are necessary at all stages of the merger, and not least during the post-merger period. Managers should prepare for surprises – these will always occur in a situation as complex as merging two companies and their employees. Nothing should be cast in stone: be willing to make changes, anticipate unexpected external events, and manage them as best as possible. Surprises need not surprise: look for the warning signs. This is another area where business intelligence in the form of scenario planning could help. In planning, the managers of the new organization should not try for absolute certainty in the integration decisions, as it is too fluid a process and waiting is often worse than at least some action.

As noted earlier, planning should start at the beginning of the deal idea stage. This includes an identification of who to fill key roles, their responsibilities, and mapping out what the future organization will look like. Business intelligence can be used to determine what changes will be necessary. The more that is done in advance of closing, the easier and faster the integration.

CONCLUSION

In summary, a merger will bring a tremendous number of changes – many unanticipated – and it is critical to have an understanding of the importance of knowing how best to work through that change process.

The monitoring should allow for flexibility in implementation. It is especially important to include the base business in the monitoring, even those areas supposedly not affected by the merger. Early warning systems should alert the transition team and integration manager to any potential problems.

CHAPTER 11

POST-ACQUISITION REVIEW

*D*o firms learn from previous acquisitions? The easiest intelligence to collect and use is the information that already exists in-house. Such knowledge can come not only from a company's own prior deals but second-hand by studying transactions of other firms. Such organizational learning can potentially lead to an improvement in acquisition success rates. It is an area where the use of the intelligence function is critical in order to gain the competitive edge.

M&A SKILL AS A CORE COMPETENCY

For some companies that acquire other companies frequently, M&A is one of their core competencies and competitive advantages. These companies, such as GE, Cisco, and Intel, even publicly trumpet their M&A expertise. Companies that have proven success in acquiring other companies do have a competitive advantage over those companies who, for whatever reason, have decided that they will only grow organically, or who have failed at prior acquisitions, have not learned from those mistakes, and are therefore doomed to repeat those errors.

To maximize the benefits from this experience, M&A skills must be institutionalized in order to retain the knowledge within the company. This is often done through a special department (often called the 'corporate development department,' but it can also be a part of a central strategy group or even the CEO's office). This is not just important for serial acquirers but for any firm that makes even occasional acquisitions, although it is certainly much more critical for those firms that do make frequent acquisitions.

Many companies lose the value of prior acquisitions by not even attempting to measure how successful the acquisitions have been. Studies consistently show that less than 50% of acquirers performed formal post-deal review or even included performance tracking in their integration.

Maersk Line: Learning from prior acquisitions

In response to high demand in the container shipping market and the need to expand capacity quickly, Maersk Line chose to grow via acquisition instead of organically. With the purchase of Royal P&O Nedlloyd (PONL) in 2005, it became the world's largest carrier. With almost double the capacity of its closest competitor, it achieved economies of scale that no other carrier could achieve.

During the 1990s, there was a remarkable expansion of international trade while the container shipping industry moved forward to expand business in emerging markets. In response to this growth, a pattern of partnerships and business integration in the shipping industry gradually developed from the alliances that began in the 1970s and 1980s to pool costs, revenues and marketing. Eventually, these alliances extended from not only vessel operations but also the shared use of terminals, joint equipment management, inland transport and logistics, joint purchasing, and procurement. Alliances, mergers, and acquisitions raised the market share of the top 20 carriers from only 26% in 1980 to 58% in 2003, according to data from the *Review of Network Economics* in 2004.

Maersk Line is a Danish shipping company which is part of the AP Møller-Maersk Group, tracing its origins to the beginning of the 20th century. In 1990, it established a collaboration with PONL on vessel employment, and the synergies realized were significant. Then, in 1993 it acquired a smaller Danish shipper (Eac-Ben) where profitability was rapidly achieved at a time when most carriers were unable to show a profit. The deals proved to the company that growth by acquisition could be highly successful and built its confidence in using M&A as a growth tool.

Only two years later, in 1995, Maersk formed an alliance with Sea-Land, an American firm and the largest carrier at the time. Complementary markets and scale synergies led to continued development of this alliance and the withdrawal of Maersk from the PONL alliance. Maersk acquired Sea-Land in mid-1999, enabling it to adopt new business practices for the industry – such as the isolation of two types of business: logistics activities and ocean carriage. The full integration of the European and American companies took a couple of years, with the challenges of merging the two cultures requiring some time.

According to several current and former employees at Maersk interviewed shortly after the acquisition, because of its experience with its earlier acquisitions, Maersk had been preparing for its next acquisition. Management had identified the need for additional ship capacity and, in May 2005, it offered to purchase PONL at a premium of 40.6%. The deal was completed in August of that year and it then controlled almost 18% of its shipping market.

> Prior to the completion of the deal, Maersk management had set up a monitoring team and monitoring program to follow up customers' contributions according to their volume commitments to ensure that expected revenue enhancement synergies were realized. Focus was on customer retention from both the Maersk and PONL sides. Control mechanisms were put in place to measure synergies. From its previous acquisitions, Maersk Line had learned that effective and frequent communication with both customers and employees was necessary in order to avoid the loss of key customers or key employees.

If you don't know what to measure, how do you know if you've succeeded? In any merger, lessons need to be learned in order to make future deals more successful. Cost-reduction benefits are more often easier to achieve than revenue-enhancing benefits. Fewer companies track revenue-enhancing benefits than cost-reduction 'benefits,' even though most pre-acquisition press releases emphasized the new business opportunities from the mergers or acquisition. Little is done to determine whether mergers result in new customers, better sales force efficiency or cross-selling, a positive effect on the product distribution channels, improved new product development, and other similar integration revenue-related benefits. The 'cost' issues have greater focus, perhaps because of their ease of measurement but still many companies do not monitor this rigorously. Headcount reductions seem to be the most common item tracked; items related to the systems supply chain, manufacturing processes, distribution, outsourcing and R&D are less frequently tracked.

POST-DEAL REVIEW TEAM

It is therefore important that the post-acquisition performance review be utilized as the final step in the merger and acquisition

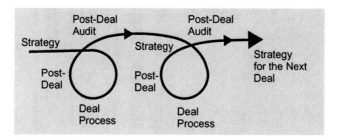

Figure 11.1 Continual need for post-deal review.

process, although in another sense it is also the first step in the planning of the next deal (see Figure 11.1). To do this effectively, the major elements of a specific and focused post-acquisition review should be in the form of a formal audit, with a review team chosen optimally from the original deal and post-merger integration teams, plus some people who were not deeply involved with the merger planning and implementation. If advisors played a significant role in the deal, they should be included as well. All members of that team must be briefed on the strategic, financial, and organizational objectives of the deal, so that they can identify where the linkages were made or neglected.

This post-acquisition performance review *must* be the responsibility of the line managers, although they can certainly use the assistance of the corporate development or strategy department (if they exist), as well as internal audit and outside advisors, consultants, and auditors.

POST-DEAL REVIEW TIMING

Adequate time must be allowed to conduct the review. The process should be in place at closing. The first review point should take place within a month of deal closing, a major review should be done at the end of the first three months or 100 days, and then at further time points post-deal depending on the

company and the type of deal. Pre-agreed performance bench-
marks should include all aspects of the deal, not just financial or
headcount numbers. There should be clear reporting on reasons
for success and failure in each area being assessed.

APPLIED LEARNING

In using the results of the reviews, past experience will become
the guide to the future. A number of possible mistakes can be
made, however. There might be the tendency to view today as
identical to the past, and thereby make inappropriate generaliza-
tions from the past to the present. Conversely, there is sometimes
the tendency to say that today is very different and the lessons
of the past do not and will not apply, therefore believing that a
new acquisition is unique in all aspects when in fact many
similarities – even if not all – exist. Experience should be used
discriminately, but it should never be ignored. This is a key lesson
from military and business intelligence.

Acquirers must also be resilient in adapting their learning to
the present. The easiest application of prior experience is clearly
for firms making multiple acquisitions within the same industry
either horizontally or even vertically. Reviews should still take
place when this is not the case. Acquirers with well-specified and
codified integration processes should be able to have significantly
improved accounting returns on assets and long-term shareholder
returns. In the studies which we have conducted, this certainly
appears to be the case.

ROLE OF ADVISORS

For firms not large enough to have corporate development departments or where acquisitions are made infrequently (in the order

of less than two or three deals annually), close advisors can be used as a repository for much of the organizational learning. This needs to be done formally, as it is not a natural role for most advisors as they may otherwise change their coverage team which will result in the loss of much of the specific company knowledge where personalities and culture play such an important role in deal success. It may be best for the firm's auditors to fill this role, as the auditors do not change as frequently as some other advisors. If they do maintain the organizational learning, it should not be done in the context of the formal accounting statement audits, but rather as a separate effort.

CONCLUSION

The ability to be a successful acquirer can and should be a competitive advantage for firms who do it well. This is best done by codifying the M&A experience to facilitate organizational learning. Business unit managers must be part of the process at all stages (although not to the degree that will totally distract them from running the business during the deal process and integration). Very senior management should focus on the high-level issues and decisions (that is, not fire fighting, problem solving, or refereeing). Such tasks can be left to the dedicated acquisition department (such as corporate development) who will shepherd the process. An effort should be made to retain these key staff members, as much of the knowledge will be retained at the individual level despite the best attempts to put it in writing. As noted earlier, M&A is an art, not a science – and the best practitioners are artists in the field of M&A, not merely finance experts, legal advisors, or negotiation specialists.

CHAPTER 12

CONCLUSIONS

*G*iven that every M&A scenario is different, so the use and application of intelligence varies remarkably between individual deals. Yet, in search of what nebulously can be termed best practice in this field, it is possible to isolate and identify an ideal common approach that can help managers ensure superior returns to shareholders off the back of M&A transactions.

While much of the book has focused around corporate entities and other institutions as remote and depersonalized participants in a highly complex commercial environment, it is important to remember, however obvious, that an organization is only ever as good as the employees that drive it forward. Thus, while it is corporate level players that are the actors *per se* on the M&A stage, it is, as Patrick Handley, a partner of Brunswick Group, notes, the staff members who provide the competitive advantage through a combination of years of relevant experience, tacit 'know-how,' and a detailed understanding of a particular situation.

As much as any other factor, hand picking the best internal and external team with the greatest amount of insight relevant to a particular M&A deal often pays the highest dividends for a company.

Yet, over and above this, there are a number of recommendations that can be made that, while not guaranteeing, may certainly aid the successful conclusion of an M&A deal. In the first instance, companies need to position information and intelligence at the very center of their organizational structure, enabling participants in an M&A scenario to tap into a wealth of tacit and codified knowledge with which to drive a deal forward. The entire team – both internal and external – must be told of the expectation that they will share any information they have gathered, whether they believe it relevant or not. Cited in the US Congress as dealing '... with all things which should be known in advance of initiating a course of action...,' intelligence enables companies to safeguard their welfare when heading into the maelstrom of an M&A deal environment by providing the most amount of foreknowledge possible. Indeed, the expression that 'to be forewarned is to be forearmed' is most apt in this context.

Johnson & Johnson's use of business intelligence

One excellent example of excellent continued use of business intelligence is Johnson & Johnson, the large US-based manufacturer of healthcare products.

In April 2005, Johnson & Johnson's acquisition of Guidant was approved by its shareholders at a cost of $25.4 billion. However, following serious operational problems that arose, Johnson & Johnson announced it would pull out of the deal. Guidant then sued Johnson & Johnson forcing it to continue, at which point Johnson & Johnson agreed to the purchase at a 15% lower price than the original. However, a second bidder suddenly entered, Boston Scientific, with a higher offer than Johnson & Johnson. This move sparked a short bidding war, with Boston Scientific finally making an offer of $27.2 billion to clinch the deal.

Johnson & Johnson wished to withdraw or at least have the deal price lowered to account for all the operational liabilities that had developed. However, once a rival entered to bid for Guidant, as a result of a possible leakage from the target's side, Johnson & Johnson were driven by the competition to increase its offer. It did not, however, increase it drastically, and it finally refused to increase it above its original offer. In comparison, Boston Scientific paid a price for the acquisition at almost 10% above Johnson & Johnson's original bid. This high bid could be seen as Johnson & Johnson's reverse white knight, since it allowed it to extract itself from its obligations to Guidant in a withdrawal that avoided being forced to overpay for the acquisition. In fact, having been outbid by Boston Scientific, Guidant even paid $705 million in termination fees to Johnson & Johnson.

Following this, in June 2006, Johnson & Johnson made an acquisition of Pfizer's consumer healthcare business, which was described by one senior manager as fitting Johnson & Johnson's strategic requirements 'like a glove.' Johnson & Johnson paid the $16.6 billion deal all in cash, but some analysts strongly felt that, at 4.3 times the earnings of Pfizer's revenues of 2005, it was an overvaluation, giving Pfizer a maximum price tag of $15 billion. However, the acquisition made Johnson & Johnson the largest worldwide supplier of over-the-counter (OTC) drugs and therefore they felt the price to be fully justified.

According to the same manager, Johnson & Johnson was extremely stringent when choosing targets; one of its most important criteria was that targets under review have a strong equity with a solid reputation in the market and no 'bad luggage,' as he phrased it. He went on to say that in its experience 'the reviewing committee is extremely rigorous: the target absolutely has to offer strategic fit and growth in line with strategy, or you can forget it.' Moreover, objectivity is crucial to ensuring all actions are directed towards the bottom line.

Johnson & Johnson was selective in its targets, it adapted its M&A behavior in direct response to the individual context, and remained firm to its goals and strategic intent. This is further backed up by the fact that in the case of Pfizer, it also went on to due diligence that rigorously assessed management. It kept a select few who it felt would add value and laid off the rest. Furthermore, in other cases, Johnson & Johnson actively sought alternatives to M&A through joint ventures, strategic alliances, and partnerships.

Furthermore, in a world that is increasingly defined by 'prescription' and heavily mandated regulation, the use of free thought and ingenuity in the gathering of information may often prove to be the defining competitive edge and recipe for success. With so much information available in the public domain, companies require simple yet innovative methods to enable them to separate the wheat from the chaff, uncovering uniquely valuable information sources that provide the most insight while offering them the edge in transactions and negotiations.

It would also be difficult to overstate the significance and value that team membership can add to an activity such as M&A. Indeed, this ties back to the comment earlier that all of the team must feel that their role in intelligence gathering is part of their core job. Knowing that they are all part of a larger network where intelligence gathering is considered a core skill will be key to enabling organizations to gather or uncover the necessary business intelligence for an M&A transaction.

Deals should hinge on commercial logic and be developed over time through the proactive use of business intelligence. Courted and serenaded by advisors who pitch opportunistic deals on an ongoing basis to executives, companies need to ensure that the M&A transactions they initiate are deeply rooted in their long-term strategy, while being constantly and dispassionately being re-evaluated to ensure that deals are still 'on track' in delivering enhanced shareholder returns.

Business intelligence is not about being more conservative in the context of M&A but instead is about making sure that the team has taken every advantage it can and has as many bargaining chips in its pocket as possible. By developing an informed comprehensive knowledge of the dynamics that surround the deal, the team can more constructively and effectively manage these dynamics on a continual basis. In short, business intelligence enables a better approach to a merger or acquisition in such a way as to bring out the best long-term value from the deal, and not simply to clinch it with little regard for how that value can most easily be realized.

In conclusion, only by employing sufficient and first-rate business intelligence – delivered by a first-rate intelligence function – will companies be able to gain the distinct competitive advantage that will enable them to achieve commercial success from mergers and acquisitions. M&A is a high risk activity for corporations in the 21st century. Notwithstanding, most companies, if not all, have no choice but to step into the M&A ring in order to guarantee their continued financial and commercial viability in a world where scale and scope arguably provide some sort of buffer against the vicissitudes of an ever-changing and often turbulent business environment. In as much as business intelligence provides a mechanism for risk management within an M&A framework, so it helps companies to beat the odds by turning deals into shareholder value-enhancing transactions.

HOW TO SURVIVE A MERGER

It is difficult in today's business environment to have a full career where an individual will not at some point experience a merger or an acquisition. Job losses – often as high as 5–15% of the employees of the combined organizations – go hand in hand with every merger or acquisition. Over 18 000 people were made redundant in the HP/Compaq 'merger' alone in just two years. It certainly is useful to know about survival techniques and tips that have proven helpful to others when faced with an upcoming or ongoing merger.

DEALING WITH STAFF

When a target is being openly considered, employees will normally be anxious about whether they will be kept or not. As a result, during the due diligence process most will attempt to be seen as acting cooperatively, but many will also try to hold onto important pieces of information for as long as possible in order to maintain control of the negotiation process, as well as to enhance their perceptions of being indispensable to the organization. This is at odds with the requirements to share knowledge as part of the business intelligence process.

Senior managers will have the responsibility to design the new organization and, using best human resources practices, will try to make an informed and fast decision about who should be kept and who should be let go. As noted earlier, when making this decision from the firm's perspective, both speed and precision are extremely important, but not necessarily 100% certainty that would introduce delays. But individual managers and employees also need to and will focus first on their own futures. Making a mistake can be extremely costly and emotionally harrowing further down the line. The process should be as quick and smooth as possible to keep anxiety at a minimum on both sides (the company and the individual employee), and to maintain commitment to a maximum also on both sides.

Senior managers must try to reassure those left behind that they will receive good remuneration packages with, if applicable, performance-related bonuses. Indeed these actions need to be directed at the full length of the remaining term of employment expected for each employee, so as to build the trust and commitment required for that length of time and to leave as good a taste as possible in their mouths. This 'good taste' is necessary as any employee may be a supplier or client someday; they could be potential re-hires.

To do this properly, there must be effective communications: from the firm's perspective, speaking to all employees clearly, directly, making intentions clear, and reassuring them, can buy much needed loyalty, time, and credibility. The second and third tiers of management should not be neglected, as one of the unfortunate facts about mergers and acquisitions is that most of the target's senior management will leave within two or three years. Exceptions exist, but rarely. From the individual's perspective, each will need to assess the veracity of statements made and their impact on them personally. This requires a certain degree of personal business intelligence gathering and social networking.

Need for longer-term management

The private equity industry understands that identifying new senior management in an acquired company is very difficult but necessary. Given that private equity firms know that they are often looking to turn a company around with new management, they usually have a pool of potential new CEOs, CFOs, COOs, and so on.

But there's a paradox: CEOs and other senior officers have a notoriously short corporate life span with any single company, yet the private equity investors will typically hold onto their investment in that company for a five to seven year holding period before an exit event such as an IPO or sale to another company. As such, ensuring that management is fit for the job and retained for five to seven years is absolutely essential, and effective management due diligence is necessary to make this happen.

'Merger' and 'acquisition' are often euphemisms for downsizing which may explicitly be one of the strategies justifying the merger. Overlaps are inevitable: no company needs two CFOs or two heads of human rescources. Promotions and demotions are inherent in the changes taking place during a merger or acquisition. So how should individuals position themselves to be best placed to avoid redundancy or even get ahead in a merger?

STAY OR LEAVE?

The first question to ask oneself is: 'Can the merger actually serve as a jump start to a new company or even career?' In answering this question, stay focused on career goals. Do you want to remain with the new company, or is this a perfect opportunity to change? The merger can often be used as the excuse to move. Fortunately as well, prospective employers will assume that every merger has the consequence that good people leave (and the market often assumes that the best people are the ones who leave first as they have the most external career opportunities and are the people who don't want to waste time to wait to see if they are retained).

Perhaps there will be an opportunity to take an attractive redundancy package. Redundancy packages can often be higher immediately after a merger than at other times because the company has taken financial provisions for such redundancies and/or you will be part of a larger group being made redundant; most acquirers also want to avoid negative publicity during a merger. A redundancy package would be especially attractive if you were considering leaving anyway, as many companies not only pay for you to leave, but offer at the same time outplacement counseling, retraining, relocation benefits, or other benefits. Most employees made redundant are also considered 'good leavers' and thus keep many of the benefits that they had accrued during their career, such as healthcare and other insurances, long-term incentive options, and even deferred cash bonuses.

> **Staff preparation in a company being acquired –
> Bankers Trust**
>
> In 1998, the senior management of Bankers Trust, the eighth largest bank in the United States, knew that it would be acquired. The principal banking regulator in the US,

the Federal Reserve Board, had told Bankers Trust management that it needed to take steps to improve its capital base and reduce risks. It was told to look for a strong partner.

Given that management knew that it would likely be acquired, preparations were made by many in the bank to reduce their personal financial risks. There was some history to this preparation, as disclosed by the equity research analysts at Sanford Bernstein.

In 1997, Bankers Trust had acquired Alex Brown, the oldest investment bank in the United States. At the time of acquisition, it became known that the top 20 executives of Alex Brown had signed employment contracts and that Bankers Trust had earmarked nearly $300 million over three years for incentive compensation of a group of several hundred Alex Brown staff members.

Given this history of retention payments and the expectation that it was to be acquired, it is not surprising that when Deutsche Bank acquired Bankers Trust just under two years later, *Bloomberg* reported that the chairman of Bankers Trust signed a contract worth $55 million over five years plus $14 million over three years in deferred compensation, and it was rumored that his severance package (so-called 'golden parachute') was $100 million when he ultimately left Deutsche Bank only a month after the deal closed in June 1999. The Bankers Trust CFO also left, reputedly with another sizeable package.

It was not only the very top staff who benefited from these retention and redundancy payments. At the time of the acquisition, Deutsche Bank announced that it expected to take a charge of DM2 billion ($1.2 million) to cover severance payments and to set aside DM700 million (almost $420 million) over three years for retention payments to retain 200 key staff.

SURVIVAL TIPS

Assuming you wish to stay with the newly merged company, what should you do? The techniques of good business intelligence applied to your own personal situation would include the following:

- **Start to prepare during the pre-merger phase.** Be part of the merger planning and design process. Get to know the other organization as well as possible using internal and external contacts and resources. This will not only give you information that will be personally useful, but also enables you to be considered more valuable, as you know the other company better than most of your colleagues.

  As part of one or more of the planning committees, you will be better able to find out when personnel and management decisions will be made, and by whom. You will be able to make connections with staff and management in the other company to gain their support as well. This is important even if your company is the larger one. In every merger, some of the managers in the new company will come from both sides, and those new managers, although typically favoring their own staff that they know so well, will want to have some representation from the other side.

  Try as well to be part of the post-merger integration team, but in this case, be careful not to be so integral and critical to that team that you cannot be assigned a good job in the new organization when one appears.
- **Don't think that your own boss will take care of you.** As with everyone else in the organization, your boss will be looking out for him/herself first. Your boss may even have less of an idea than you do as to how decisions will be made. This is a situation that is more likely to occur when official lines of communication break down as they often do in the

period of uncertainty immediately following the announcement of a merger or acquisition. In any case, you cannot
necessarily trust your own boss because your boss may just
be uninformed or made redundant.

- **Stay around the office.** Become more visible. Be the
hardest worker or at least perceived to be such. Don't take
vacation during key periods of decision making, stop working
from home, and avoid unnecessary business trips (external
industry conferences, for example, unless you need these for
networking and intelligence gathering).

  You will not only want to be around the office to hear
any rumors about changes to be made or potential job opportunities, but you will also want to demonstrate that you are
invaluable. This is the time to pull out all the stops and
produce. Many others in the company will be slacking off as
this is a time when morale generally declines in an organization and when people spend hours swapping rumors.

- **Your own team may be your most valuable asset.** They
may be questioned by the transition or integration team about
your ability to assume a new role or even to keep your
current role as you are in competition with your counterparts
in other firms. Your own team may have sources of information that aren't communicated by your network or by your
manager; receptionists, secretaries, and personal assistants
often know the most about what's happening! Additionally,
you'll feel better if you are doing your best for your staff. In
addition, you may need them in the new organization and
you don't want them to consider leaving prematurely.

- **Network incessantly, both internally and externally.**
This is important both to gather intelligence about what is
to happen, and also to gain support as decisions are made.
Often, those outside the company will know more (and
will be more objective) than many internally will. Also, let
others know your accomplishments, talents, and what you've

done for the company. This is not the time to be falsely modest.

- **Keep your clients and keep them happy.** If you have external relationships, make sure that they are loyal to you personally as the salesperson. The company will be less willing to make you redundant for fear of losing your clients – and their revenue.

    Support and middle-office staff should think of the front office as their client. As support staff are most at risk of redundancy after a merger, try to link yourself with some client-facing teams; at least get those who you support to speak up positively on your behalf.

- **Be flexible.** Be willing to move or change jobs. The best positions (or at least the ones to be retained in the new organization) may be in a different location or different department. Show adaptability to a new corporate culture, manager, travel, job requirements, hours, or other business practices.

- **Prepare for the worst, even if you think your job is secure.** When rumors about a merger or acquisition appear, take them seriously. As anyone is potentially at risk (remember, the decision on who to keep is often political and not based on merit), take defensive actions on the home front such as cutting unnecessary personal expenditures, reducing debts, and saving money: now is not the time to remodel the kitchen or move house.

    Call headhunters (especially those that have contacted you in the past) and update your CV. Read the job advertisements. Such preparation is especially important if your company is the smaller one in an acquisition.

    If rumors start appearing or your company is actually in play (and even if it isn't and you are in a position to do so), have your employment contract revised to include a golden parachute or silver parachute if possible.

- **Be positive about the new company.** Be future oriented and focus on what the new organization needs. No one wants to work long term with someone who hangs on to or pines for the past, or with someone who continually reminds people why things were better in the old organization. A positive outlook about yourself and your place in the company can also be important at easing your own anxieties about work and the merger.

There are no guarantees that a job can be retained or found in the newly combined company, but an application of these recommendations should improve the odds immensely. Good luck!

BIBLIOGRAPHY AND REFERENCES

Note: we have organized this bibliography by chapter for ease of use, but many of the references apply to multiple chapters and even the entire subject.

CHAPTER 1   THE NEED FOR INTELLIGENCE IN MERGERS AND ACQUISITIONS

Bekier, M.M., Bogardus, A.J. and Oldham, T. (2001) Why mergers fail. *The McKinsey Quarterly*, Number 4

Bleeke, J. and Ernst, D. (1995) Is your strategic alliance really a sale? *Harvard Business Review*, January/February

Bower, J. (2001) Not all M&As are alike. *Harvard Business Review*, March/April

Cook, M. and Cook, C. (2001) Anticipating unconventional M&As: the case of Daimler Chrysler. *Competitive Intelligence Magazine*, Volume 4, Number 1, 19–22

Darveau, L. (2001) Forecasting an acquisition. *Competitive Intelligence Magazine*, Jan/Feb, Volume 4, Number 1, 13–17

Ghadar, F. (2000) The dubious logic of global megamergers. *Harvard Business Review*, July/August

McGonagle, J.J. Jr. and Vella, C.M. (2003) A case for competitive intelligence. *Information Management Journal*, Volume 36, Number 4, 35–40

Miller, S. (2001) The urge to merge. *Competitive Intelligence Magazine*, Jan/Feb, Volume 4, Number 1, 3

Schweizer, P. (1996) The growth of economic espionage. *Foreign Affairs*, Volume 75, Number 1, 9–14

Stone, E. (2000) Protecting yourself from M&A disasters. *Journal of Corporate Accounting & Finance*, Jan/Feb, Volume 11, Issue 2, 13–16

Weiss, A. (2003) The urge to merge – and the role of CI. *Competitive Intelligence Magazine*, Volume 6, Number 3, 11–14

CHAPTER 2   BUSINESS INTELLIGENCE

Ashby, W.R. (1956) *An Introduction to Cybernetics*. Chapman & Hall

Bartram, P. (1998) The spying game. *Director*, Volume 51, Issue 9

Beer, S. (1972) *Brain of the Firm: A Development in Management Cybernetics*. McGraw-Hill

Betts, R. (1978) Analysis, war and decision: why intelligence failures are inevitable. *World Politics*, Volume 31, Number 1, 61–89

Blenkhorn, D. and Fleisher, C. (2005) *Competitive Intelligence and Global Business*. Praeger Publishers, Westport, Connecticut

Brady, C. (1993) Intelligence failures: plus ça change. . . . *Intelligence and National Security*, Volume 8, Number 4

Brittin, M. (1991) *How to Develop your Competitor Intelligence System: Five Case Studies*. Headland Press, Cleveland

Cohen, W.M. and Levinthal, D.A. (1990) Absorptive Capacity: A New Perspective on Learning and Innovation, *Administrative Science Quarterly*, Volume 35, Number 1, 128–152

Day, G.S. and Schoemaker, P.J.H. (2006) *Peripheral Vision: Detecting the Weak Signals that will Make or Break your Company*. HBR Press

Dhar, V. and Stein, R. (1997) *Seven Methods for Transforming Corporate Data into Business Intelligence*. Prentice Hall, Upper Saddle River, New Jersey

Eels, R. and Nehemkis, P. (1984) *Corporate intelligence and espionage: a blueprint for executive decision making*. Macmillan Press, New York

Gates, B. (2000) *Business @ the Speed of Thought: Succeeding in the Digital Economy*. Business Plus Press

Gilad, B. and Herring, J. (1996) *The Art and Science of Business Intelligence Analysis*. JAI Press, London

Gordon, I. (1989) *Beat the Competition! – How to Use Competitive Intelligence to Develop Winning Business Strategies*. Basil Blackwell, Oxford

Greene, R. (1966) *Business Intelligence and Espionage*. Dow Jones-Irwin, Homewood, Illinois

Kahaner, L. (1996) *Competitive Intelligence – How to Gather, Analyse and Use Information to Move your Business to the Top*. Simon & Schuster, New York

Kurtz, J. (2006) *Business Wargaming*. KappaWest, Laguna Hills, California

Lowenthal, M. (2003) *Intelligence – From Secrets to Policy*. CQ Press, Washington D.C.

Salmon, R. and Linares, Y. (1999) *Competitive Intelligence – Scanning the Global Environment*. Economica, London

Smith, P. (1970) *Industrial Intelligence and Espionage*. London Business Books Limited, United Kingdom

West, C. (2001) *Competitive Intelligence*. Palgrave, Basingstoke, Hampshire

CHAPTER 3 DESIGNING THE ACQUISITION PROCESS

Albizzatti, N.J., Christofferson, S.A. and Sias, D.L. (2005) Smoothing postmerger integration. *McKinsey Quarterly*, Autumn

Auerbach, A. (1988) *Mergers and Acquisitions*. University of Chicago Press, Chicago

DePamphilis, D. (2001) *Mergers, Acquisitions and Other Restructuring Activities*. Academic Press, London

Dinkin, D. and O'Connor, A. (2001) The big deal: getting M&A right from pre-deal through post-deal. *Accenture – The Point*, Volume 1, Issue 1, 1–6

Jemison, D. and Sitkin, S. (1986) Acquisitions: the process can be a problem. *Harvard Business Review*, March/April

Temple, P. and Perk, S. (2001) *Mergers and Acquisitions*. Routledge, London

Weston, J.F., Mitchell, M.L. and Mulherin, J.H. (2001) *Takeovers, Restructuring, and Corporate Governance*. 3rd Edition, Prentice-Hall

CHAPTER 4 CONTROLLING THE ADVISORS

Harding, D. and Rovit, R. (2004) Building deals on bedrock. *Harvard Business Review*, September

Henry, B.R. (1995) Antitrust and CI: notifying the government about a proposed merger, acquisition, or joint venture: the Hart-Scott-Rodino Act. *Competitive Intelligence Review*, Volume 6, Number 4, 67–69

Rankine, D. and Howson, P. (2006) *Acquisition Essentials: A Step-By-Step Guide to Smarter Deals.* FT Prentice Hall

Wasserstein, B. (2000) *Big Deal 2000: The Battle for Control of America's Leading Corporations.* Warner Books

CHAPTER 5 IDENTIFYING THE BEST TARGETS

Campbell, A., Goold, M. and Alexander, M. (1995) Corporate strategy: the quest for parenting advantage. *Harvard Business Review*, March/April

Carey, D. (2000) Lessons from master acquirers: a CEO roundtable on making mergers succeed. *Harvard Business Review*, May/June

Grant, R. (2005) *Contemporary Strategy Analysis.* Blackwell Publishing, Oxford

Henry, B.R. (1994) Antitrust and CI: mergers, acquisitions, and joint ventures. *Competitive Intelligence Review*, Volume 5, Number 2, 45–47

Johnson, L. (2003) Bricks and mortar for a theory of intelligence. *Comparative Strategy*, Volume 22, 1–28

Lisle, C. and Bartlam, J. (1999) Can the target pass the competitive intelligence test? *Mergers and Acquisitions*, Volume 33, Number 4, 27–32

Porter, M. (1980) *Competitive Strategy.* Free Press, New York

Porter, M. (1987) From competitive advantage to corporate strategy. *Harvard Business Review*, May/June

CHAPTER 6 THE BEST DEFENSE

Gelb, B.D., Saxton, M.J., Zinkhan, G.M. and Albers, N.D. (1991) Competitive intelligence: insights from executives. *Business Horizons*, Jan/Feb, 43–47

Gaughan, P. (2007) *Mergers, Acquisitions, and Corporate Restructuring.* 4th Edition, John Wiley & Sons, New York

Hitt, M.A., Harrison, J.S. and Ireland R.D. (2001) *Mergers and Acquisitions: A Guide to Creating Value for Stakeholders.* Oxford University Press, Oxford

Weiss, A. (2003) The urge to merge – and the role of CI. *Competitive Intelligence Magazine*, Volume 6, Number 3, 14

CHAPTER 7 DUE DILIGENCE

Bacon, C. (2004) Next Generation Due Diligence. *Mondaq Business Briefing*, 1 October

Brady, C. and Lorenz, A. (2005) *End of the Road: The True Story of the Downfall of Rover.* FT/Pearson

Dishman, P. (2001) Two tools for M&A analysis. *Competitive Intelligence Magazine*, Volume 4, Number 1, 23–26

Grogan, N. and Christian, G. (2005) Access to documents in a competition context. *Competition Law Journal*, Volume 4, Issue 4

Hester, J. (2003) Corporate finance – integrity checks halt M&A deals. *Accountancy Age*, 6 November

Howson, P. (2003) *Due Diligence – The Critical Stage in Mergers and Acquisitions.* Gower Publishing Limited, Aldershot

Husey, D. and Jenster P. (1999) *Competitor Intelligence – Turning Analysis into Success.* John Wiley & Sons, Chichester

Janis, I.L. (1972) *Victims of Groupthink: A Psychological Study of Foreign-Policy Decisions and Fiascoes.* Houghton Mifflin

Kadlec, D.J. (2000) *Masters of the Universe: Winning Strategies of America's Greatest Dealmakers.* Collins

Marrs, S. (2000) Inside story on trade secrets. *ABA Journal*, October, 77

McGonagle, J.J. Jr. and Vella. C.M. (1986) Competitive intelligence: plugging information voids. *Mergers & Acquisitions*, Volume 21, Number 1, 43–47

Nolan, J. (1999) *Confidential: Uncover your Competitors' Top Business Secrets Legally and Quickly – and Protect your Own.* HarperBusiness, New York

Ojala, M. (2006) Due diligence research. *Online Magazine*, March/April, 44–46

Reid, T. (1985) *Legal Industrial Espionage: A Sourcebook and Guide to Finding Company Information.* Eurofi (UK), Northill

Sammon, W.L., Kurland, M.A. and Spitalnic, R. (1984) *Business Competitor Intelligence – Methods for Collecting, Organizing, and Using Information.* John Wiley & Sons, New York

Stewart, A. (2001) Applying competitive intelligence to mergers and acquisitions, pp. 149–158 in *Managing Frontiers in Competitive Intelligence*, Blenkhorn, D. and Fleisher, C. (eds), Quorum Books, Westport, Connecticut

Whalley, M. (2000) *International Business Acquisitions: Major Legal Issues and Due Diligence*. Kluwer Law International, Boston

CHAPTER 8 VALUATION, PRICING, AND FINANCING

Arzac, E. (2005) *Valuation for Mergers, Buyouts and Restructuring*. John Wiley & Sons, Inc., Hoboken, New Jersey

Bieshaar, H., Knight, J. and van Wassenaer, A. (2001) Deals that create value. *The McKinsey Quarterly*, Number 1

Copeland, T. and Koller, T. (2000) *Valuations: Measuring and Managing the Value of Companies*. John Wiley & Sons, New York

Evans, F. and Bishop, D. (2001) *Valuation for M&A, Building Value in Private Companies*. John Wiley & Sons, New York

Isaacs, R. (2004) A field day for spies: while a deal advances. *Mergers & Acquisitions: The Deal Maker's Journal*, 1 January

Koller, T., Goedhart, M. and Wessels, D. (2005) *Valuation: Measuring and Managing the Value of Companies*, University Edition. 4th Edition. John Wiley & Sons, Inc., Hoboken

Sirower, M. (1999) Stock or cash? The trade-offs for buyers and sellers in mergers and acquisitions. *Harvard Business Review*, November/December

Springsteel, I. (1996) SHHHH! Information leaks are expensive for acquisition-minded firms, but they can be plugged. *CFO*, Volume 12, Issue 10

CHAPTER 9 NEGOTIATION AND BIDDING

Bernhardt, D. and Eger, M. (1995) M&A and competitive intelligence. *International Law Firm Management*, Volume 12, 11–15

Bris, A. (1998) *When Do Bidders Purchase a Toehold? Theory and Tests*, October. Available at SSRN: http://ssrn.com/abstract=139824

Bruner, R. (2004) *Applied Mergers & Acquisitions*, University Edition. John Wiley & Sons, Hoboken, New Jersey

Brady, C. and Brady, T. (2000) *Rules of the Game – Business: A Player's Guide*. Prentice Hall, Harlow

De Smedt, S., Tortorici, V. and van Ockenburg, E. (2005) Reducing the Risk of Early M&A Discussions. *McKinsey Quarterly*, Number 17, Autumn

Evans, E. (1998) *Mastering Negotiation*. Thorogood, London

Minford, J. (2002) *Sun-Tzu – The Art of War*. Penguin Books, London

Rothberg, H.N. and Erickson, G.S. (2004) *From Knowledge to Intelligence: Creating Competitive Advantage in the Next Exonomy*. Butterworth-Heinemann

CHAPTER 10 POST-MERGER INTEGRATION

Ashkenas, R. and Francis, S. (2000) Integration managers: special leaders for special times. *Harvard Business Review*, November/December

Ashkenas, R.N., DeMonaco, L.J. and Francis, S.C. (1998) Making the deal real: How GE Capital integrates acquisitions, *Harvard Business Review*, Jan/Feb

Clemente, M. and Greenspan, D. (1998) *Winning at Mergers and Acquisitions*. John Wiley & Sons, New York

Cooke, T. (1988) *International Mergers and Acquisitions*. Basil Blackwell, Oxford

Davis, S. (2000) *Bank Mergers: Lessons for the Future*. Macmillan Press Ltd, Basingstoke

Donahue, K. (2001) How to ruin a merger: five people-management pitfalls to avoid. *Harvard Management Update Article*

Drucker, P. (1986) *The Frontiers of Management: Where Tomorrow's Decisions are Being Shaped Today*. Dutton Adult

Gaughan, P. (2005) *Mergers: What Can Go Wrong and How to Prevent It*. John Wiley & Sons, Inc., Hoboken

Galpin, T. and Herndon, M. (2000) *The Complete Guide to Mergers and Acquisitions: Process Tools to Support M&A Integration at Every Level*. Jossey-Bass, San Francisco

Haspeslagh, P.C. and Jemison, D.B. (1991) *Managing Acquisitions: Creating Value Through Corporate Renewal*. Free Press, New York

Lee, M. and Mirvis, P. (2001) Making mergers and acquisitions work: strategic and psychological preparation. *The Academy of Management Executives*, Volume 15, Number 2, 80–94

Tetenbaum, T. (1999) Beating the odds of merger & acquisition failure: seven key practices that improve the chance for expected integration and synergies. *Organizational Dynamics*, Autumn, 22–35

Wharton Leadership Digest (2000) Leadership Interview: John Ross, Chief Executive of Deutsche Bank Americas, Volume 4, No 6

CHAPTER 11   POST-ACQUISITION REVIEW

Moeller, S. (2007) *Case Studies in Mergers & Acquisitions, Spring 2007.* Pearson Custom Publishing, Harlow

Simon, N.J. (2000) Managing the CI department: successful merger challenges. *Competitive Intelligence Magazine*, Volume 3, Number 4, 52–53

Sudarsanam, S. (2003) *Creating Value from Mergers and Acquisitions.* Pearson Education Limited, Harlow

WEBSITES

Note: websites are known to change and some require registration or subscription; the ones included here are most useful at the time of publication of this book in addition to those shown in the chapters.

www.acquisitions-monthly.com (Acquisitions Monthly)
www.aurorawdc.com (Aurora WDC)
www.marketing-intelligence.co.uk (AWARE)
www.corpfin.co.uk (Corpfin Worldwide)
www.dealogic.com/mergers.aspx (Dealogic Mergers & Acquisitions)
www.factiva.com (Factiva)
www.mergerstat.com (FactSet Mergerstat)
www.mergermarket.com (Mergermarket.com)
www.m-a-monitor.co.uk (M&A Monitor)
www.pharmaceuticalalliance.com (Johnson & Johnson)
www.scip.org (Society of Competitive Intelligence Professionals)
www.thomsonmergers.com (Thomson Mergers)

INDEX

Index compiled by Terry Halliday

Lightning Source UK Ltd.
Milton Keynes UK
UKOW041433260513

211231UK00001B/4/P